Clifford & Barbara
Dawson

FIGHTING FOR YOUR MARRIAGE

Fighting *for*

Howard   Scott   Susan L.
Markman   Stanley   Blumberg

With a foreword by Dean S. Edell, M.D.

Your Marriage

POSITIVE STEPS
FOR PREVENTING
DIVORCE AND
PRESERVING
A LASTING LOVE

JOSSEY-BASS PUBLISHERS • SAN FRANCISCO

Substantial discounts on bulk quantities of Jossey-Bass books are available to corporations, professional associations, and other organizations. For details and discount information, contact the special sales department at Jossey-Bass Inc., Publishers. (415) 433-1740; Fax (800) 605-2665.

For sales outside the United States, please contact your local Simon & Schuster International office.

Manufactured in the United States of America.

Library of Congress Cataloging-in-Publication Data

Markman, Howard, date.
 Fighting for your marriage: positive steps for preventing
divorce and preserving a lasting love/Howard Markman, Scott Stanley,
Susan L. Blumberg.
  p. cm.—(The Jossey-Bass social and behavioral science
series)
 Includes bibliographical references and index
 ISBN I-55542-700-6 (cloth)
 ISBN 0-7879-0280-2 (paperback)
 1. Marriage. 2. Interpersonal relations. 3. Interpersonal
communication. I. Stanley, Scott, date. II. Blumberg, Susan
L., date. III Title. IV. Series
HQ734. M347 1994   94-9277
306.81—dc20

HB Printing 10 9 8 7 6 5 4 3 2   FIRST EDITION
PB Printing 10 9 8 7 6 5 4 3 2 I

To my family—Fran, Mathew, and Leah,
for the joy of being together, their support, and understanding,
and the gentle reminders that there is life
away from the computer and phone;
and to my parents,
Claire and Arnold Markman,
and my brother Barry,
for being there and caring

—HM

To Nancy,
for all your love and patience
as we walk this path together;
to Kyle and Luke,
for the laughter and the joy;
and to Mom and Dad,
for believing in me, always

—SS

To Savanna McCain and Chuck Lobitz,
who taught me what I could do;
and to Lewis,
whose love and endless support
make everything possible

—SLB

Contents

PART THREE: ENHANCEMENT

Foreword

NOTHING HAS THE POTENTIAL to make us more miserable or more ecstatic than marriage; yet we enter the institution without any training whatsoever. We are required to demonstrate some proficiency when obtaining a driver's license, but marriage licenses can be had for a signature.

Here is a manual, a user's guide, for one of life's great adventures. Markman, Stanley, and Blumberg offer us their experiences as scientists who study relationships. Their program is based on objective research about strategies that increase communication and intimacy.

Fighting for Your Marriage marks a turning point in relationship self-help books. It is essential reading for couples who care.

Dean S. Edell, M.D.
Medical journalist

Acknowledgments

T HE PREP APPROACH, as described in this book, is built on foundations provided by many other contributors to the fields of behavioral marital therapy, psychoeducational approaches to marriage and family relationships, and personal relationships in general. In particular, we want to acknowledge the influence of Clifford Notarius (coauthor with Howard Markman of *We Can Work It Out: Making Sense of Marital Conflict*),whose work at Catholic University of America has profoundly influenced material in the book and whose friendship has been an invaluable support. In addition, there are numerous researchers and theorists in the field whose work has been extremely important to us, including Don Baucom, Steven Beach, Andy Christensen, Steven Duck, Norm Epstein, Frank Fincham, Frank Floyd, John Gottman, Bernard Guerney, Kurt Hahlweg, Kim Halford, Amy Holtzworth-Munroe, Jill Hooley, Ted Huston, Ted Jacob, Neil Jacobson, Danielle Julian, Gayla Margolin, Sherrod Miller, Pat Noller, Dan O'Leary, Gerald Patterson, Cas Schaap, and Robert Weiss.

We also have had the good fortune to connect over time with many people who have supported us in meaningful ways as our work has developed, including William Coffin and his colleagues in the U.S. Navy, and Kathryn Barnard, Michael Cassidy, Lynn Davis, Robert

Emde, Scott Halford, Swanee Hunt, Richard Hunt, and Philip Yun. All deserve our thanks for their encouragement in expanding our ability to meet the needs of couples.

Over the years, we have been assisted by a set of bright and energetic research assistants, consultants, and colleagues as we have developed and evaluated the PREP approach. We express our strongly felt appreciation to Mari Clements, Wayne Duncan, Joyce Emde, Amy Galloway, Paul Howes, Lisa LaViolette Hoyer, Donna Jackson, Karen Jamieson-Darr, Holly Johnson, Matthew Johnson, Shelle Kraft, Douglas Leber, Hal Lewis, Kristin Lindahl, Savanna McCain, Nancy Montgomery, Naomi Rather, Mari Jo Renick, Dawn Richards, Christopher Saiz, Daniel Trathen, Brigit VanWidenfelt, and Wendy Wainright.

Most of the research reported in this book has been funded by the University of Denver, the National Institute of Mental Health, and the National Science Foundation. We are grateful for the support from these institutions, which has enabled us to develop the research basis for the program presented in *Fighting for Your Marriage*. In particular, we would like to single out Daniel Ritchie, chancellor of the University of Denver, for taking a special interest in our work and being a major source of emotional support and encouragement. The emphasis in our book on preventing problems before they develop—in addition to treating them—is one shared by the National Institute of Mental Health, and we express our gratitude for its backing of our research program on the possibilities of preventing divorce and marital distress.

The cartoons in the book are the work of our friend and collaborator, Ragnar Storaasli. Not only has Ragnar conducted many of the research analyses that underlie the findings in the book, but he has a wonderful knack for humorously capturing some of the key issues that affect relationships. We thank him for his efforts in all of these arenas. We also would like to thank Sandra Rush for her input on early drafts of the manuscript.

Our editor at Jossey-Bass, Alan Rinzler, has been supportive throughout—and critical when necessary. All told, he's been a major contributor to the quality of the book. He has pushed us in our goal to make *Fighting for Your Marriage* as effective as possible for couples. We thank Alan and the staff at Jossey-Bass for their support and expertise.

Finally, we want to express our deep sense of appreciation to the couples and families in our research projects who have shared their lives with us. These people have opened their hearts and their relationships to our interviewers and video cameras. They have shared their struggles and successes, and we hope that the knowledge presented here represents some small compensation to these couples, without whom the book could never have been written.

We would also like to acknowledge the role that our clients and seminar participants have played in shaping the ideas and case histories we present. By using composites and altering details, we have disguised the identities of the couples in the vignettes. Nevertheless, the stories told by many couples over the years are so strikingly similar that the themes in the case histories we include will speak to a variety of people. We can all learn from each other.

The book you are about to read rests on this foundation of support and assistance. We share a desire that you will use the knowledge we've gained over the years through our research to create the type of relationship you want.

Introduction

GOOD MARRIAGES TAKE WORK. Contrary to popular belief, it's not how much you love each other that can best predict the future of your relationship, but how conflicts and disagreements are handled. Unfortunately, conflict is inevitable—it can't be avoided. So if you want to have a good marriage, you'd better learn to fight right.

This book will teach you how to fight *for* your marriage. It's designed to provide you with the specific tools that twenty years of research have shown can make a real difference in your current and future happiness. At the same time, we'll help you to maintain and enhance intimacy, fun, commitment, friendship, and sensuality in your marriage.

THE RISKS OF MARRIAGE

Most people want a satisfying marriage that lasts a lifetime. Yet, couples marrying today have a 50 percent chance of getting divorced. In fact, the divorce rate increased in 1992 for the first time in five years. Many couples who don't divorce wind up staying together but remain unhappy for years. *We believe that marriage is the most risky undertaking routinely taken on by the greatest number of people in our society.* What starts out as a

1

relationship of great joy and promise can become the most frustrating and painful endeavor in a person's lifetime.

The damaging effects of destructive marital conflict and divorce on spouses and children are incalculable. These effects include economic, medical, and mental health problems. For example, marital problems are one of the top causes of depression, and depression is the most common mental health problem in our society. Marital distress and divorce cause distracted and poorly motivated workers, which leads to great losses in productivity in our society. Divorce is also a leading cause of poverty in America, dividing families and leaving many children in poor, single-parent homes. More recently, the powerful effects of marital distress on physical health also have been documented. Marital distress can lead to high blood pressure, the decline of our immune system, and gastrointestinal, respiratory, and urinary problems. And these are only some of the problems it causes. A recent National Institute of Mental Health committee concluded that marital problems are a major risk factor for myriad mental and medical health problems.

WHY THIS BOOK?

We have written this book to help you create and sustain a satisfying marriage. Our approach is based on the Prevention and Relationship Enhancement Program (PREP™) and fifteen years of research at the University of Denver. PREP is a program we developed to help couples beat the odds. In PREP workshops, couples are taught the skills and attitudes associated with good relationships through specific steps and exercises. Because of its roots in solid research and its straightforward approach, PREP has received a great deal of attention from couples across the country, professionals in the field of marital counseling, and the media.

PREP is one of the most extensively researched programs for couples ever developed. More studies are being planned all the time by us and others who are interested in the PREP approach. This research has shed light not only on the greatest risk factors for marital failure but also on the most promising avenues to help you lower the risks in your relationship. The bad news is that marriage in our culture is a

risky business, and the costs of marital failure are staggering. The good news is that in this book we present powerful, proven strategies for you to beat the odds, strategies based on research and our PREP workshops for couples.

We have trained mental health professionals from around the world and leaders of institutions such as the U.S. Navy Family Service Centers, the Catholic church, and various Protestant churches. While it would be nice to be able to work with you personally, we recognize that most of you will not have the opportunity to attend one of our workshops, or one led by those we have trained. However, this book presents PREP as we present it in our workshops. We've written it in the same form as the manual couples receive in our workshops, but also as a stand-alone book designed to present the material in an effective manner. One of our primary goals is to give solid information to as many couples as possible about what they can do to prevent marital distress and divorce.

The techniques and strategies in this book are based on the most up-to-date research in the field of marriage. We base our suggestions on solid research rather than "pop-psych" speculation. This means that we don't just assume what may help couples but use research and testing to see what really works. Although we'll discuss the problems and patterns that can destroy relationships, this book is less about what goes wrong and more about the specific things you can do to achieve and maintain a successful, satisfying relationship.

WHAT OUR RESEARCH REVEALS

Our program incorporates principles based on couples' research done in the United States and around the world, and we have benefited from the findings of many colleagues whose research has preceded, accompanied, and followed ours. For example, a great deal of evidence shows major differences in the ability of distressed couples and happier couples to communicate well and handle conflict. This yields very specific ideas about teaching couples to handle issues more constructively.

This book is not just about communication and conflict, however. PREP also focuses on topics such as commitment and dedication, forgiveness, friendship, and fun. Wherever possible, we try to tell you about interesting and well-founded research in the field that can help you strengthen your relationship. You may be thinking, "Who cares about research?" We think you'll appreciate how compelling good research can be when it provides useful insights about your relationship.

The most important research on the PREP approach has been conducted at the University of Denver. Our research has been supported by National Institute of Mental Health, National Institute of Health, and National Science Foundation grants and has resulted in over fifty scientific and professional publications. A careful analysis of years of research—comparing couples who are having significant problems to couples who are happy together—resulted in PREP and, now, in this book.

In one of our key studies, we've followed a sample of 150 couples for thirteen years, both before they got married and after. These couples have come into our lab yearly and have given us a massive amount of information about satisfaction, adjustment, the intensity of their problems, commitment, demographic information, sexual satisfaction, violence and abuse, family development, and sensual and sexual enhancement, among other issues. We've also asked couples to talk with each other about such issues, with their conversations recorded on videotape. These videotaped conversations are subjected to many hours of analysis to assess different communication styles. Using the data, we can track the factors that best predict future marital success and failure.

·In our research, using only data from before couples married, we have been able to predict with 82 to 93 percent accuracy which of them will go on to be divorced and which will stay happy. Other studies in this field have also found that it's possible to predict which relationships are most likely to fail in the future. While this kind of finding can be intimidating to some couples, we see such studies as very helpful. Knowing more about how marriages fall apart over time gives us a much clearer idea of where couples should focus their attention. This kind of research has not quite reached the point where a couple can take a simple paper-and-pencil test for marital success, but these studies do shed a great deal of light on which factors place couples at the greatest risk for failure.

HOW ARE THINGS GOING FOR YOU?

Consider the following quiz, developed in our research project. While this is not an actual quiz we give to couples, these statements focus on the best predictors of marital distress and divorce. Everyone may occasionally answer true to some of these statements, but a persistent pattern of true answers over time can be a warning signal that a relationship needs help. Answer true or false to the following:

1. Little arguments escalate into ugly fights with accusations, criticisms, name calling, or bringing up past hurts.

2. My partner criticizes or belittles my opinions, feelings, or desires.

3. My partner seems to view my words or actions more negatively than I mean them to be.

4. I do not feel valued by my partner.

5. I don't feel it is "safe" to share my true feelings, thoughts, and desires in our relationship.

6. I think seriously about what it would be like to date or marry someone else.

7. I feel lonely in this relationship.

8. When we argue, one of us withdraws—that is, doesn't want to talk about it anymore—or leaves the scene.

As you read this book, you will understand not only why these statements are important, but what you as a couple can do about building and maintaining the healthy patterns associated with good relationships. Remember: it's not how much you love one another, how good your sex life is, or what problems you have with money that best predicts the future quality of your marriage. As noted at the outset, the best predictor of marital success is the way you handle conflicts and disagreements. The key is for you to develop constructive tactics and ground rules for handling the conflicts and disagreements that are inevitable in any significant relationship.

Can this book really help? Absolutely. In 1980, a long-term study of the effects of the PREP program began at the University of Denver. We wanted to see if premarital couples could be taught skills and strategies that would prevent significant relationship distress from developing in the first place. Results have shown that couples receiving PREP—compared to those who did not receive the program—have happier marriages years later with significantly reduced chances of a breakdown in the relationship or divorce. Up to eight years after com-

pleting the program, PREP couples are still communicating significantly better than the other couples. PREP couples also report significantly fewer instances of physical aggression in the years following training.

In the newest study on PREP, Susan Blumberg recently completed the first phase of a major project contrasting PREP with a modified version of Engaged Encounter for engaged and newly married couples. Engaged Encounter is a popular program for couples that doesn't emphasize specific skills to the degree that PREP does.

Upon completion of the programs, the couples who participated in PREP were able to communicate more effectively than those who participated in Engaged Encounter. PREP couples also maintained their high levels of satisfaction to a greater degree. This study highlights not only the importance of raising key issues for couples but also the need to provide the skills for dealing with the issues most effectively. That's what we'll try to do here.

Although you may not be taking a PREP workshop, you'll find all the key information and techniques presented here.

WHO IS THIS BOOK FOR?

The time-tested techniques of this book can be used by any couple—from the newly engaged to long-time partners—who want to solve problems or prevent them from happening. This book is for anyone interested in marriage, whether you're newlyweds, married twenty years, or trying marriage for a second or third time. Some of you may be having significant problems at this time in your marriage. Others may have a happy relationship now, but may be interested in preventing the kinds of problems encountered by all too many couples in our culture.

PREP was originally devised as a program to help premarital couples prevent serious relationship problems from developing in the first place, but in working with couples in the program, we've found that the techniques are also effective for couples in distressed relationships. Whether or not you're having serious problems at this point, the information and specific techniques in the book will be both useful and beneficial for your relationship.

HOW TO GET THE MOST
OUT OF THIS BOOK

This book starts with the basics, presented in a step-by-step manner, and builds to integrate a variety of good information for making marriage all that it can be. We believe that learning how to have a good relationship is largely a skill, like any other skill, that you can learn together as a couple. To help you do this, we provide specific instructions for exercises that can be practiced at home. Hence, this is a hands-on, "just do it" kind of book.

Ideally, a couple should work through this book together. This could mean reading each chapter together or individually, then meeting together to discuss it or practice the skills being taught. However, one person can follow our principles and start a chain reaction that can be beneficial to both partners.

Often, one partner may buy our book and hope to get the other interested. If this is your situation, we have a suggestion or two. First, be enthusiastic about your desire to work through the book together. Make the point that this is something you want to do for "us." Reluctant spouses are less likely to respond to pressure. Second, suggest that your partner leaf through the book and get a feel for it. We believe that many people are resistant to reading self-help books out of a concern that a lot of the material will be more of the latest hype from the "guru-of-the-month" club. If this is a concern, you'll find this book refreshing in the no-nonsense, commonsense, concrete ideas that are presented. A lot of self-help books help people understand themselves or their partner but do little to help them actually change patterns. All the insight and good intentions in the world won't help if your relationship doesn't change. In our workshops, we give homework. In this book, you should do the exercises at the end of each charpter. There's no more effective way to get the most out of the ideas we present.

OVERVIEW OF THE BOOK

Like our PREP workshops, the material presented in this book is organized in three parts, each with a number of chapters. These parts represent the following steps:

1. Practicing communication and conflict management

2. Adopting the attitudes and actions of strong relationships

3. Establishing and enhancing relationships for the long term

In Part One, we'll introduce a number of very effective skills for handling conflict and disagreements. These skills will suggest behaviors that may be very different from the way you normally might do things, but that's the point. Like any skill, these new suggestions will become easier with practice. With each skill or principle, we'll also tell you about the underlying theory and research so that you understand why it works. You'll find that these techniques are not really difficult to understand, but they'll take work for you to master as a couple. You'll be asked to practice a number of new skills and exercises together. We believe that it will be worth your effort to make what you learn here a part of your relationship.

In Part Two, we'll concentrate on the ways in which successful couples think about and view their relationships. Whereas Part One focuses a lot on behavior, this part focuses more on thinking patterns and motivation. It puts the emphasis on your individual responsibility to think and act in ways that promote the health of your relationship. You'll be asked to think about expectations, commitment, and forgiveness. As in the rest of the book, our goal is to help you consider these important dimensions in a useful, no-nonsense manner that we believe can strongly affect your relationship for the good.

Part Three will help you explore a number of important dimensions that relate to the reasons why people get married in the first place: friendship, fun, physical intimacy, and purpose in life. These chapters have two key goals: (1) to help you enhance such important dimensions and (2) to help you learn powerful strategies to protect these delightful aspects of your relationship from the less positive things that happen in life and love, such as stress and conflict.

We hope you'll find great benefit in the program presented in this book. Now let's begin with Chapter One, where you'll learn more about fascinating research on how couples handle conflict and how we think you can best "fight for your marriage."

HANDLING CONFLICT

1

Four Key Patterns That Can Harm a Relationship

ONE OF THE MOST POWERFUL THINGS you can do to protect your marriage is to learn constructive ways to handle conflict, differences, and disagreements. Researchers from two major research labs in the United States found that the likelihood of divorce can be predicted by studying how couples handle conflict. In this chapter, we will focus on four specific patterns of conflictual interactions that often lead to marital problems:

1. Escalation

2. Invalidation

3. Withdrawal and avoidance

4. Negative interpretations

Once you understand these patterns, you can learn to prevent them from taking over your relationship. As we describe them, we'll also provide some ideas for counteracting them. In later chapters, we will focus in much greater depth on how you can protect your relationship from such negative patterns.

If you're currently happy together, you can use the PREP approach to prevent these patterns from developing in the first place. If you're

experiencing relationship problems, we want to motivate you to fight more constructively, so that issues actually get resolved. Let's start by looking at the four predictive patterns.

ESCALATION: WHAT GOES AROUND COMES AROUND

Escalation occurs when partners negatively respond back and forth to each other, continually upping the ante so that conditions get worse and worse. Often, negative comments spiral into increasing anger and frustration. Couples who are happy now and likely to stay that way are less prone to escalation; if their arguments start to escalate, they're able to stop the negative process before it erupts into a full-blown, nasty fight. The escalation process is clearly seen in the interactions of a couple who participated in our PREP research and programs.

Ted, a thirty-four-year-old construction worker, and Wendy, thirty-two, who runs a catering business out of their home, were married for eight years when we first saw them. As with many couples, their fights started over small issues:

TED: [*sarcastically*] You'd think you could put the cap back on the toothpaste.

WENDY: [*equally sarcastically*] Oh, like you never forget to put it back.

TED: As a matter of fact, I always put it back.

WENDY: Oh, I forgot just how compulsive you are. You're right, of course!

TED: I don't even know why I stay with you. You are so negative.

WENDY: Maybe you shouldn't stay. No one is barring the door.

One of the most damaging things about arguments that are escalating out of control is that partners tend to say things that threaten the very lifeblood of their marriage. As frustration and hostility mount, partners often try to hurt each other by hurling verbal (and sometimes physical) weapons. You can see this pattern with Ted and Wendy, where the stakes quickly rose to include threats of ending the relationship. Once very negative, verbally abusive comments are made, they're hard to take back. The damage can be undone, but it takes a lot of work. Saying "I was just kidding when I said you should move out" may not cut it, because it doesn't address the hurt feelings.

Partners can say the nastiest things during escalating arguments, but such remarks often don't reflect what they actually feel about the other. You may believe that people reveal their "true feelings" in the midst of fierce fights, but we don't think that this is usually the case. Instead, they mostly try to hurt the other person and to defend themselves. One of the biggest problems with this scenario is that the comments that hurt the other person the most tend to be confidences that were shared at earlier, intimate moments. Hence, in the heat of escalation, the weapons chosen are often based on intimate knowledge of the partner.

In Wendy and Ted's argument, for example, Wendy mentioned Ted's being compulsive because she really wanted to hit him below the belt. At a more tender moment between them, he once shared his concerns about being so driven and said that he'd learned this style to please his father when he was growing up. While you may think that Wendy was provoked in this argument, nevertheless, the escalation quickly led to her use of intimate knowledge to gain the upper hand. Such tactics are tantamount to marital terrorism and cause great pain and damage in the relationship. When escalation includes the use of intimate knowledge as a weapon, the threat to the future likelihood of tender moments is great. Who's going to share deep feelings if the information may be used later when conflict is out of control in the relationship?

You may be thinking, "We don't fight like cats and dogs—how does this apply to us?" In fact, escalation can be very subtle. Voices don't have to be raised for you to get into the cycle of returning negative for negative. Yet research shows that even subtle patterns of escalation can lead to divorce in years to come. Consider the following conversation between Max and Donna, newlyweds in their twenties, who are just starting out in an apartment in Denver:

MAX: Did you get the rent paid on time?

DONNA: That was going to be your job.

MAX: You were supposed to do it.

DONNA: No, you were.

MAX: Did it get done?

DONNA: No. And, I'm not going to, either.

MAX: [muttering] Great. Just great.

If you could actually listen to this argument, you would not hear raised voices. In fact, if you heard this conversation through a wall, without being able to tell what was being said, the tone could sound quite casual. However, you can see the negative-to-negative character of this conversation. That is escalation as we define it in our research.

Even escalation at this low level is destructive over time. Being newlyweds, Donna and Max are very happy with their marriage. Imagine, however, years of small arguments like this one taking a toll on their marriage, eroding the positive things that they now share.

The more arguments escalate, the more at risk couples are for future problems. It's very important for the future health of your relationship to learn to counteract whatever tendency you have for your arguments to escalate. If they don't escalate very much, great! Your goal is to learn to keep things that way. If they do escalate a fair amount, your goal is to recognize this problem and to stop it.

SHORT-CIRCUITING ESCALATION

All couples have arguments that escalate from time to time, but some couples steer out of the pattern more quickly, and much more positively. Compare Ted and Wendy's argument, earlier, with Maria and Hector's. Maria, a forty-five-year-old sales clerk for a jewelry store, and Hector, a forty-nine-year-old attorney who works for the Justice Department, have been married twenty-three years. They came to one of our workshops in Vail, Colorado, referred by a local marital therapist who felt they could benefit from our weekend communication workshop. Like Ted and Wendy, they also tended to argue about everyday events, as in this example:

MARIA: [annoyed] You left the butter out again.

HECTOR: [irritated] Why are little things so important to you? Just put it back.

MARIA: [softening her tone] Things like that are important to me. Is that so bad?

HECTOR: [calmer] I guess not. Sorry I was snotty.

Notice the difference. Like Wendy and Ted's argument, Hector and Maria's argument showed escalation, but they quickly steered out of it. When escalation sequences are short-circuited, it's usually because one partner backs off and says something to de-escalate the argument, thus breaking the negative cycle.

Maria and Hector each did something constructive to end the escalation. For her part, Maria softened her tone rather than getting defensive. For his part, Hector made the decision to back off and acknowledge Maria's point of view. Softening your tone and acknowledging your partner's point of view are powerful tools you can use to defuse tension and end escalation. As we go on, we'll be teaching you powerful and specific ways to do just this.

INVALIDATION: PAINFUL PUT-DOWNS

Invalidation is a pattern in which one partner subtly or directly puts down the thoughts, feelings, or character of the other. Sometimes such comments, intentionally or unintentionally, lower the self-esteem of the targeted person. Invalidation can take many forms. Let's listen in on two other arguments between Ted and Wendy and between Maria and Hector.

WENDY: [*very angrily*] You missed your doctor's appointment again! You're so irresponsible. I could see you dying and leaving me, just like your father.

TED: [*bruised*] Thanks a lot. You know I'm nothing like my father.

WENDY: He was a creep and so are you.

TED: [*dripping with sarcasm*] I'm sorry. I forgot my good fortune to be married to such a paragon of responsibility. You can't even keep your purse organized.

WENDY: At least I am not so obsessive about stupid little things.

TED: You're so arrogant.

•   •   •

MARIA: [*with a tear*] You know, I'm really frustrated by the hatchet job Bob did on my evaluation at work.

HECTOR: I don't think he was all that critical. I'd be happy to have an evaluation as positive as that from Fred.

MARIA: [*with a sigh and turning away*] You don't get it. It upset me.

HECTOR: Yeah, I see that, but I still think you're overreacting.

While both these examples show invalidation, the first example is much more caustic than the second. With Wendy and Ted, you can feel the belligerence and contempt seeping through. The argument has settled into an attack on character. And although Hector and Maria do not show the same nastiness expressed by Ted and Wendy, Hector is subtly putting down Maria for the way she's feeling. He may even think that he's being constructive or trying to cheer her up by saying, in effect, "It's not so bad." Nevertheless, this kind of communication is also invalidating. Maria feels more hurt now because Hector has said, in effect, that her feelings of sadness and frustration are inappropriate.

Another subtle form of invalidation occurs when you are expecting praise for some positive action that is ignored by your partner, while some minor problem is highlighted. For example, suppose that you worked hard all afternoon to reorganize and clean up the kitchen, and your spouse came home and complained because you didn't get to the store. You're going to feel pretty invalidated. Going out of your way to do something positive, then being ignored or criticized for your efforts, can be very painful and frustrating.

Invalidation hurts. It leads naturally to covering up who you are and what you think, because it becomes just too risky to do otherwise. People naturally cover up their innermost feelings when they believe that they will be "put down." Our research shows that invalidation is one of the very best predictors of future problems and divorce. Interestingly, the amount of validation in a relationship doesn't say as much about its health as the amount of invalidation does. Invalidation is a highly toxic poison to the well-being of your relationship.

PREVENTING INVALIDATION

In either argument above, both couples would have done better if each partner had shown respect for and acknowledged the other's viewpoint. Note the difference in how these conversations could have gone:

WENDY: [*very angry*] I'm very angry that you missed the doctor's appointment again. I worry about you being around for me in the future.

TED: [*bruised*] It really upset you, didn't it?

WENDY: You bet. I want to know that you're going to be there for me, and when you miss an appointment that I'm anxious about, I worry about us.

TED: I understand why it would make you worried when I don't take care of myself.

.   .   .

MARIA: [*with a tear*] You know, I'm really frustrated by the hatchet job Bob did on my evaluation at work.

HECTOR: That must really tick you off.

MARIA: Yeah, it does. And, I also get worried about whether I'll be able to keep this job. What would we do?

HECTOR: I didn't know you were so worried about losing your job. Tell me more about how you are feeling.

In these examples, we have replayed the issues but with very different outcomes for both couples. Now we see ownership of feelings, respect for each other's character, and an emphasis on validation. By *validation*, we mean that the one raising the concern is respected and heard. You don't have to agree with your partner to validate his or her feelings. Validation is a powerful tool that you can use both to build intimacy and to reduce anger and resentment. But it takes discipline, especially when you're really frustrated or angry. In later chapters we'll teach you some very effective ways to enhance validation.

WITHDRAWAL AND AVOIDANCE: HIDE AND SEEK

Withdrawal and *avoidance* are different manifestations of a pattern in which one partner shows an unwillingness to get into or stay with important discussions. *Withdrawal* can be as obvious as getting up and leaving the room or as subtle as "turning off" or "shutting down" during an argument. The withdrawer may tend to get quiet during an argument or may quickly agree to some suggestion just to end the conversation, with no real intention of following through.

Avoidance reflects the same reluctance to participate in certain discussions, with more emphasis on preventing the conversation from happening in the first place. A person prone to avoidance would prefer it if the difficult topic never came up, and if it did, might manifest the signs of withdrawal described above.

Let's look at this pattern as it was played out in a discussion between Paula, a twenty-eight-year-old realtor, and Jeff, a thirty-two-year-old loan officer. Married for three years, they have a two-year-old baby girl, Tanya, whom they both adore. They were concerned that the tension in their relationship was starting to affect their daughter:

PAULA: When are we going to talk about how you're handling your anger.

JEFF: Can't this wait? I have to get these taxes done.

PAULA: I've brought this up at least five times already. No, it can't wait!

JEFF: [*tensing*] What's to talk about, anyway? It's none of your business.

PAULA: [*frustrated and looking right at Jeff*] Tanya is my business. I'm afraid that you may lose your temper and hurt her, and you won't do a darn thing to learn to deal better with your anger.

JEFF: [*turning away and looking out the window*] I love Tanya. There's no problem here. [*leaving the room as he talks*]

PAULA: [*very angry now, following Jeff into the next room*] You have to get some help. You can't just stick your head in the sand.

JEFF: I'm not going to discuss anything with you when you are like this.

PAULA: Like what? It doesn't matter if I'm calm or frustrated—you won't talk to me about anything important. Tanya is having problems and you have to face that.

JEFF: [*quiet, tense, fidgeting*]

PAULA: Well?

JEFF: [*going to the closet and grabbing sweater*] I'm going out to have a drink and get some peace and quiet.

PAULA: [*voice raised, angry*] Talk to me, now. I'm tired of you leaving when we're talking about something important.

JEFF: [*looking away from Paula and walking toward the door*] I'm not talking, you are. Actually, you're yelling. See you later.

Many couples do this kind of dance when it comes to dealing with difficult issues. One partner *pursues* dealing with issues (Paula) and one *avoids* or *withdraws* from dealing with issues (Jeff). This common scenario is very destructive to the relationship. As with the other patterns presented, it doesn't have to be this dramatic to predict problems to come. It's one of the most powerful predictors of unhappiness and divorce.

The *pursuer* is the one in the relationship who most often brings issues up for discussion or calls attention to the need to make a decision about something. The *withdrawer* is the person who tends to avoid these discussions or pull away during them. Studies show that men tend to take the withdrawing role more frequently with women tending to pursue. However, in many relationships this pattern is reversed. It is also common for partners to switch these roles, depending on the topic. For example, one of you may handle the budget and be more likely to pursue in discussions about money-related problems. Your partner may handle issues about the children's schooling more often, and so may be more likely to pursue in talking about these concerns. Nevertheless, relative to females, males are more likely to take the withdrawing role across a range of issues.

AVOIDING WITHDRAWAL

Research clearly shows that male withdrawal and avoidance are clear predictors of problems now and in the future. In the next chapter, we'll tell you why men are more likely to take the role of withdrawer and what withdrawal is all about. If you're seeing this pattern in your relationship, keep in mind that it will likely get worse if you allow it to continue. That's because as pursuers push more, withdrawers withdraw more, and as withdrawers pull back, pursuers push harder. Furthermore, when issues are important, it should be obvious that trying to avoid dealing with them will only lead to damaging consequences. You can't stick your head in the sand and pretend that important or bothersome problems are not really there.

In the case of withdrawal and avoidance, the first and best step you can take right now is to realize that you are not independent of each another. Your actions cause reactions, and vice versa. For this reason, you will have much greater success if you work together to change or prevent the kinds of negative patterns discussed here. Withdrawers are not likely to reduce avoidance unless pursuers pursue less or more constructively. Pursuers will find it hard to cut back on pursuing unless withdrawers deal more directly with the issues at hand.

Here's one way that Jeff and Paula were able to deal with their dilemma after taking one of our workshops. Before things got out of hand the next time, Jeff decided to take a more constructive approach:

JEFF: Okay. I can see you're really frustrated about this, and we need to talk it out.

PAULA: Right!

JEFF: We do need to talk about it, but I'm really not up to it right now. How about we agree that we'll sit down, face to face, and talk about Tanya tonight after she falls asleep.

PAULA: Will you really do that?

JEFF: Yes, if you'll give me some space on this until then.

PAULA: Okay. I'll go for that. Tonight, as soon as Tanya falls asleep, we talk.

JEFF: You can count on it.

This is a much more constructive pattern. They agreed to a plan that gives each something they want. Jeff got some time to calm down and think about how he sees the issues concerning Tanya. Paula got the talk she was seeking, but at a time when Jeff could participate constructively. Paula had to back off from pursuing for the moment and Jeff agreed to quit avoiding the conversation. This plan worked well for them because they both followed through and did what they agreed to do, working as a team to overcome the negative pattern.

We'll get much more specific about ways to combat these patterns in the next few chapters. For now, try to agree that if you're having trouble with pursuit and/or withdrawal, you will work together to change the pattern.

PHYSICAL VIOLENCE AND HEALTHY WITHDRAWAL

At times, withdrawal is better than the alternative, particularly if the conflict is likely to escalate to the point of physical aggression. Physical violence is a pervasive problem in our culture. Approximately 25 percent of couples report incidents of pushing, shoving, or hitting within the previous year. Both men and women in these relationships resort to physical tactics from time to time, although it is potentially more dangerous for the husband to become violent and control his wife fear and threats. For many couples, physical aggression is the outgrowth of poor handling of escalation and withdrawal.

For some couples, there is a much more dangerous pattern, in which the husband batters the wife and his intention is to wear down, subjugate, and dominate his partner. If this sounds like your situation, please get help. In an emergency, you can call the police. Short of that, help can be found by calling organizations that help women find safety and obtain advice for dealing with domestic violence. Most communities have shelters or advocacy groups; phone numbers for such resources can be obtained by calling your local police or mental health agency. This book is designed, in part, to help couples handle conflict, but conflict at this physically and emotionally dangerous level requires professional help and legal intervention.

If you have a pattern of occasional physical aggression consisting of pushing, shoving, or slapping, the PREP approach can teach you how to cut the escalation cycles that lead up to such actions and how to use a constructive form of mutual, agreed upon withdrawal—Time Out. As we go on, we'll teach you techniques for handling escalation and withdrawal in the most productive manner. Nevertheless, if you are worried about physical danger, please seek additional help.

NEGATIVE INTERPRETATIONS: WHEN PERCEPTION IS WORSE THAN REALITY

Negative interpretations occur when one partner consistently believes that the motives of the other are more negative than is really the case. This can be a very destructive pattern in a relationship, and it will make any conflict or disagreement harder to deal with constructively.

You can see the effects of negative interpretations in the discussions of two of our research couples, but to different degrees. Margot and David have been married twelve years and they are generally happy with their relationship. Yet their discussions have been plagued at times by a specific negative interpretation. Every December they've had trouble deciding whether to travel to Margot's parents' home for the holidays. Margot believes that David dislikes her parents, but in fact, he is quite fond of them in his own way. She has this mistaken belief because of a few misunderstandings early in the marriage that

David has long since forgotten. Here's how a typical discussion around their issue of holiday travel plans goes:

MARGOT: We should start looking into plane tickets to go visit my parents this holiday season.

DAVID: [thinking about their budget problem] I was wondering if we can really afford it this year.

MARGOT: [in anger] My parents are very important to me, even if you don't like them. I'm going to go.

DAVID: I'd like to go, really I would. I just don't see how we can afford a thousand dollars in plane tickets and pay the bill for Joey's orthodontist, too.

MARGOT: You can't be honest and admit you just don't want to go, can you? Just admit it. You don't like my parents.

DAVID: There's nothing to admit. I enjoy visiting your parents. I'm thinking about money here, not your parents.

MARGOT: That's a convenient excuse. [storming out of the room]

Even though David really does like to visit Margot's parents, her negative interpretation has become too powerful and he cannot penetrate it. What can he say or do to make a difference as long as she believes so strongly that he dislikes them? If a negative interpretation is strong enough, nothing will change it. In this case, David wants to address the decision they must make from the standpoint of the budget, but Margot's interpretation overpowers their ability to communicate effectively and come to a decision that makes both of them happy. Fortunately for them, this problem is relatively isolated and not a consistent pattern in their marriage.

When relationships become more distressed, the negative interpretations create an environment of hopelessness and demoralization. Alfred and Eileen are a couple who were high school sweethearts, have been married eighteen years, and have three children, but they have been very unhappy in their marriage for more than seven years, in part due to the corrosive effect of strong, negative interpretations. While there are positive things in their marriage, almost nothing either of them does is recognized positively by the other, as seen by this recent conversation about parking their car:

ALFRED: You left the car out again.

EILEEN: Oh. I guess I forgot to put it in when I came back from Madge's.

ALFRED: [with a bit of a sneer] I guess you did. You know how much that irritates me.

EILEEN: [exasperated] Look, I forgot. Do you think I leave it out just to irritate you?

ALFRED: [coldly] Actually, that's exactly what I think. I've told you so many times that I want the car in the garage at night.

EILEEN: Yes, you have. But I don't leave it out just to tick you off. I just forget.

ALFRED: If you cared what I thought about things, you'd remember.

EILEEN: You know that I put the car in nine times out of ten.

ALFRED: More like half the time, and those are the times I leave the garage door up for you.

EILEEN: Have it your way. It doesn't matter what reality is. You'll see it your way.

This may sound like a minor argument, but it isn't. It represents a long-standing tendency for Alfred to interpret Eileen's behavior in the most negative light possible. For the sake of argument, assume that Eileen is absolutely correct when she says that she simply forgot to put the car in the garage and that this only happens about one in ten times. Alfred sees it differently, especially in his interpretation that she leaves the car out mostly to upset him.

A marriage would truly be in terrible shape if either partner routinely and intentionally did things just to frustrate the other person. Much more frequently, the actions of one partner are interpreted negatively and unfairly. This is a sign of a relationship heading for big trouble in the future. Negative interpretations are very destructive, in part because they're very hard to detect and counteract after they become cemented into the fabric of a relationship. This intractability has its roots in the way we form and maintain beliefs about others.

Both solid research and experience tell us that people tend to see what they expect to see in others and in situations. In fact, we have a very strong tendency toward "confirmation bias," which consists of looking for evidence that confirms what we already think is true about a person or situation. We can be wrong in our assumptions, but we all have formed beliefs and expectations about why those we know well do what they do.

For example, if you believe that your neighbor Bill can never say anything nice to you, then no matter what he actually may say, you will interpret his comments in light of your expectations. He could say, "Gee, you sure did a nice job on that project," and you might think to yourself, "He's only trying to manipulate me, what does he want now?" If Bill was sincere, your strong assumption will wipe out his good intent. No one is immune from looking for information to confirm her or his expectations about others.

In the example above, Alfred has the expectation: "Eileen doesn't care one bit about anything that's important to me." This assumption colors the good things that do happen. In distressed relationships, partners have a tendency to discount the positive things they see, attributing them to causes such as chance rather than to any positive characteristics of the partner. Because of Alfred's negative interpretations, he attributes the times Eileen does put the car in the garage to his own action of leaving the door open and not to her intention to put it there. She can't win this argument, and they won't be able to come to an acceptable resolution with his negative mind-set.

BATTLING NEGATIVE INTERPRETATIONS

We are not advocating some kind of unrealistic "positive thinking." You can't just sit around and wish that your partner would change truly negative behaviors, but you may need to consider that your partner's motives are more positive than you are willing to acknowledge.

The bottom line with negative interpretations is that positive behavior is viewed negatively, and negative behavior is seen as an extension of character flaws, even if the actual intention was positive. We can show you how to work as a couple to overcome negative patterns such as escalation and invalidation, but negative interpretations are something you have to confront within yourself. Only you can control how you interpret your partner's behavior.

First, you have to ask yourself if you might be being overly negative in your interpretation of your partner's actions. Second—and this is hard—you must push yourself to look for evidence that is contrary to the negative interpretation you usually take. For example, if you believe that your partner is uncaring and generally see most of his or her actions in that light, you need to look for evidence to the contrary. Does your partner do things for you that you like? Could this be because she or he is trying to keep the relationship strong? It's up to you to consider your interpretation of behavior that others may see as obviously positive.

Of course, negative interpretations can be accurate. But suppose you begin to suspect that you're being hard on your partner. A third constructive step you might take is to ask yourself if you might have any personal reasons for maintaining a pattern of negative interpretation with your spouse. If you're being unfair, there must be some reason. Perhaps you learned a certain style of thinking growing up. Perhaps you have some deeper need to see yourself as the partner who truly cares about the relationship. Perhaps you want to feel sorry for yourself and think of yourself as a kind of martyr. This type of self-reflection can be difficult, but it may be very productive if you can discover why you might persist in seeing things negatively.

In Alfred's case, he grew up in a home with judgmental, perfectionist parents. Negative interpretations come easily to him. It was not at all unusual for him to hear his father say, "If you cared at all about what's important to me, you'd have played better in that game." Like his father, Alfred developed a pattern of interpreting the motivations of others negatively unless they performed to meet his perfectionist standards. It doesn't matter how he came to think this way, only Alfred can really confront his internal bias against Eileen. The way he thinks is his responsibility, not hers. If he doesn't deal with this pattern—and Eileen doesn't deal with areas where she has similar problems—their marriage is certain to fail.

As you work through this book and are considering positive changes in your relationship, make sure you try to give your partner the benefit of the doubt in wanting to make things better. Don't allow inaccurate interpretations to sabotage the work you're trying to accomplish.

HOW POSITIVE FEELINGS ERODE IN MARRIAGE: THE LONG-TERM EFFECT OF NEGATIVE PATTERNS

Contrary to popular belief, positives in marriage do not slowly fade away for no reason in particular. We believe that the chief reason that marriages fail at alarmingly high rates is that conflict is handled poorly, as evidenced by such patterns as those described in this chapter. Over time, these patterns steadily erode all the good things in the relationship.

For example, when couples routinely resort to escalation when problems arise, they may come to the conclusion that it's just as easy not to talk at all. After all, talking leads to fighting, doesn't it? When partners become more concerned with getting their own way, invalidation becomes a weapon easily taken in hand. Over time, no issue seems safe.

Not only do many couples deal with issues poorly; they also may not set aside time to discuss them or come to any agreement about how they will be handled. Even in what starts out as the best of marriages, these factors can lead to growing distance and a lack of confidence in the relationship. Remember Jeff and Paula, earlier in this chapter? Though they are a genuinely caring couple, their inability to discuss tough issues—in this case, his anger—has caused a rift that will widen and perhaps destroy the marriage if nothing is done.

When negative patterns are not changed, real intimacy and a sense of connection die out, and couples settle for frustrated loneliness and isolation. If you want to keep your relationship strong or renew one that is lagging, you must learn to counteract destructive patterns such as those we have described. Fortunately, this can be done. You can prevent the erosion of happiness in your relationship for the years to come.

In this chapter we have described four patterns in handling conflict that predict future marital discord and divorce. We've made the point that certain ways of dealing with conflict are particularly destructive in a relationship. How can couples manage their tendencies toward destructive patterns and limit the damage they cause? We'll suggest a specific set of agreed-upon rules and strategies for handling conflict and difficult issues in your relationship.

Keep in mind that most couples show some of these patterns to some degree. It isn't important whether you currently show some of these patterns as long as you decide to do something to protect your relationship from them. The exercises that follow are a first step toward doing this. We hope that these questions will shed further light on how your relationship is affected by negative patterns. That in turn will help you replace such patterns with the positive behaviors and attitudes we will demonstrate later in the book.

Sometimes, the process of considering questions like the ones in the exercises and reflecting on where your relationship stands at this point causes anxiety or sadness. While it may not be pleasant to think about negative patterns, we believe that it will help you as you move ahead in this book and learn constructive ways to keep your marriage strong. In the next chapter, we deepen our discussion of how couples handle conflict, but show how the major difference between men and women in marriage is not how they handle intimacy, or how they make love—but how they make war.

Exercises

Please take a pad of paper and write down your answers to these questions independently from your partner. When you have finished, we suggest that you share your perceptions. However, if this raises conflict, put off further discussion of your answers until you have learned more about how to talk safely about the tough topics in the next few chapters. Before getting into specific questions about the four negative patterns, consider the following one about your overall impression of how you handle conflict together: When you have a disagreement or argument, what typically happens? In answering this question, think about the four key patterns described earlier.

ESCALATION

Escalation occurs when you say or do something negative, your partner responds with something negative, and off you go into a real battle. In this snowball effect, you become increasingly angry and hostile as the argument continues.

1. How often do you think you escalate arguments as a couple?

2. Do you get hostile with each other during escalation?

3. What or who usually brings an end to the fight?

4. Do one or the other of you sometimes threaten to end the relationship when angry?

5. How do each of you feel when you are escalating as a couple? Do you feel tense, anxious, scared, angry, or something else?

INVALIDATION

Invalidation occurs when you subtly or directly put down the thoughts, feelings, actions, or worth of your partner. This is different from simply disagreeing with your partner or not liking something he or she has done. Invalidation includes belittling or disregarding what is important to your partner, out of either insensitivity or outright contempt.

1. Do you often feel invalidated in your relationship? When and how does this happen?

2. What is the effect on you?

3. Do you often invalidate your partner? When and how does this happen?

4. What do you think the effect is on him or her? On the relationship? What are you trying to accomplish when you do this? Do you accomplish that goal?

WITHDRAWAL AND AVOIDANCE

Men and women often deal quite differently with conflict in relationships. Most often, men are more prone to withdraw from and women more prone to pursue discussion of issues in the relationship.

1. Is one of you more likely to be in the pursuer's role? Is one of you more likely to be in the withdrawer's role?

2. How does the withdrawer usually withdraw? How does the pursuer usually pursue? What happens then?

3. When are you most likely to fall into this pattern as a couple? Are there particular issues or situations that bring out this pattern?

4. How are you affected by this pattern?

5. For some couples, either or both partners tend to pursue or both tend to withdraw at the same time. Is that true for your relationship? Why do you think this happens?

NEGATIVE INTERPRETATIONS

Negative interpretations occur when you interpret the behavior of your spouse's much more negatively than they intended. It is critical that you open yourself to the possibility that your view of your partner could be unfair in some areas. These questions will help you reflect on this.

1. Can you think of some areas where you consistently see your partner's behavior as negative? What are the advantages to you in making these interpretations?

2. Reflect on this awhile. Do you really think that your negative view of your partner's behavior is justified?

3. Are there some areas where you have a negative interpretation, but where you are open to considering that you may be missing evidence to the contrary?

4. List two issues where you're willing to push yourself to look for the possibility that your partner has more positive motivations than you have been thinking he has. Next, look for any evidence that is contrary to your interpretation.

2

The Differences Between
Men and Women in Conflict

IN THE LAST CHAPTER, we discussed the importance of how couples handle conflict in predicting the success of their relationship and highlighted male withdrawal as one of the major danger signs for couples. In this chapter, we take a closer look at male withdrawal and focus on important differences in how men and women deal with conflict. In doing so, we also look at how men and women differ in their approaches to intimacy. We think many of the characteristic differences between women and men are not the ones people commonly think of. Through a better understanding of these differences, we hope to change the battle of the sexes into a team sport.

WHAT DO WOMEN
AND MEN WANT OUT
OF MARRIAGE?

Sometimes you can tell what people want by looking at what they complain about. Women often voice concerns about withdrawn, avoidant husbands who won't open up or talk about their views or feelings. In such cases, women usually feel shut out and they begin to feel that their husbands don't care about the relationship. In fact, this is the primary complaint we hear from women who come in for marital counseling. For many women, a lack of talking equals a lack of caring. It's very important to women for their husbands to communicate often and openly.

On the other hand, men often complain that their wives get upset too much, griping about this or that and picking fights. Men may feel hassled and want peace—often at any price. In one way or another, this is what we most commonly hear men asking for when they come in for marital counseling. It seems very important to them to have harmony and calm in their relationships with their wives.

That's the way it is for Mel and Sandy, a couple who had been married ten years when we saw them. Mel was the manager of a restaurant and Sandy was a schoolteacher who was taking a few years off to be at home with their children while they were young. As with many couples, money was tight. Mel worked long hours to make ends meet. Sandy was torn between her desire to be home with the kids and her wish to be back teaching, bringing in some income. Sandy deeply desired to talk with Mel about her conflicting feelings, but he never seemed interested in hearing what was on her mind. Her frustration grew daily. She felt that he was avoiding talking with her about anything more important than the weather. The following conversation was typical, taking place one Saturday morning as the kids were out playing:

SANDY: [sitting down by Mel and looking at him] I sure wish I could relax about money. When I see you worrying so much, it's just . . . I wonder if I'm doing the right thing, you know, being here at home.

MEL: [not looking up from the paper] It'll all work out.

SANDY: [She thinks, "He doesn't want to hear it. I wish he'd put that darn paper down."] I don't know. Am I really doing the right thing taking off from teaching? I think about it every day. Some days, I . . . you know, I'm not sure.

MEL: [He tenses, while thinking, "We always end up fighting when we talk about money. Why is she bringing this up now? I thought we'd settled this."] I really think you are doing the right thing. It's just harder to make the budget work, but we'll get back on track. I don't think we need to hash it out again.

SANDY: [She thinks, "Why can't he relax and open up more? I want to talk and know he's listening."] I can tell you really don't want to talk about it. It bugs me that you can't talk with me about this. You always either change the subject or get real quiet.

MEL: [He takes a deep breath and lets out a loud sigh. He wants to say something to stop the escalation, but no good idea comes to mind. He says nothing. He feels tense.]

SANDY: [feeling very frustrated, with growing anger.] That's exactly what I mean. You just close me out, again and again, and I'm tired of it!"

MEL: [He thinks, "I knew it. We always fight when we talk about money."] Why do you do this? I'm just sitting here relaxing. It's the only time I have all day to sit still, and you pick a fight. I hate this! [He throws the paper down, gets up from the table, and walks into the living room.]

If we summed up the concerns bluntly, Sandy wants Mel to "open up" and he wants her to "back off." At face value, it sounds as though they have very different goals for their relationship. Such patterns are commonly explained by saying that she wants intimacy and he doesn't. However, if you look underneath this pattern, you usually see something very different.

Many partners and therapists have concluded that men are less interested in intimacy and seek to avoid it. Our research and clinical experience suggests otherwise. Moreover, we don't believe that women desire conflict or take delight in stirring up turmoil. We believe that men and women want most of the same things in a relationship: respect, connection, intimacy, friendship, peace, and harmony. Our beliefs are not fueled by armchair speculation but are based on many studies of men and women in marriage and on our experience with couples in the PREP program.

WHAT IS "INTIMATE" TO YOU?

Research shows that women tend to define intimacy in terms of verbal communication, whereas men are more likely to define it in terms of shared activities. This is a critical point to keep in mind. When a wife asks her husband to spend some time talking about feelings, she may be showing her preference for intimacy, but so is a husband who asks his wife to take a walk or make love. These preferences parallel upbringing: little girls spend much more energy mastering verbal intimacy and little boys become intimate through activities, especially through play that has rules, such as sports.

Even in their goals for therapy, men and women are not as different as it may appear. Whereas a man's number-one goal may be to reduce conflict and a woman's to improve communication, we often find that her second most important goal is to reduce conflict and his is to communicate better. So even in the typical goals for marital counseling, what men and women want is similar—both want improved communication and reduced conflict—but they differ in the priority attached to each goal. Thus, the key difference between males and females regarding intimacy is one of preference, not interest or even capacity. In fact, one important study in the field showed that, when conditions are right, men are nearly as capable of verbal intimacy as women. This study has such interesting implications that we'll describe it for you in detail.

The study was conducted in the late 1980s at the University of Denver by Judy Schwartz and her colleagues. Young adults were asked to come to the research lab with their best same-sex friend to participate in a study on relationships. The partners were asked to sit down in a comfortable room and talk with each other as they might in other situations. The conversations were audiotaped and transcribed. The researchers were interested in the topics of conversation as they related to intimacy as well as in how the same-sex friends talked to each other.

As might have been expected, women were more likely to talk about intimate topics such as relationships, feelings, and family issues. Men were more likely to talk about sports, cars, and women. However, this was not the end of the study. After the first conversation, the researchers came in and asked the partners to have another discussion, but this time to "be intimate." Once again the conversations were recorded and transcribed. The transcripts were then rated by another sample of young adults. What do you think the psychologists found?

Believe it or not, the raters could not tell from reading the transcripts whether the conversation was between two males or two females. Thus, when both sexes were instructed to be intimate, the conversations of males with their best friends and females with their best friends were indistinguishable. This study indicates that males have the capacity to be intimate but may not choose to do so in the same way as females.

Some of the work of Lillian Rubin makes this point in a slightly different way. She describes interviewing a couple about their relationship. Each partner was interviewed separately. Dr. Rubin first talked to the wife, who said, "One of the things that drives me crazy about our relationship is that he just wants to spend all his time watching television. Even if I'm in the room with him, he doesn't talk. Sometimes I want to go over and pick up his softball bat and bop him

over the head." On the other hand, when Dr. Rubin talked to the husband, he said, "One of my favorite things about our marriage is that we can just sit together, to watch television, hold hands, with no pressure to talk, and at these times I feel really close to her." Unbeknownst to his wife, he valued their relationship, and especially these moments. Unbeknownst to him, she hated the very kind of experience he prized in the relationship.

This vignette illustrates not only that men and women have different preferences for intimacy, but that they may define the same intimate experience differently. Still, we assert that the capacity for, and interest in, intimacy is similar for men and women. The key is that men and women differ more in their *preference* for a type of intimacy.

Consequently, it's not fair or wise for either of you to look down on the other's preference for intimacy. Couples in relationships that are working well have learned to use their understanding of their similarities and differences to work as a team rather than as enemies. They've usually developed the capacity to connect on several dimensions of intimacy, including verbal communication, shared activity, and sensual partnership, to name a few. We'll help you enhance all of these dimensions as we go on.

CONFLICT: THE REAL DIFFERENCE

If men and women both want intimacy and are only different in the type they prefer, why do so many couples have trouble preserving, protecting, and nurturing intimacy? Conflict! The important difference between men and women lies not in their desire for intimacy, but in how they handle conflict. One key is how the experience of intimacy is affected by conflict and, even more, by potential conflict. We believe that when men go into a conflict-management mode, they limit their choices concerning intimacy because they're overly focused on preventing conflict from erupting. They tend to avoid or withdraw from it at all costs.

The reason is that most men do not handle marital conflict as well as most women. You may ask, "But men seem so calm and women seem so emotional during arguments. How can it be said that men handle conflict less well?" This statement may surprise you, but we can back it up. One of our colleagues, John Gottman, stated it this way: "In a sea of conflict, women swim and men sink." It's not that women like conflict, but they seem much better equipped to handle it in marriage.

ARE MEN REALLY LESS EMOTIONAL?

No! Reconsider the case of Mel and Sandy. When they have arguments, Mel appears fairly calm and Sandy appears very emotional. In fact, Mel usually looks totally shut down, much to Sandy's chagrin. She wants him to respond and he looks almost dead to her. But to say that Mel isn't emotional during these conflicts is to rely on a limited definition of what *emotional* means.

Suppose we hooked Sandy and Mel up to equipment designed to measure physiological reactions to stress, such as variations in blood pressure, heart rate, or galvanic skin response. These are ways of gauging a person's *inside* emotional state, no matter how outwardly expressive he or she may be. Studies using such equipment have found that men may be responding intensely on the physiological level even though they outwardly display little emotion. This is why Mel can seem very calm one minute, then blow up the next, when he's reached his limit. While it may not be obvious on the outside, the pressure is building on the inside.

We can conclude from this type of research that many men are very emotional, whether they show it or not. One study showed that the degree of physiological arousal men feel just contemplating talking to their wives at the end of the day strongly predicts divorce. In other words, the more anxious and aroused you are just imagining a conversation with your partner, the greater the risk of divorce in the future.

Hence, even though there does seem to be a difference in they way men and women express emotion, it's not accurate to think that men do not respond emotionally, especially to conflict. Could this high degree of physiological arousal help explain the common occurrence of men shutting down in conversations with their partners? We believe so, and we'll explain why. To better understand this, we need to discuss both biological and socialized or cultural differences in males and females.

WHY ARE YOU LIKE THAT?

Biologically, important differences exist between males and females, especially in their vulnerability to stress. In general, males are more physiologically vulnerable than females at every point in the life span. Males are more likely to die before birth, are more likely to die at any age, and are generally more susceptible to all sorts of stress-related damage and diseases.

One of the reasons for this is that males go through a crucial, extra step in biological development. At the point of conception, everyone is either male or female genetically. If you have two X chromosomes (XX), you are genetically female. If you have an X and a Y chromosome (XY), you are genetically male. As the fetus develops, males and females look identical and essentially are, until hormonal changes in the womb give the developing XY fetus the characteristics of a male. In other words, it takes an extra set of steps in the womb to develop male characteristics. And in nature, extra steps result in increased biological (and psychological) vulnerability.

Another sign of vulnerability is that at the point of conception in early embryonic development, 52 percent of the newly formed zygotes are males-to-be and 48 percent are females-to-be. Yet at birth, the ratio is approximately fifty-fifty. Thus, males are even more likely to die before birth than females. They are also more likely to suffer from biologically based disorders during the early years of childhood, especially in the psychological realm. For example, males are four or five times more likely to experience childhood autism and various forms of learning disabilities, including attention deficit disorder.

If you add this all up, it seems that instead of being the stronger sex, males are physiologically weaker on a host of dimensions. Sure, they tend to be physically stronger, but they are not more durable. And with research showing that they often experience higher levels of physiological stress during conflict with their partners, we can see a clear motivation for them to avoid or withdraw from conflict. In the average relationship, females are probably more resilient, and therefore less inclined to shy away from talking out conflicts.

We have talked with many men who report a very unpleasant sense of tension and anxiety during conflict with their wives. They bottle up these unpleasant feelings, without finding any appropriate outlet to express their feelings. In Mel and Sandy's case, Mel only expressed his frustration when he could no longer hold it in. Even when he did this, he was still trying to shut the conversation down. On the other hand, women who are more expressive and more physiological resilient have less reason to avoid discussing the issue in question, at least in a physically safe relationship. They simply don't feel the same pressure favoring avoidance that men do.

Biology isn't the only relevant factor in explaining these gender differences in handling conflict. Upbringing plays an important role as well. There is ample reason to believe that women are more comfortable with verbal relationships than men are. This may partially explain why women prefer verbal intimacy more than men in the first place. Women have typically practiced verbal skills with their family and friends since childhood. It's not that men haven't done this, but little girls are socialized to do much more. Dealing with issues verbally as they grow up gives them greater confidence in handling conflicts through communication when they become adults.

The common reaction for anyone dealing with a situation that causes anxiety and in which one feels inadequately skilled is avoidance or withdrawal. Hence, when men and women get into conflict, men are more prone to make the wrong choice to deal with it—withdrawal.

THE EFFECT OF RULES IN CONFLICT

There are three main areas in which we tend to think of men as proficient at some kinds of conflict: sports, military, and business. What do these involvements have in common? How are they different from conflict in marriage? *Rules!*

Sports, the military, and many business settings have relatively clear sets of expectations about how conflict is to be played out. Sports are particularly important in our culture in socializing men. Although women are becoming more and more involved in sports all the time, this has historically been an area where men are socialized about conflict. Sports are regulated by rules. There are even rules for what is and isn't acceptable in war, such as the Geneva Convention.

Research indicates that when conflict arises in a game, girls are more likely to break off the activity and boys are more likely to try to work through the conflict to keep the game going. They do this by resorting to rules or by creating new rules to resolve conflicts. This does not suggest that the girls are avoiding the conflict, but rather that the relationship is more important than the game for them, whereas for the boys the game *is* the relationship; it results in activity-oriented intimacy. A few personal examples with Howard's son, Mathew, and his classmates demonstrate these points.

Mathew was playing a game of basketball during lunch with a number of second-graders from his class. One of the boys was dribbling toward the basket and took about four steps between dribbles as he went in for a lay-up. Mathew immediately said, "No basket—traveling" and an argument broke out among the boys.

The argument basically had two components. First, a few of the boys didn't know the rules of basketball. These boys asked "What's traveling? Why does traveling mean that we didn't get a basket?" Another group of boys, who were more familiar with the rules of bas-

IN THERE... WITH THE REST OF THE BRAINTRUST.

ketball, tried to remember how many steps the rules allow before traveling is called. They also tried to establish how many steps the scorer had actually taken before making his basket.

One of the fifth-grade monitors heard the ruckus on the basketball court and came over. He explained to the boys who didn't know the rule that it was real, and he explained to the boys who weren't sure what the rule was that two steps was the limit. The monitor ruled that the basket didn't count since everyone agreed that the scorer had taken more than two steps. This shows how boys tend to be socialized by resorting both to rules and to those they think know the rules for conflict management.

Note the contrast in the way two girls in Mathew's class resolved a disagreement that emerged as they were planning the design of a dinosaur. Part of the project called for making a dinosaur that moved and naming it. Jackie wanted to call the dinosaur a Creatasaurus. Julie didn't like that name but couldn't come up with an alternative. Jackie started to talk about why she thought it should be called a Creatasaurus, and even though her position mad͏' ͏se to Julie, Julie said it just wasn't a name that she liked. The girl͏ ͏d to talk things out and avoid damage to their relationship; ther͏ ͏r a few minutes of trying to talk it out, Julie suggested that they decide which parts of the dinosaur should move and worry about the name later. They went off together and engaged in this new task.

As they were working on deciding which part of the dinosaur should be movable, Mathew came over and suggested that one of the girls could serve as the source of movement. The girls agreed that this might work, then went on to talk about their idea of trying to use some mechanical parts to move the arms up and down. Rather than discussing the girls' idea, Mathew said that he thought that using mechanical parts was against the rules. The girls weren't sure this was so and still wanted to talk about their various options, but Mathew wasn't interested in talking and went to get Julie's mother to ask her exactly what the rules said.

This example shows some of the precursors of male-female differences in marriage, with Mathew resorting to rules and external sources and the girls trying to talk things out. These experiences offer insights into a paradox. Culturally, we tend to think of men as more oriented toward conflict, not avoiding it, as so often seems to be the case in marriage. We might think that the experiences men have as boys would offer some guidance they could use as adults in handling marital conflicts, but although the presence of rules in games allows boys to cope with conflict, the absence of rules for dealing with emotional conflict in marriage sets the stage for men to withdraw. Women, who are not socialized to look to rules and who are freer to engage in the verbal process, usually don't have the same problems with conflict in marriage.

The emotional, rather than intellectual, nature of much relationship conflict is at the heart of the problem. If marital conflict didn't arouse emotion (an unreasonable expectation), there would be less avoidance and withdrawal. In settings where men are more used to dealing verbally with conflict, such as the work environment, conflict is more likely to be intellectually, not emotionally, expressed.

Men seem to be very comfortable dealing with problem-solving tasks that are kept on an intellectual level, both inside and outside of marriage. In fact, many women complain that men are too intellectual, while men complain that women are too emotional. This has led many people to conclude that men are more rational than women when dealing with problems, but there's no evidence that this is actually the case. Such differences seem to be related to emotional expressiveness, not rationality. Men may seek to keep discussions with their wives on an intellectual level to avoid the perceived complications of emotion.

It's evident that there are few rules or widely accepted methods designed to help men and women deal with emotional conflict in marriage. We're not saying that none exist, but it's difficult for many couples to understand them. We suggest that many men, and women too, can handle conflict and differences better when the rules are clearly spelled out.

Rules are agreed-upon techniques and strategies for dealing with conflict in marriage. For example, in the next chapter we'll teach you the rules for a very powerful communication technique. The rules do not remove the conflict or solve the problem, but they set the stage for the discussion. They provide agreed-upon guidelines for what is in bounds and what is out, who can speak when and in what way, and how both will take turns listening to each other. As you'll see, the kinds of rules we emphasize don't take the emotion out of the issues being discussed, but they're of great help in making it manageable.

When you've agreed on such rules and strategies ahead of time—and have mastered them in practice—you'll find that you can increase your ability to deal with issues without avoidance, withdrawal, escalation, or invalidation. In one sense, the next few chapters present what we think of as a sort of Geneva Convention for couples. We're not implying that marriage is war, but it sure can look like it when couples haven't learned to handle their conflicts with skill and respect.

All couples will experience disagreements and conflicts. This means that all of them will experience negative emotions such as anger, hostility, mistrust, fear, and sadness. A major task for partners in a close relationship, therefore, is to be able to handle these negative feelings constructively, without high levels of conflict or the loneliness of avoidance.

In light of the gender differences we have discussed, a major determinant of the future of marriage is whether wives can bring up issues—including negative feelings—constructively and whether husbands can respond by listening and talking, rather than avoiding and shutting down. An even better situation occurs when withdrawing partners can learn to raise issues on their own and not discuss a matter solely because their partners have brought it to light.

Agreed-upon rules for handling conflict can greatly facilitate your ability as a couple to handle conflict in a manner that protects intimacy and promotes growth in your relationship. You may be thinking that this sounds like a rigid approach, but as you'll see, it's not. It's just that the kinds of rules we're going to suggest are very effective in helping couples keep poorly handled conflict from destroying the great things in the relationship.

In Chapter Three, we'll begin this process by presenting the rules for the Speaker-Listener Technique, and in Chapter Four, we'll offer an effective method for solving problems. When couples regularly use such rules and techniques for dealing with the issues in their relationships, they develop an increased sense of confidence.

🐾 Exercises

The exercises we suggest here call for reflection. Mostly, we want you to think about the questions below, perhaps putting your thoughts down on a separate pad of paper, and plan some time to talk together about your own perceptions of how these patterns work for you. Most of the exercises in this book will have you focus together on your relationship. Here, we ask that you look at your individual styles.

1. You were asked in the last chapter to consider who withdraws more and who pursues more. Here, we ask you to reflect on why you do what you do, whichever role you identify with more. If you tend to avoid or withdraw, why do you do this? How does your physiology or upbringing fit in with your pattern? If you tend to pursue, why? What are you seeking when you pursue?

2. After reflecting on your own understanding of what you do in your relationship, plan some time together to discuss your perceptions. You should focus on this being an open, nonconflictual talk. Share with each other your own perceptions of why you do what you do, not why you think your partner does what he or she does.

3

Communicating Clearly and Safely: The Speaker-Listener Technique

DO YOU REALLY WANT to communicate well? Most couples do, but many have never learned to communicate when it counts most—in conflict. As you learned in the first two chapters, handling conflict well is critical to the future of your marriage. And communicating well is critical to handling conflict. There are two keys: making it clear and making it safe.

In this chapter, we'll learn the Speaker-Listener Technique. When you use this technique, your communication is protected against destructive patterns, making possible clear and safe communication that can bring you closer together.

MAKING IT CLEAR: THE PROBLEM OF FILTERS

Have you ever noticed that what you're trying to say to your partner can be very different from what he or she hears? You may say something you think is harmless and suddenly your spouse is mad at you. Or you may ask a question such as "What do you want for dinner?" and your partner starts complaining that you're not doing your share of the work.

We've all experienced the frustration of being misunderstood. We think we're being clear, but our partner just doesn't seem to "get it." Or we "know" what our partner said yesterday, but today he or she says something that seems completely different. Like the rest of us, Tanya and Wellington can relate to this common problem. They married five years ago. Tanya works as a reservation agent for an airline and Wellington is an accountant for a major firm. Their jobs leave them exhausted at the end of each day. They don't have any children yet, so they can usually crash when they get home.

One Thursday night, Wellington came home first and read the paper while he was waiting for Tanya. He was thinking, "I sure am wiped out. I bet Tanya is, too. I'd really like to go out to eat and just relax with her tonight." Good idea, right? This is what happened with his idea:

WELLINGTON: [*He's thinking he'd like to go out to dinner with Tanya, as she comes in the door.*] What should we do for dinner tonight?

TANYA: [*She hears "When will dinner be ready?"*] Why is it always my job to make dinner?

WELLINGTON: [*He hears her response as an attack and thinks, "Why is she always so negative?"*] It's not always your job to make dinner. I made dinner once last week!

TANYA: [*The negative cycle continues, as Tanya tends to feel that she does everything around the house.*] Bringing home hamburgers and fries is *not* making dinner, Wellington.

WELLINGTON: [*With his frustration mounting, Wellington gives up.*] Just forget it. I didn't want to go out with you anyway.

TANYA: [*Tanya's confused. She can't remember him saying anything about going out.*] You never said anything about wanting to go out.

WELLINGTON: [*He feels really angry.*] Yes I did! I asked you where you wanted to go out to dinner, and you got really nasty.

TANYA: I got nasty? You never said anything about going out.

WELLINGTON: Did too!

TANYA: You're never wrong, are you?

Sound familiar? You can see where things went wrong for them. Wellington had a great idea, a positive idea, and yet conflict ruined the evening. Wellington was not as clear as he could be in telling Tanya what he was thinking. This left a lot of room for interpretation, and interpret is what Tanya did. She assumed that he was asking—no, telling—her to get dinner on the table as she walked in the door.

This kind of miscommunication happens in relationships all the time. Many of our biggest arguments begin with a failure to understand what our partner is saying, in a way that fosters anger. What gets in the way? *Filters.*

Filters change what goes through them. A furnace filter takes dust and dirt out of the air. A filter on a camera lens alters the properties of the light passing through it. A coffee filter lets the flavor through and leaves the grounds behind. As with any other filter, what goes into our communication filters is different from what comes out.

We all have many kinds of filters packed into our heads, which affect what we hear, what we say, and how we interpret things. They're based on how we're feeling, what we think, what we've experienced in our life, and our family and cultural backgrounds, among other factors. In this chapter, we emphasize four types of filters that can affect couples as they struggle for clear communication:

1. Inattention

2. Emotional states

3. Beliefs and expectations

4. Differences in style

INATTENTION

A very basic kind of filter has to do with whether you have the attention of the person with whom you're trying to speak. Both external and internal factors can affect attention. External factors could include noisy children, a hearing problem, a bad phone line, or the background noise at a party. You're not likely to have a good conversation about an important matter with a crying child or a blaring television set in the room. For important talks, when you really need to communicate well, find a quiet place if you can, and don't answer the phone. Make it easier to pay attention to one another and get rid of external filters.

Internal factors affecting attention include feeling tired, thinking about something else, mentally forming a rebuttal, and being bored. These internal factors distract you from the conversation. It's common for one partner to think—correctly—that the other isn't paying attention. There are many times in relationships when you say something only to find, in frustration, that your partner didn't hear it. When one partner believes that this happens consistently, feelings of invalidation grow.

Sometimes, the listener who doesn't hear is rude or really doesn't care what the speaker has to say. In most cases, however, we don't think that this is the best explanation. Choosing to believe this about your partner can be a destructive interpretation if you're wrong. More often, the listener is tired or preoccupied, distracted by an internal filter. Psychological studies reveal that people differ in their ability to attend to several things at once. Often, the unhearing listener is focused on something else and truly doesn't hear what is being said. People also differ in their ability to break off their focus on one stim-

ulus and turn their attention to another. And for everyone, the ability to switch or maintain attention suffers greatly with fatigue.

So be sure you have your partner's attention when you're trying to get your point across. It is just as rude to begin a point when your partner is focused on something else as it is for your partner not to respond. Let's look at an example with Madeline and Jacob. Madeline is watching her favorite show on TV, and Jacob wants to discuss plans for the weekend:

JACOB: You know, I think we should try a long bike ride on Overland Trail this weekend. The weather is supposed to be great.

MADELINE: [staring at the TV] Uh huh.

JACOB: We could pack lunches, leave early, and get out there before the crowds.

MADELINE: [staring at the TV] What? Oh, that might be okay.

JACOB: What time do you think we could leave?

MADELINE: [turning to Jacob for a moment] What do you mean?

JACOB: [with some irritation] Saturday. What time do you want to leave Saturday?

MADELINE: [confused] Leave where?

JACOB: Didn't you hear anything I just said?

MADELINE: Well, I thought I did. What did you say?

Both partners could have done more to limit the frustration resulting from this conversation. Jacob picked a bad time to talk, right in the middle of Madeline's show. He'd have been better off to wait for a commercial and then say, "I'd really like to talk about what we're going to do on Saturday. Could we talk now, or should we wait till after your show?" And even if he had spoken during the show, Madeline could have said, "I'd like to talk that over with you, but I'm focused on this show right now. Let's talk about it at the commercial." It really doesn't take much more than such simple strategies to limit the frustration from filters of inattention.

We recommend that you accept lapses in attention as part of life. Sometimes they'll affect your communication in frustrating ways. Try not to make too much of them. The key is to make sure you have your partner's attention and give your attention when it counts the most.

EMOTIONAL STATES

Emotional states or moods become filters that affect communication. For example, a number of studies demonstrate that we tend to give people the benefit of the doubt more frequently when we're in a good mood and less frequently when we're in a bad mood. If you're in a bad mood, you are more likely to perceive whatever your partner says or does negatively, no matter how positive he or she is trying to be. Have you noticed that sometimes, when your spouse is in a bad mood, you get jumped on no matter how nicely you say something?

The best way to keep this kind of filter from damaging your relationship is to acknowledge when you're aware that one is operating. Here's an example. It's dinnertime. The kids are hungry and complaining. Steve just got home and is reading the mail, while Melissa is cooking macaroni in the kitchen:

STEVE: This bill for the phone company got missed again. We better get this paid.

MELISSA: [*snapping with anger*] I'm not the one who forgot it. Can't you see I have my hands full? Do something helpful.

STEVE: I'm sorry. I should have seen you were busy. Rough day?

MELISSA: Yes. I had a very frustrating day. I don't mean to snap at you, but I've had it up to here. If I am touchy, it's not really anything you've done.

STEVE: Maybe we can talk about it some after dinner.

MELISSA: Thanks.

Without using the term *filter*, Steve and Melissa were acknowledging that one was there. Melissa had a bad day and was on edge. They could have let this conversation escalate into an argument, but Steve had the good sense to see he'd raised the issue at the wrong time. He decided not to get defensive and chose to validate Melissa in her frustration.

Melissa responded by essentially telling Steve that she had a filter going—her bad mood. Furthermore, since she was in the middle of getting dinner ready, it was a bad time for Steve to get her attention. Once Steve became aware of her mood, he could interpret her behavior in light of it and understand that her negative mood was not his fault. Knowing this reduced the likelihood that he would become defensive in reaction to her mood. Many kinds of emotional filters can exist in any one person. If you are angry, worried, sad, or upset about anything, it can color your interpretation of what your partner says and your response to it.

BELIEFS AND EXPECTATIONS

Many very important filters arise from how you think about your relationship and what you expect from it. As we mentioned in the first chapter, research and experience tell us that people tend to see what they expect to see in others. This kind of expectation becomes a filter that distorts communication. Studies show that expectations not only affect our perceptions but can influence the behavior of others. For example, if you believe that someone is an extrovert, that person is more likely to sound like an extrovert when talking with you, even if she or he is introverted. We "pull" from others behavior that's consistent with what we expect.

The next example shows how difficult it can be to get around such filters. Alonzo and Heidi are a couple who came to one of our workshops. They were having problems deciding what to do for fun when they had free time. With three children in elementary school, free time without the kids was very valuable. But they rarely were organized enough to get out and do something, so they both were frustrated. This conversation was typical for them. Note that they both acted as if they could read each other's mind :

ALONZO: [He really wants to go bowling but thinks that Heidi is not interested in going out and doing anything fun together.] We have some free time tonight. I wonder if we should try to do something.

HEIDI: [*She thinks that she'd like to get out but hears the tenta-tiveness in his voice and believes that he really doesn't want to go out.*] Oh, I don't know. What *do* you think?

ALONZO: Well, we could go bowling, but it could be league night and we might not get in anyway. Maybe we should just stay in and watch "Home Improvement."

HEIDI: [*She thinks, "Aha, that's what he really wants to do."*] That sounds good to me. Why don't we make some popcorn and watch some tube?

ALONZO: [*He's disappointed, and thinks, "I knew it. She really doesn't like to get out and do things that are fun."*] Yeah, okay.

In this conversation, there was no escalation, invalidation, or with-drawal. Nevertheless, they didn't communicate well because of their filters. Alonzo's belief that Heidi doesn't like to go out colored the entire conversation—so much so that the way he asked her to go out led her to think that he wanted to stay in. He "knew" that she really didn't want to go; this constitutes mind reading. Mind reading occurs when you assume that you know what your partner is thinking or feel-ing. It's a common form of filtering based on your predetermined beliefs and expectations.

DIFFERENCES IN STYLE

Everyone has a different style of communicating and different styles can lead to filtering. Perhaps one of you is much more expressive and the other is more reserved. You may have some trouble understanding each other because you use such different styles. Styles are determined by many influences, including culture, gender, and upbringing. Some-times, differences in style that are rooted in family backgrounds can cause serious misunderstandings, becoming powerful filters that dis-tort communication.

Sue and Tom come from very different families. His family has always been very expressive, showing great intensity when they're emo-tional. It's just their way. Sue's family has always been more reserved. As a result, a slight rise in voice could mean great anger in her family, whereas it would hardly be noticed in his. In many conversations, therefore, Sue overinterprets the intensity of Tom's feelings, and Tom underestimates Sue's feelings, as in this example:

TOM: What did it cost to get the muffler fixed?

SUE: Four hundred and twenty-eight bucks.

TOM: [*intense, quickly getting red*] What? How could they possibly charge that much. That's outrageous.

SUE: [*lashing out*] I wish you could stop yelling at me! I've told you over and over that I cannot listen to you when you are yelling!

TOM: I am not yelling at you. I just can't believe that it could cost that much.

SUE: Why can't we have a quiet conversation like other people? My sister and brother-in-law never yell at each other.

TOM: They don't talk about anything, either. Look, $428 is too much to pay, that's all I'm reacting to.

SUE: Why don't *you* take the car in next time. I'm tired of being yelled at for things like this.

TOM: Honey, look. I'm not upset at you. I'm upset at them. And you know I can get pretty hot, but I'm not trying to say you did anything wrong.

SUE: [*calming down*] It seems that way sometimes.

TOM: Well, I'm not upset at you. Let me give that place a call. Where's the number?

Tom and Sue are caught up in a misunderstanding based on differences in style. But in the conversation above, they do a great job of not allowing things to escalate. As in preceding examples in which a conversation got back on track, one partner figures out that a filter is distorting the intended message and takes corrective action. Here, Tom forcefully clarifies that he is not mad at Sue.

Becoming more aware of the effects of your differing communication styles can go a long way toward preventing misunderstandings. Give some thought to these differences between you and your partner.

FILTERS AND MEMORY: THAT'S NOT WHAT YOU HEARD!

Some of the biggest arguments couples have are about what was actually said in the past. How often have you wished that you had a tape recording of an earler conversation? This happens to all of us. These differences in memory occur in great measure because of the variety of filters that operate in all relationships. Any of the filters discussed here can lead to differences—and arguments—about what was actually said or done in the past.

Read again the conversation earlier in this chapter between Wellington and Tanya. Notice that they ended up arguing about what Wellington actually said at the start of the conversation. He truly thought he asked her out to dinner, but what he said was vague. She truly thought he told her to get dinner on the table, which also was not what he said. Without a tape recording, no amount of convincing could get either one to back off from their version of the story.

We recommend two things that can save your relationship from such fruitless arguments about the past. First, don't assume that your memory is perfect. Accept that it isn't. Countless studies in the field of psychology show how fragile human memory is and how susceptible it is to motivation and beliefs. This is a tremendous problem in our legal system, and it's just as great a problem in relationships. Accept that you both have filters, and that plenty of room exists for something to be said or heard differently from what was intended.

Second, when you disagree, don't persist in arguments about what one of you said in the past; you'll get nowhere. Memory matching is a game that produces no winners. Instead, accept that you each remember the conversation differently and that filters were in force on both sides. Then move forward by focusing on what you think or feel about the issue right now. If Wellington and Tanya had taken this advice, their conversation might have continued in this way:

TANYA:	Hold on a second. This is getting us nowhere.
WELLINGTON:	You're right. I'm really tired.
TANYA:	Me too.
WELLINGTON:	Look, whatever I said, I really just wanted to ask you to go out to dinner with me. I think we could use the time together to relax.
TANYA:	I like that. Where do you want to go?

Notice that the conversation shifts away from what was actually said to what is going on now, bringing them back together and salvaging their evening. This can't happen unless each person is willing to have the perspective—and humility—to back off from the impasse and focus on what is desired now. Don't get stuck in the past, even if it was five minutes ago. Deal with what you think and feel in the present.

We all have filters. Either we react to them with little awareness, which can cause damage to the relationship, or we learn to look for them when conversations go awry. Try to get in the habit of announcing your filter when you're aware that you might have one, for example, "I know I'm sensitive about sex, so I may not be real clear in what I'm trying to tell you right now." We all have different moods, levels of attention, beliefs. We also have differences in experience and upbringing that can result in filters to clear communication. After discussing the importance of safety in your relationship, we'll show you a very effective communication technique for reducing the effect of filters on your important discussions.

MAKING IT SAFE: THE VALUE OF STRUCTURE

To have a great marriage, both of you must be able to express your beliefs, concerns, and preferences clearly, without damaging the relationship in the process. The patterns we discussed in Chapter One can make it unsafe to express your views about what's most important to you. Filters compound the problem, making it a wonder that couples can communicate about anything truly important.

Unless you feel emotionally safe, you're not likely to share important thoughts or feelings with your partner. For many couples, the relationship ends up feeling more like a mine field than a safe haven. People generally don't share openly with anyone, including a spouse, without some feeling of safety. Are marriages necessarily safe? No. Most married people want the safe haven of a friendly relationship, but many of them just don't get or remain there.

To play it safe, people often decide not to share important parts of their life like personal dreams, sexual desires, or feelings. In a way, the belief that a relationship isn't safe becomes yet another kind of filter, as you learn to hide what you think, feel, and want. If your relationship does feel safe for sharing your heart and soul, learn to keep it that way. If it's not safe, learn to make it that way. We'll help you get started.

By "safe," we do not mean risk-free. If you're going to share what you're concerned with, hurt by, or hoping for, you're going to take risks. There is a direct relationship between risk and reward in much of life. You can't be accepted deeply without offering something deep for your partner to accept. Conversely, you can take the risk, share deeply, and be rejected. This hurts a lot, because you've chosen to risk a deeper part of yourself in the relationship. But if it goes well, you find a deep, soul-satisfying acceptance of who you are, warts and all.

When you disagree, or think you do, more is at stake and more can go wrong. For your relationship to grow through conflict, instead of being damaged by it, it's necessary to use agreed-upon strategies and techniques for keeping conversations safe and under control. This doesn't mean that conversations will always be pleasant, but that you work at keeping escalation, invalidation, withdrawal, and negative interpretations from surfacing.

Using agreed-upon strategies and techniques adds structure to your interaction. This is exactly what is done in work and political settings. Consider for a moment what the U.S. Congress would look like if there were no rules for how and when things could be shared. With adequate structure, you can manage conflict with less chance of damage to your relationships. To show you how to do this, we'll first describe how a nuclear reactor works to demonstrate the benefits of structure. We'll then present a structured way to communicate that can make any conversation safer and clearer.

THE NUCLEAR REACTOR MODEL

Nuclear reactors are structures for harnessing the heat produced by radioactive material so that its energy can be used constructively. Figure 3.1 is a simple depiction of a reactor, showing the radioactive material confined in a vessel. Reactors make usable energy by generating heat, which is used to make steam, which is then used to propel turbines, which in turn spin generators, which make electricity. Heat is produced in the vessel as radioactive particles bounce around inside it, hit each other, and break apart, releasing tremendous energy and heat. These particles are released from the radioactive material as it decays.

There are two extremes in the reactor that the engineers wish to prevent. This is where the reactor is like your relationship. First and foremost, they want to prevent meltdowns. Meltdowns result when the heat gets away from the engineers, destroying the reactor and possibly contaminating the landscape for years to come. On the other hand, the engineers don't want the reactor to be so cold that no heat is produced, which would defeat the whole purpose.

To maintain control over the reaction, the engineers can raise and lower control rods to manage the amount of heat the reactor generates. Control rods work by absorbing the particles that are flying around so that fewer of them hit other particles and less friction is produced. The lower the rods, the cooler the temperature, since more of the reaction is stopped. The control rods are the engineers' way of *structuring* the reaction. The more structure there is, the slower the reaction and the less heat. The less structure there is, the greater the reaction and the more heat. But what does all this mean for you?

Your relationship is like a nuclear reactor in the following ways:

1. Certain issues generate heat.

2. This heat either can be used constructively or can lead to destructive consequences that are hard to clean up.

3. You can control how much structure you need to deal with a particular issue, just as the engineers can control the rods in the reaction.

If a topic is very hot for you, you should use more structure to handle

LESS STRUCTURE
MORE HEAT

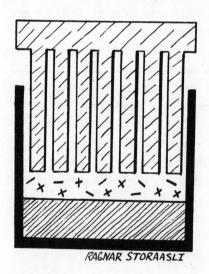

MORE STRUCTURE
LESS HEAT

RAGNAR STORAASLI

Figure 3.1 Control Rods (Structure) Slow Action and Decrease Heat in Nuclear Reactor Model.

the conversation; this is like lowering the control rods. This means using all of the rules we'll teach you in this book. When less is at stake, or you're not in conflict, you don't need much structure. Just communicate in whatever way you're most comfortable, since using structure at these times would make things cooler than they need to be.

THE SPEAKER-LISTENER TECHNIQUE

The Speaker-Listener Technique offers couples an alternative mode of communication when issues are hot or sensitive, or when they are likely to get that way. Any conversation in which you want to enhance clarity and safety can benefit from this technique. However, we don't expect couples to use the technique during normal conversations. Many (though not all) couples can decide whether to go out for Chinese food without it, but but when it comes to handling sensitive issues concerning money, sex, or in-laws, for example, having the safety net that such a technique provides can be a real comfort. However, in order to use these skills to talk through difficult issues, you'll need to learn them when things are going well.

We've found particular success with the Speaker-Listener Technique because it's so simple and effective. The technique works because you both follow certain rules, which we'll now describe.

RULES FOR BOTH OF YOU:

1. *The Speaker has the floor.* Use a real object to designate the "floor." In seminars, we hand out pieces of linoleum or carpet for couples to use as the floor. You can use anything, though: the TV remote control, a piece of paper, a paperback book—anything at all. If you don't have the floor, you're the Listener. As Speaker and Listener, you follow the rules for each role.

2. *Share the floor.* You share the floor over the course of a conversation. One person has it to start and may say a number of things. At some point, you switch roles and continue as the floor changes hands.

3. *No problem solving.* When you use this technique, you're going to

focus on having good discussions, not trying to come to solutions prematurely.

RULES FOR THE SPEAKER:

1. *Speak for yourself. Don't try to be a mind reader.* Talk about your thoughts, feelings, and concerns, not your perceptions of the Listener's point of view or motives. Try to use "I" statements, and talk about your own point of view. "I think you're a jerk" is not an "I" statement. "I was upset when you forgot our date" is.

2. *Don't go on and on.* You'll have plenty of opportunities to say all you need to say. To help the Listener listen actively, it will be very important to confine what you say to brief manageable statements. If you're in the habit of giving monologues, remember that having the floor protects you from interruptions, so you can afford to pause and be sure that your partner understands you.

3. *Stop and let the Listener paraphrase.* After you've talked a short while, stop and allow the Listener to paraphrase what you just said. If the paraphrase wasn't quite accurate, you should politely restate what was not heard the way it was intended to be heard. Your goal is to help the Listener hear and understand your point of view. This is not a test—help make sure that the Listener really hears you.

RULES FOR THE LISTENER:

1. *Paraphrase what you hear.* You must paraphrase what the Speaker is saying. Briefly repeat back what you heard the Speaker say, using your own words if you like, and make sure that you understand what was said. The key is to show your partner that you are listening by restating what you heard. If the paraphrase is not quite right (which happens often), the Speaker should gently clarify the point being made. If you truly don't understand some phrase or example, you may ask the Speaker to clarify, but you may not ask questions on any other aspect of the issue unless you have the floor.

2. *Focus on the Speaker's message. Don't rebut.* In the Listener's role, you may not offer your opinion or thoughts. This is the hardest part of being a good Listener. If you're upset by what your partner

says, you need to edit out any response you may want to make and pay attention to what your partner is saying. Wait until you get the floor to make your response. As the Listener, your job is to speak only in the service of understanding your partner. Any words or gestures that would show your opinion are not allowed, including making faces!

Before showing how this technique works in a conversation, we want to give you some ideas about what good paraphrases can sound like. Suppose that your spouse says to you, "I really had a tough day. Mom got on my case about how I handled the arrangements for Dad's party. Ugh!" Any of the following might be an excellent paraphrase:

"Sounds as though you had a really tough day."

"So, your mom was critical of how you handled the party, and really got on you about it."

"Bad day, huh?"

Any one of these responses conveys that you've listened and displays what you understood. A good paraphrase can be short or long, detailed or general. If you're uncertain how to get a paraphrase started, it can help to begin with "What I hear you saying is . . ." Then fill in what you just heard your partner say. Another way to begin a paraphrase is with the words "Sounds like . . ."

When using the Speaker-Listener Technique, the Speaker is always the one who determines if the Listener's paraphrase was on target. Only the Speaker knows what the intended message was. If the paraphrase was not quite on target, it's very important that the Speaker gently clarify or restate the point rather than responding angrily or critically. One more key point: when you're in the Listener's role, be sincere in your effort to show that you are listening carefully and respectfully. Even when you disagree with the point being made by your partner, your goal is to show respect for—and validation of—his or her perspective.

Show respect and listen well. If you disagree, wait until you have the floor to express your point of view.

USING THE SPEAKER-LISTENER TECHNIQUE

Here's an example of how this technique can change a conversation that is going nowhere into a real opportunity for communication. Peter and Tessie are in their mid thirties, with four children aged two to ten. For years they've had a problem dealing with issues. Peter consistently avoids discussing problem areas, and if he's cornered by Tessie, he withdraws by pulling into himself. They know they need to communicate more clearly and safely on tough topics and have agreed that the structure of the Speaker-Listener Technique might help.

In this case, Tessie and Peter have been locked in the pursuer-withdrawer cycle over the issue of Jeremy's preschool. However, they've been practicing the Speaker-Listener Technique and are ready to try something different. Let's see what happens:

TESSIE: I'm really getting tired of leaving Jeremy's preschool up in the air. We've got to deal with this, now.

PETER: [not looking up from the TV] Oh?

TESSIE: [walking over and standing in front of the TV] Peter, we can't just leave this decision hanging in the air. I'm getting really ticked about your putting it off.

PETER: [recognizing this would be a wise time to act constructively and not withdraw] Time out. I can tell we need to talk, but I've been avoiding it because it seems that talking just leads to fighting. Let's try that Speaker-Listener Technique we've been practicing.

Using the Speaker-Listener Technique isn't a normal way to communicate, but it is a relatively safe way to communicate on a difficult issue. Each person will get to talk, each will be heard, and both will show their commitment to discussing the problems constructively. When the person who usually withdraws moves toward the pursuer in this manner, the effect on the relationship is often very positive. The action attacks the foundation of the pursuer's belief that the withdrawer does not care about the relationship.

The conversation proceeds, with Peter picking up a piece of carpet they use for the "floor."

PETER: (Speaker) I've also been pretty concerned about where we send Jeremy to preschool, and I'm not even sure this is the year to do it.

TESSIE: (Listener) You've been concerned, too, and you're partly not sure he's ready.

PETER: (Speaker) Yeah, that's it. He acts pretty young for his age, and I'm not sure how he would do, unless the situation were just right.

Note how Peter acknowledges that Tessie's summary is on the mark before moving on to another point.

TESSIE: (Listener) You're worried that he wouldn't hold his own with older-acting kids, right?

Tessie is not quite sure she has understood Peter's point, so she makes her paraphrase tentative.

PETER: (Speaker) Well, that's partly it, but I'm also not sure if he's ready to be away from you that much. Of course, I don't want him to be too dependent, either.

Note how Peter gently clarifies. He's moving forward in the conversation, rather than backward. In general, whenever you, as the Speaker, feel that clarification is needed, use your next statement to restate or expand upon what you're trying to get across.

TESSIE: (Listener) So, you're feeling torn about him needing me a lot and him needing to be more independent.

PETER: (Speaker) That's right. Here, you take the floor.

They pass the floor.

TESSIE: (now the Speaker) Well, I appreciate what you're saying. Actually, I hadn't realized you'd thought this much about it. I was worried that you didn't care about it.

As the Speaker, now, Tessie validates Peter in the comments he's made.

PETER: (Listener) Sounds as though you're glad to hear that I'm concerned.

TESSIE: (Speaker) Yes. I agree that this isn't an easy decision. If we did put him in preschool this year, it would have to be just the right place.

PETER: (Listener) You're saying that it would have to be just the right preschool for it to be worth doing this year.

TESSIE: (Speaker) Exactly. It might be worth trying if we could find a great environment for him.

Tessie feels good with Peter listening so carefully, and she lets him know it.

PETER: (Listener) So you'd try it if we found just the right setting.

TESSIE: (Speaker) I *might* try it. I'm not sure I'm ready to say I *would* try it.

PETER: (Listener) You're not ready to say you'd definitely want to do it, even with a perfect preschool.

TESSIE: (Speaker) Right. Here, you take the floor again.

They pass the floor again.

As you can tell, Peter and Tessie have been practicing quite a bit. They're both doing an excellent job following the rules and showing concern and respect for each other's viewpoints. Couples can have discussions like this on difficult topics, even when they disagree. The key is making it safe and showing respect for your partner's thoughts, feelings, and opinions.

THE ADVANTAGES OF USING THE SPEAKER-LISTENER TECHNIQUE

The Speaker-Listener Technique has many advantages over unstructured conversation in discussing difficult issues. Most important it counteracts the destructive styles of communication described in Chapters One and Two—escalation, invalidation, pursuit and withdrawal, and filters:

1. *Escalation.* It's nearly impossible to escalate if you both follow the rules and work at showing respect. You can't scream at one another if you have to stop every few sentences and ask for a paraphrase! The momentum of escalation is stopped dead.

2. *Invalidation.* The simple process of paraphrasing intervenes effectively with invalidation because the Speaker gets immediate feedback. You can enhance the validation by saying "I understand" or "I see what you mean" at the end of a paraphrase or when you get the floor. This doesn't mean that you agree, just that you can see the situation from the other person's perspective. Save agreement or disagreement for your turn as Speaker. *You don't have to agree with your partner to be a good listener!*

3. *Pursuit and Withdrawal.* For the spouse who tends to withdraw from conversations in which conflict is possible, the structure of this technique makes it much safer to remain in the conversation. When you have a clear sense that both of you are committed to keeping things from getting out of hand, there's less to be anxious about, because conflict is less likely to occur in an unmanageable way. For the spouse who is usually in the role of pursuer, structure in conversations ensures that you will be heard and issues will be addressed. If you're the withdrawer, as you feel safer and more willing to address issues, withdrawing becomes less useful or necessary. This moves you both closer to a win-win situation and away from hopeless win-lose cycles.

4. *Filters.* The Speaker-Listener Technique makes it much easier to identify filters as soon as they come up. They will be evident in the paraphrases. The Speaker will then have a nonthreatening opportunity to say, "That's not quite what I said. I said 'such and so.' Could you paraphrase again, please?" All manner of filters can be reduced using this technique, especially negative interpretations.

Our research shows that couples benefit from learning to use structure when handling conflict. This makes a great deal of sense. Agreed-upon rules like the Speaker-Listener Technique add some degree of predictability, which reduces anxiety and avoidance and helps both partners to win rather than lose when dealing with conflict. Instead of fighting each other, you need to work together to fight negative patterns. As the technique becomes more comfortable, you'll be able to take full advantage of many other ideas presented in this book.

When you choose to use the skills and ground rules we present for handling conflict, you're choosing to use more structure. As with the engineer for a nuclear reactor, one of the most important things you can do as a couple is to learn when you need more structure and when you need less. If you practice, you'll learn as a couple how and when to lower the control rods to handle the tough times. Practice is the key. If you want to strengthen your marriage and reduce your chances of divorce, learn to move toward each other and deal constructively with those issues that have the potential to drive you apart. We'll cover many other important principles in this book, but none is more critical.

In the next chapter, we'll teach you a structured model for solving problems. If you work at it, you will find that using it and the Speaker-Listener Technique in combination can make a tremendous difference in your ability to deal with whatever issues you must face as a couple.

 ## Exercises

The Speaker-Listener Technique does not work miracles, but it does work well. If it's going to be useful, you have to practice. Like any new skill, you'll likely be a bit unsure at the start. You need to learn this technique so well together that the rules are automatic when you have something really difficult to discuss.

If you were learning to play tennis, you would not try to perfect your backhand at center court at Wimbledon. Instead you would hit backhands against the back wall for hours to get it just right. Trying to learn a new skill under a high-stress situation is not advisable. Hence, we suggest that you follow the suggestions below to learn the Speaker-Listener Technique.

1. Practice this technique several times a week for fifteen minutes or so each time. If you don't set aside the time to practice, you will never find this technique very helpful.

2. For the first week, try the technique with only nonconflictual topics. Talk about anything of interest to either of you: your favorite vacation ever, news, sports, your dreams for the future, concerns you have at work, and so on. Your goal here is not to resolve some problem but to practice new skills.

3. After you have had three successful practice sessions on nonconflictual topics, choose areas of minor conflict to discuss. Sometimes couples are poor at knowing what will and will not trigger a fight. If the discussion gets heated on a topic you choose, drop it. (It won't go away, but you can deal with it when you've practiced more together.)

   Practice several discussions in which you both exchange some thoughts and feelings on these minor issues. Don't try to solve problems; just have good discussions. Your goal is to understand each other's point of view as clearly and completely as possible. In the process, you may solve some problems, because all that was needed was to understand what the other person was thinking. That's okay, but don't set out—or intentionally try—to find solutions. You're focusing on good discussions right now. You'll learn and practice problem solving in the next chapter.

4. When you are doing well on the last assignment, move up to tougher and tougher issues. As you do, remember to work at sticking to the rules. It works if you work at it.

4

Problem Solving

I N THE LAST CHAPTER, we focused not on solving problems, but on the need for clear and safe communication when it counts most. If you're progressing in your ability to talk about things effectively, you're better prepared for what we'll now say about solving problems.

We all want to solve problems that affect our relationships. This is natural. But we've waited to discuss this subject until now because most couples try to solve problems prematurely, before they've developed a thorough, mutual understanding of the issues at hand. Understanding, *before* solving, is crucial for maintaining respect and connection in your relationship. In this chapter, we present a straightforward approach to problem solving that can help you through those times when you really need practical, workable solutions.

THREE KEY ASSUMPTIONS

We'd like to describe three key, research-based assumptions before presenting the specific steps that can help you solve problems effectively in your relationship:

I. All couples have problems.

2. The couples who are best at working through their problems work together as a team, not against each other as adversaries.

3. Most couples rush to find quick solutions that don't take into account the real concerns of each partner and therefore don't produce lasting solutions.

Let's explore these three points.

ALL COUPLES HAVE PROBLEMS

Have you ever wondered why some couples seem to sail through marital life? It's not that they don't have problems. Although the nature of the problems change for couples over time, all couples encounter problems.

During their engagement, couples report that their key problem areas are jealousy and in-laws. These issues reflect the core task they have early in their relationship of establishing boundaries with others. By the first year of marriage, they report other problems as being more important, such as communication and sex. These are issues central to how the partners interact with each other. Even with this simple data, it is clear that communication becomes a greater concern for couples over time. And whether they're in a new or long-standing relationship, most couples report money as a top problem, no matter how much they have.

So while the nature of the conflicts may change over time, all couples report problems that reflect a core set of issues they have to resolve. Granted, some couples are dealt a more difficult hand in life than others. However, our observations of couples in PREP and in our research dovetail to indicate that those who handle problems well tend to display a common set of skills—skills that can be learned.

YOU NEED TO WORK TOGETHER AS A TEAM

Some couples combine their mutual respect and skill to produce a powerful sense that they are a team working together to find solutions that will enhance their life. You have a choice when dealing with a problem. Either you will nurture a sense that you are working together against the problem or you will operate as if you are working against each other. This principle holds true for all problems, great or small.

For example, Jeremy and Lisa, a newlywed couple in their late twenties, received the fees for a weekend version of our program as a wedding gift from Jeremy's family. They were talking about how to handle the feeding of their newborn baby (Brent) while Lisa was working at the local hospital where she is a pediatric nurse. Jeremy recently lost his job as an executive when his firm merged with another, but he was confident of finding another position in the near future. The following conversation illustrates that, for them, teamwork generally flows naturally:

LISA:	The biggest concern I have is about breast-feeding.
JEREMY:	What do you mean? Can't he do that when you're at home— with me giving him a bottle during your shift?
LISA:	No. That's not going to work because I'll swell up while I'm away. I make milk whether or not he drinks it, you know.
JEREMY:	I had no idea that would be a problem. You mean you can't go through your shift without him nursing?
LISA:	Not without exploding.
JEREMY:	Ouch! What can we do to make this work out?
LISA:	Well, either Brent nurses on my break or I need to pump.
JEREMY:	What's better for you? I could help either way.
LISA:	Would you be willing to bring him over to work at lunchtime? If he'd nurse well then, that would tide me through the day, and you could give him bottles the rest of the time.
JEREMY:	Sure. I'd be glad to bring him over. No biggie with me out of work for now.
LISA:	That would help a lot. I'd also get to see him during the day. Let's give it a try this week.

Notice how Jeremy and Lisa are working together. They are listening to each other, with a sense of respect and cooperation. This is the way they have learned to approach all kinds of problems—as challenges to be met together. Since they're able to handle this issue so well, there's no particular need in this conversation to use a more structured approach, such as the Speaker-Listener Technique.

Contrast the tone of Lisa and Jeremy's discussion with that of Shandra and Eric. Shandra, the owner of her own dry-cleaning business, and Eric, a real estate agent, are the parents of two middle schoolers. They have repeated arguments about housework, which generally go like this:

SHANDRA: [*calmly*] We need to do something about keeping the house looking better. It's such a mess most of the time. . . .It's depressing.

ERIC: [*a bit annoyed*] Look, that's your job. My work keeps me out a lot more than you. I just don't have the time, and you know it! Keeping the place picked up is more your job than mine.

SHANDRA: [*hurt and angered*] Says who? There's a lot more to do than you seem to think. And did you forget that I work, too? Besides, you don't even clean up after yourself!

ERIC: I'd do more around here if you could generate more money in your business. . . .You know, when you're home, you spend lots of time watching the tube—you could use your time better.

SHANDRA: [*anger growing*] I need some breaks. And I work just as hard as you outside the home. You need to do your share.

ERIC: You said I wouldn't have to do any more work around here when you began devoting more time to your business. That was a deal.

SHANDRA: [*looking him in the eye, and very angry*] That was when you used to do a lot more than you do now.

ERIC: [*turning away and indicating that the conversation is over for him*] I don't agree and I'm not talking about it anymore. A deal's a deal.

This discussion ends with Shandra discouraged and Eric annoyed that she even brought up the problem. They show a definite lack of teamwork. Eric refuses to accept any role in dealing with this problem.

He sees Shandra as trying to take something away from him, not as a partner working to make life as good as it can be for both of them. Likewise, Shandra sees Eric as the problem, not as a teammate who is working with her.

All too often, people approach problems as if their partner is the enemy to be conquered. For such couples, issues are approached as if there will be a winner and a loser. Who wants to lose? That kind of attitude is guaranteed to produce tension and conflict. People don't get married to have an enemy to struggle with for years—although, sadly, many couples end up in this type of brutal situation.

The good news here is that you don't have to be locked into the cycle of one partner trying to win at the expense of the other. *You can learn how to work as a team.* But even when couples work well as teams, many fail to take the necessary time to move toward solid, lasting solutions to problems.

DON'T RUSH TO FIND SOLUTIONS

Many well-intentioned attempts at problem solving fail because couples don't take time to understand the problem together; this prevents them from working out a solution that both partners can support. If you're deciding which movie to see, not much is at stake in rushing to a solution—except maybe the prospect of sitting through a boring film. But if you're deciding something more important, such as how to parent or to divide up the household responsibilities, it's critical to take the time to develop a mutually satisfying solution.

Two major factors propel couples to rush to solutions: time pressure and conflict avoidance.

Time Pressure

Most of us are not all that patient. We want it now. Unfortunately, quick fixes seldom last. This tendency reflects the hurried pace of our lives. We usually don't take the time to plan what we're doing in our family relationships. We've had many colleagues visit us from Europe over the years, and they often comment about how crazy we are in America. They see us as rushed and always busy, with little attention left for the really important things. When this time pressure is combined with our desire to be in control of our lives, we experience an overwhelming desire to solve problems quickly and move on to the next challenge.

But when it comes to dealing with important issues in families, hasty decisions are often poor decisions. We must be committed to spending the time to work things out if we're going to make good decisions together. One colleague recently remarked that "time is the currency of the nineties." Failing to spend enough of this currency on marital and family relationships becomes a major problem for many people.

Conflict Avoidance

The following example is fairly typical in describing how, because of a desire to avoid further conflict, a couple can rush to a solution that is destined to fail. Frances and Bjorn have been married twenty-four years, with one child through college and one a senior in high school. Bjorn is an insurance salesman and Frances works as a nearly full-time volunteer with a local religious charity. They've always had enough money, but things have gotten much tighter with college bills piling up. An issue for Bjorn is that Frances devotes so much time to a job that doesn't pay. The following conversation is typical of their attempts to solve the problem:

BJORN: [*testily*] I noticed that the VISA bill was over $600 again. I just don't know what we're going to do to keep up. It worries me. I'm doing all I can, but . . .

FRANCES: [*gives no indication that she's paying attention to Bjorn*]

BJORN: [*frustrated*] Did you hear me?

FRANCES: Yes. I didn't think we spent that much this time.

BJORN: [*really annoyed now*] How many clothes did Jeanne need, anyway?

FRANCES: [*annoyed, but calm*] Well, we figured she needed one really nice outfit for applying for jobs. I guess we got more extras than I thought, but it was all things she can use. It's very important to her to look good on interviews. And you know, the sooner she gets a job, the better off our budget will be.

BJORN:	[*settling down a bit*] I understand, but this kind of thing adds to my worry. [*long pause*] We aren't saving anything at all for retirement, and we aren't getting any younger. If you had some income coming in for all your work, it would help a lot.
FRANCES:	Why don't we just get rid of that credit card. Then you wouldn't have to worry about it anymore.
BJORN:	We could do that, and also plan to put aside an extra $150 a month in my retirement plan. That would help a lot to get us going in the right direction. What about a part-time job?
FRANCES:	I can think about it. What I'm doing seems a lot more important. For now, let's try to get rid of the credit card and save more. That sounds good. Let's try it out.
BJORN:	Okay, let's see what happens.

End of discussion. The one good thing about this discussion is that they had it. However, what are the chances that they came to a satisfactory resolution of their money problem? Two months later, nothing was changed, no more was saved, the credit card was still being used, interest was accruing, and they were no closer to working together on the budget. In addition, they didn't really address Bjorn's central concern about Frances's volunteer job.

One of the main difficulties is that there are no specifics about how their agreement will be implemented. Bjorn and Frances are not generally into quick fixes, but they do rush to solutions at times because they hate conflict. For them, this conversation was a relatively big fight. Both were eager to get back to being nice to each other after a disagreement.

Finding a solution can be a relief when you and your spouse are talking about an issue that causes some anxiety. However, when you settle on a solution prematurely, you're likely to pay for the lack of planning with more conflict later. The good news is that once you agree on a solution to a nagging issue, it will be under rule control and will stop being a cause of ongoing conflict. *Rule control* means that you've agreed together on a principle or rule to guide you whenever this issue comes up in the future.

HOW TO SOLVE YOUR PROBLEMS

The approach we take here to solving problems—consistent with the general PREP approach—is structured. In other words, we recommend a specific set of steps that successful problem solvers follow. The steps we present are modified and adapted from ideas presented in earlier works, especially *We Can Work It Out: Making Sense of Marital Conflict* (Notarius and Markman, 1993), and *A Couple's Guide to Communication* (Gottman, Notarius, Gonso, and Markman, 1976). While these steps are very straightforward, don't be misled by the simplicity of the approach. You must be willing to work together, be creative and flexible, and be willing to experiment with change. Under these conditions, you'll be able to discover solutions to most of the problems you have to grapple with together.

The steps to handling problems well include:

I. Problem Discussion

II. Problem Solution

A. Agenda setting

B. Brainstorming

C. Agreement and compromise

D. Follow-up

PROBLEM DISCUSSION

Problem discussion is critical to handling problems well. In this step, you're laying the foundation for the problem solution to come. Although you may not agree about how to solve the problem, a good discussion can lead to a clear sense that you're working together and respecting each other.

Whether the problem is large or small, you shouldn't move on to problem solution until you both understand and feel understood by your partner. This means that you have each expressed your significant feelings and concerns on the topic and believe that the other person has clearly seen your point of view. We recommend you use the Speaker-Listener Technique for this step. Placing a premium on validation in this phase results in an atmosphere of mutual respect, which allows the problem solution to proceed much more smoothly.

In all the examples so far, the couples experienced greater pain and distance because they failed to take the time to discuss the issues before coming to an agreement. We have repeatedly seen that when it's preceded by good discussion, problem solving can often go quickly and smoothly, even for difficult issues. With all the relevant facts and feelings on the table, the foundation is laid for working as a team.

During problem discussion, it is likely that one or both of you may have a specific gripe that needs to be expressed. When this is the case, it's very important for each of you to present your feelings and concerns constructively. One way to do this is to use what Gottman, Notarius, Gonso, and Markman call an XYZ statement in their book *A Couple's Guide To Communication* (1976). With the XYZ statement, you put your gripe or complaint into this format:

"When you do X in situation Y, I feel Z."

When you use an XYZ statement, you're giving your partner usable information: the specific behavior, the context in which it occurs, and how you feel when it happens. This is much preferred to what often is offered: a vague description of the problem and some character assassination instead of an "I" statement.

For example, suppose that you have a concern about your partner making a mess at the end of the day. Which of the following statements do you think gives you a better shot at being heard?

"You are such a slob."

"When you drop your pack and jacket on the floor (X) as you come in the door at the end of the day (Y), I feel angry (Z)."

Or, suppose that you are angry about a comment your spouse made at a party last Saturday night. Here's a contrast:

"You are so inconsiderate."

"When you said that what I did for work wasn't really that hard (X) to John and Susan at the party last Saturday (Y), I felt very embarrassed (Z)."

Unless you're careful, it's all too easy to fall into a nonspecific attack on character. Such statements are guaranteed to cause defensiveness and escalation. The XYZ statements are far more constructive: a specific behavior is identified in a specific context. The "I feel Z" part requires you to take responsibility for your own feelings. Your partner doesn't "make" you feel anything in particular—you are in charge of how you feel.

Keep in mind that no one really likes to hear a gripe or criticism, no matter how constructively it is expressed. But unless you are hiding out in avoidance, there are times when you need to voice a concern, and you need to do it without fostering unneeded conflict. The XYZ format will help you do just that.

Before we turn to problem solution, remember that with problem discussion, you are really laying the foundation for productive problem solving as a team. So we repeat—*do not move from discussion to solution unless you both agree that the issue or problem in question has been fully discussed.* In many instances, however, you'll find that after an excellent discussion, there's really no problem solving to be done. Just having a good discussion is enough. In fact, in our PREP seminars, we often shock couples by announcing that our experience indicates that approximately 70 percent of the issues couples deal with don't really need to be solved, just well discussed. "How can that be?" they ask.

It's hard for couples to appreciate this point without experiencing the power of a problem discussion that leaves you with what therapists call an "ah-ha!" experience. After such a discussion, there's often nothing left to resolve. That's because we often want something much more fundamental in our relationships than solutions to problems.

In one study, we asked partners in all types of relationships what they wanted out of their relationship. What do you think they told us? Financial security? No. Good sex? No. Emotional security? No. The major desire people have is for their partner to be a friend. When we ask, "What is a friend?" people tell us that a friend is someone who listens, who understands, who validates. This kind of listening and validation occur in good problem discussions. Most of the time, what partners want most when they are upset is not agreement or even change, but just to feel heard and understood.

Howard Markman had the opportunity to be on "The Oprah Winfrey Show" a couple of years ago. Oprah disagreed with him about many issues concerning relationships, and as the show progressed, he was convinced that he'd never be asked back. When the idea that good problem discussion often eliminates the need for problem solution came up, Oprah started by saying that she disagreed with the 70 percent estimate. Howard thought, "Here we go again!" But to his surprise, Oprah went on to say, "Doctor Markman, in my experiences, I believe 90 percent of the problems do not need to be solved!" Don't rely on our estimates or Oprah's; find out for yourself how powerful good discussions are for resolving the issues that come up in your relationships. (And by the way, Howard has been back on the show since then.)

Nevertheless, we recognize that there are many times when your discussion of problems or issues will naturally lead to the next step—working together to find specific solutions. When you need to come up with a specific solution, the steps of the problem-solution phase can help you get there.

PROBLEM SOLUTION

We have found the following steps to work very well for couples, provided that the work of problem discussion has been done.

Setting Agendas

The first step in problem solution is to set the agenda for your work together. The key here is to make very clear what you are trying to solve at this time. Often, your discussion will have taken you through many facets of an issue. Now you need to decide what to focus on. The more specific the problem you are tackling now, the better your chances of finding a workable and satisfying solution. Many problems in marriage seem insurmountable, but they can be cut down to size if you follow these procedures.

For example, you may have had a problem discussion about money that covered a range of issues, such as credit card problems, checkbooks, budgets, and savings. As you can see, the problem area of money can contain several more specific problem areas to consider, so it's necessary to take apart a large problem such as this and focus on the more manageable pieces, one at a time. It is also wise to work on an easier piece of a problem first. For example, you might initially decide who should balance the checkbook each month, then deal with budget plans later. Be sure to set a specific time to talk about those issues.

At times, your problem discussion will have focused from start to finish on a specific problem. In this case, you won't have to define the agenda for problem solving. You might be working on the problem of where to go for the holidays—your parents' home or that of your spouse's parents. There's no way to divide this problem into smaller parts, so you'll set the agenda to work on all of it.

Brainstorming

As far as we know, the process referred to as brainstorming has been around forever. However, it seems to have been refined and promoted by the National Aeronautics and Space Administration during the early days of the U.S. space program. They needed a way to bring together the many different engineers and scientists who were looking for solutions to the varied problems of space travel. Their method worked for NASA and came to be used frequently in business settings. We've found that it works very well for couples, too. There are several rules regarding brainstorming:

- Any idea can be suggested. One of you should write down the ideas.

- Don't evaluate the ideas during brainstorming either verbally or nonverbally (this includes making faces!).

- Be creative. Suggest what comes to mind.

- Have fun with it, if you can. This is a time for a sense of humor; all other feelings should be dealt with in problem discussion.

The best thing about this process is that it encourages creativity. If you can edit out your tendency to comment critically on the ideas that are presented, you'll encourage each other to come up with some great stuff. Wonderful solutions can emerge from considering the points made during brainstorming. Following the rules helps you resist the tendency to settle prematurely on a solution that isn't the best you can find.

Agreement and Compromise

In this step, the goal is to come up with a *specific* solution or combination of solutions that you both *agree* to try. We emphasize the word agree because the solution is not likely to help unless you both agree to try it. We emphasize specific because the more specific you are about the solution, the more likely it is that you'll follow through. This is the time to discuss the ideas you came up with during the brainstorming step. Explore combinations of ideas that you each think might work well. This isn't the time for heavy discussions, but rather for working toward a specific solution.

Although it is easy to see the value of agreement, some people have trouble with the idea of compromise. To some, it sounds more like lose-lose than win-win. Obviously, compromise implies giving up something you wanted in order to reach an agreement. But we do mean to emphasize using it in a positive manner.

Marriage is about teamwork. Two separate individuals may see things differently and might make different decisions. But often the best solution will be a compromise in which neither of you gets everything you wanted. The reason is that you won't have a great marriage if you get your way all the time. Our goal is to help you win as a team, with solutions that show mutual respect and bring you closer as a couple. Sure, at times you may give up a little as an individual, but if you can gain as a couple, the exchange can be more than worth it.

Follow-Up

Many couples make an agreement to try a particular solution to a problem. It is just as important to follow up to see how the agreement is working out. Following up has two key advantages. First, solutions often need to be "tweaked" a bit to work in the long term. Second, following up builds accountability. Often, we don't get serious about making a change unless we know there is some point of accountability in the near future.

Sometimes a lot of follow-up is needed in the problem solution phase; at other times, it's not really necessary. You reach an agreement and it works out, and nothing more needs to be done.

Some couples choose to be less formal about follow up, but we think they're taking a risk. Most people are so busy they don't plan the next step, and nothing happens. There's an old-but-true saying: "If you fail to plan, you plan to fail." Set a specific time (in a week or a month) to sit down and say how well something is working or discuss any small changes needed to help it work better.

Writing down what you have agreed on can help you in following up. This can clear up any differences in memory later on, as well as serving as a reminder to talk about how the solution is working out. However, we caution you not to go so far as to think of these agreements as contracts. The legal metaphor may not enhance your sense of working together as a team. If you do like the term *contract*, make your solutions "good faith" agreements, in which you each try your best to keep up your end no matter what your partner does.

A DETAILED EXAMPLE: BJORN AND FRANCES

It did not take Frances and Bjorn very long to realize that their problem-solving attempts concerning the credit card, her volunteer work, and their retirement savings were not working. They decided to try the steps we're suggesting here.

First, they set aside the time to work through the steps. Depending on the problem, these steps may not be very time-consuming, but specifically setting aside time is very wise. Let's follow Bjorn and Frances through the steps:

PROBLEM DISCUSSION USING THE
SPEAKER-LISTENER TECHNIQUE

FRANCES: (Speaker) I can see that we really do have to try something different. We aren't getting anywhere on our retirement savings.

BJORN: (Listener) You can see we aren't getting anywhere, and you're concerned, too.

FRANCES: (Speaker) [letting Bjorn know he had accurately heard her] Yes. We need to come up with some plan for saving more and for doing something about the credit cards.

BJORN: (Listener) You agree we need to save more, and can see that how we spend on the credit cards may be part of the problem.

FRANCES: (Speaker) I can also see why you're concerned about my volunteer work—when I could be spending some of that time bringing in some income. But my volunteer work is really important to me. I feel like I'm doing something good in the world.

BJORN: (Listener) Sounds like you can appreciate my concern, but you also want me to hear that it's really important to you—it adds a lot of meaning to your life. [Here, he validates her by listening carefully.]

FRANCES: (Speaker) Yeah. That's exactly what I'm feeling. Here, you take the floor, I want to know what you're thinking.

FLOOR SWITCH.

BJORN: (Speaker) I've been anxious about this for a long time. If we don't save more, we're not going to be able to maintain our life-style in retirement. It's not all that far away.

FRANCES: (Listener) You're really worried, aren't you?

BJORN: (Speaker) Yes, I am. You know how things were for Mom and Dad. I don't want to end up living in a two-room apartment.

FRANCES: (Listener) You're worried we could end up living that way, too.

BJORN: (Speaker) I'd feel a lot better with about three times as much saved.

FRANCES: (Listener) Too late now. [She catches herself interjecting her own opinion.] Oh, I should paraphrase. You wish we were much further along in our savings than we are.

BJORN: (Speaker) [This time, he feels he is really getting her attention.] I sure do. I feel a lot of pressure about it. I really want to work together so we can both be comfortable. [This lets her know he wants to work as a team.]

FRANCES: (Listener) You want us to work together, reduce the pressure, and plan for our future.

BJORN: (Speaker) [suggesting some alternatives] Yes. We'd need to spend less to save more. We'd need to use the credit cards more wisely. I think it would make the biggest difference if you could bring in some income.

FRANCES: (Listener) You feel that to save more we'd need to spend less with the credit cards. More important, you think it's pretty important for me to bring in some money.

BJORN: (Speaker) Yes. I think the income is a bigger problem than the outgo.

FRANCES: (Listener) Even though we could spend less, you think we may need more income if we want to live at the same level in retirement. Can I have the floor?

BJORN: (Speaker) Exactly! Here's the floor.

FLOOR SWITCH.

FRANCES: (Speaker) [responding to Bjorn's clarification] Sometimes I think that you think I'm the only one who overspends.

BJORN: (Listener) You think that I think you are mostly at fault for spending too much. Can I have the floor again?

FLOOR SWITCH.

BJORN: (Speaker) Actually, I don't think that, but I can see how I could come across that way. [*validating Frances' experience*]. I think I overspend just as often as you do. I just do it in bigger chunks.

FRANCES: (Listener) Nice to hear that. [*validating his comment and feeling good about hearing him taking responsibility*] You can see that we both spend too much, just differently. You buy a few big things we may not need and I buy numerous smaller things.

BJORN: (Speaker) Exactly. We're both to blame and we can both do better.

FRANCES: (Listener) We both need to work together.

FLOOR SWITCH.

FRANCES: (Speaker) I agree that we need to deal with our retirement savings more radically. My biggest fear is losing the work I love so much. It's been the most meaningful thing I've done since the kids got older.

BJORN: (Listener) It's hard to imagine not having that—it's so important to you.

FRANCES: (Speaker) Exactly. Maybe there's some way to deal with this so I wouldn't lose all of what I'm doing, but where I could help us save what we need for retirement at the same time.

BJORN: (Listener) You're wondering if there could be a solution that would meet your needs and our needs at the same time.

FRANCES: (Speaker) Yes. I'm willing to think about solutions with you.

They discontinue the Speaker-Listener Technique.

BJORN: Okay.

FRANCES: So, are we both feeling understood enough to move on to the problem-solution step?

BJORN: I am, how about you?

FRANCES: [*she nods her head, yes*]

Here, they are agreeing together that they have had a good discussion and are ready to try some problem solving. They are consciously turning this corner together to move into problem solving.

PROBLEM SOLUTION
Bjorn and Frances now go through the four steps of problem solution.

Agenda Setting
Here, the important thing is for them to choose a specific piece of the whole issue that was discussed. This increases their chances of finding a solution that will really work:

FRANCES: We should agree on the agenda. We could talk about how to get more into the retirement accounts, but that may not be the place to start. I also think we need a discussion to deal with the issue of how we spend money and the credit cards.

BJORN: You're right. We're going to need several different stabs at this entire issue. It seems we could break it all down into the need to bring in more and the need to spend less. I don't want to push, but I'd like to focus on the "bring in more" part first, if you don't mind.

FRANCES: I can handle that. Let's problem-solve on that first, then we can talk later this week about the spending side.

BJORN: So, we're going to brainstorm about how to boost the income.

Brainstorming
The key here is to generate ideas freely.

FRANCES: Why don't you write the ideas down? You have a pen handy.

BJORN: Okay. You could get a part-time job.

FRANCES: I could ask the board of directors about making some of my work into a paid position. I'm practically a full-time staff member anyway.

BJORN: We could meet with a financial planner so we had a better idea what we really need to bring in. I could also get a second job.

FRANCES: I could look into part-time jobs that are similar to what I'm already doing, like those programs for kids with only one parent.

BJORN: You know, Jack and Marla are doing something like that. We could talk to them about what it's about.

FRANCES: I feel this list is pretty good. Let's talk about what we'll try doing.

Agreement and Compromise

Now they sift through the ideas that were generated in Brainstorming. The key is to find an agreement that both can get behind.

BJORN: I like your idea of talking to the board. What could it hurt?

FRANCES: I like that, too. I also think your idea of seeing a financial planner is good. Otherwise, how do we really know what the target is if I'm going to try to bring in something extra? But I don't think it's realistic for you to work more.

BJORN: Yeah, I think you're right. What about talking to Marla and Jack?

FRANCES: I'd like to hold off on that. That could lead them to try and get me involved, and I'm not sure I'm interested.

BJORN: Okay. What about seeing if there are any kinds of part-time jobs where you could do something that has meaning for you and make some bucks, too?

FRANCES: I'd like to think about that. It'd be a good way to go if they don't have room in the budget where I am now. I sure wouldn't want to do more than half-time, though. I'd hate to give up all of what I'm doing now.

BJORN: And I wouldn't want you to. If you could make a part-time income, I'll bet we could cut back enough to make it all work.

FRANCES: So how about I talk to the board, you ask Frank about that financial planner they use, and I'll also start looking around for part-time jobs.

BJORN: Great. Let's schedule some time next week to talk about
                how we're moving along for the solution we need.

FRANCES: Agreed.

They set a time to meet and follow up.

Follow-Up

At the end of the week, Frances and Bjorn meet to discuss what they're
finding out and what to do next. To her surprise, the board member
she talked with seemed eager to try to work something out. She'd also
started looking into various part-time jobs that would meet her needs.
Meanwhile, Bjorn has scheduled a meeting for them with a financial
planner for the following week.

In this case, the solution was a process made up of a series of smaller steps and agreements. Things were now moving on an issue that was
a problem between them for a long time, mostly because it felt good to
work together and they were no longer avoiding a tough issue.

Later, they went through the steps again and came to a specific
agreement about spending less. They decided how much less to spend
and agreed to record all the credit card purchases in a checkbook reg-
ister so they would know how they were doing compared to their target. In contrast to their problem solving about income, which was a
process that lasted for several weeks, the solution on spending was
implemented right away.

We'd like to tell you that this model always works this well, but
there are times when it doesn't. What do you do then?

WHEN IT'S NOT
THAT EASY

In our experience with couples, there are a few dilemmas that commonly come up in dealing with problems:

   I. Friction is likely and discussions can heat up. If they become so
      tense that you resort to negative behavior, it's time for a Time
      Out. We'll have more on that in the next chapter. If you can get
      back on track by staying with the structure (for example, the

Speaker-Listener Technique), great. If not, you need a break until you can be constructive again.

2. Sometimes, negative feelings can arise during the problem-solving phase. They need to be talked out. To do this, it's usually best to cycle back to problem discussion. Simply pick up the floor again and resume your discussion. It's better to slow things down than to continue to press for a solution that may not work.

3. The best solution you can reach during a session may not always be the best solution for the whole problem. At times, you should set the agenda just to agree on the next steps toward the best solution. For example, you might brainstorm about the kind of information you need to make your decision.

Your agreement phase could focus on who will gather specific pieces of information and when you will meet again to work on a decision based on what you find out. This is what Bjorn and Frances did in the example above. They broke down a very complex problem into much smaller pieces.

Remember this tactic when the problem seems too big or you don't know what to do next. If you use it consistently, you will increase your chances of regular, effective problem solving.

WHEN THERE'S NO SOLUTION

Although some problems don't have mutually satisfying solutions, there are far fewer unresolvable problems than couples sometimes think. If you've worked together for some time using the structure we suggest and no solution is forthcoming, either you can let this lack of a solution damage the rest of your marriage, or you can plan how to live with the difference. Sometimes couples allow the rest of a good marriage to be damaged by insisting on a resolution to a specific unresolved conflict.

For example, Phil and Deanne had recurrent nasty arguments about Deanne's smoking. Phil had been a smoker for many years, then quit. Now Deanne's smoking seemed to drive him crazy. This had become a power struggle in which both had developed filters about the problem.

Each felt unloved by the other because of the lack of a solution, and each interpreted the other's stubbornness as rejection. They had the choice to either deal with reality as it was or allow the accumulated frustration to damage everything else that was good in their marriage.

If you have an area that seems unresolvable, you can use the agenda in the problem-solution step to protect the rest of the marriage from the fallout from that one problem area. You literally "agree to disagree" constructively. This kind of solution comes about through both teamwork and tolerance. You can't always have your spouse be just the way you want him or her to be, but you can work as a team to deal with the differences.

Phil and Deanne decided to try the model, focusing on ways to protect the marriage. After an excellent discussion in which each really listened to what the other had to say, they were able to work toward a solution that limited the damage. Phil agreed not to pester Deanne and she agreed to smoke only in a certain room, and to smoke less when they were together. This problem could have led to the death of their marriage, but they refused to let that happen.

Here, we have given you a very specific model that will work well to help you preserve and enhance your teamwork in solving the problems that will come your way in life. We don't expect couples to use such a structured approach for minor problems, but we do expect that most couples could benefit from this model when they're dealing with more important matters, especially those that can lead to unproductive conflict. This is one more way to add structure when you need it most to preserve the best in your relationship.

In the next chapter, we'll build further on the techniques presented so far to help you prosper in your relationship together. The ground rules we present help you take control of the conflict in your relationship rather than allowing it to take control of you.

Exercises

There are three separate assignments for this chapter. First, we want you to practice making XYZ statements. Second, we invite you each to rate some common problem areas in your

relationship. Third, we ask you to practice the problem-solving model presented in this chapter. Remember, good ideas won't help unless you're motivated to put them into practice.

XYZ STATEMENTS: CONSTRUCTIVE GRIPING

1. Spend some time thinking about things that your partner does that bother you in some way. On a separate piece of paper, list your concerns as you normally might state them. Then practice putting your concerns into the XYZ format: "When you do X in situation Y, I feel Z."

2. Next, repeat the first exercise, but list the things your partner does that please you. You will find that the XYZ format also works well for giving positive, specific feedback, for example: "When you came home the other night with my favorite ice cream, I felt loved." Try sharing some of the positive thoughts with your spouse.

PROBLEM-AREA ASSESSMENT

The following inventory is a simple measure of common problem areas in relationships. It was originally developed by Knox in 1971, and we've used it for years in our research as a simple but very relevant measure of the problem areas in couples' relationships. As we'll explain, filling these forms out will help you practice the problem-solving skills we have presented. You should each fill out your own form independently.

PROBLEM INVENTORY

Consider the following list of issues that all relationships must face. Please rate how much of a problem each area currently is in your relationship by writing in a number from 0 (not at all a problem) to 100 (a severe problem). For example, if children are a slight problem in your relationship, you might enter 25 next to "children." If children are not a problem, you might enter a 0, and if children are a severe problem, you might enter 100. If you wish to add other areas that aren't included in our list, please do so in the blank spaces provided. Rate each area on a separate scale of 1 to 100 and be sure to rate all areas.

_____ money   _____ in-laws

_____ recreation   _____ alcohol and drugs

_____ jealousy   _____ sex

_____ communication   _____ children (or potential
                                           children)

_____ friends   _____ religion

_____ careers   _____ other (relatives,
                                           housework, etc.)

_____   _____

_____   _____

_____   _____

PROBLEM INVENTORY

Consider the list below of issues that all relationships must face. Please rate how much of a problem each area currently is in your relationship by writing in a number from 0 (not at all a problem) to 100 (a severe problem). For example, if children are a slight problem in your relationship, you might enter 25 next to "children." If children are not a problem, you might enter a 0, and if children are a severe problem, you might enter 100. If you wish to add other areas that aren't included in our list, please do so in the blank spaces provided. Rate each area on a separate scale of 1 to 100 and be sure to rate all areas.

_____ money

_____ recreation

_____ jealousy

_____ communication

_____ friends

_____ careers

_____ in-laws

_____ alcohol and drugs

_____ sex

_____ children (or potential children)

_____ religion

_____ other (relatives, housework, etc.)

_____

_____

_____

_____

_____

_____

PRACTICE PROBLEM SOLVING

For practicing this model, it's critical that you follow these instructions carefully. When you're dealing with real problems in your relationship, the chances of conflict are significant, and we want you to practice in a way that enhances your chances of solidifying these skills.

1. Set aside uninterrupted time to practice. Thirty minutes or so should be sufficient to begin using the sequence on some of the problems you want to solve.

2. Look over your problem inventories together. Make a list of those areas where you both rated the problem as being less serious. These are the problem areas we want you to use first to practice the model. Practice with very specific problems and look for very specific solutions. This will boost your skills and help you to gain confidence in the model.

3. We recommend that you set aside time to practice the problem-discussion and the problem-solution sequence several times a week for two or three weeks. If you put in this time, you'll gain skill and confidence in handling problem areas together.

4. Keep this chapter open while you're practicing, and refer back to the specific steps that are recommended.

5

Ground Rules for Handling Conflict

A S WE'VE SEEN in previous chapters, upbringing, gender differences, and personal choices made during arguments can put couples at risk if they don't learn to manage the inevitable conflicts and differences that arise in marriage. Without using some skill to overcome negative patterns, the resulting anger, contempt, and hostility can seriously damage the love and commitment in your relationship. Now that you understand some powerful techniques for communicating and solving problems, we turn to our five ground rules for protecting your relationship from mishandled conflict.

We call these principles ground rules to highlight their importance for your marriage. Used properly, these rules can help you control the difficult issues in your relationship rather than having the issues control you. We end Part One of the book with this topic for two reasons. First, the ground rules sum up many of the key points we have made so far. Second, these rules will give you the opportunity to agree on how you want to change the way in which you will communicate and handle conflict together.

In sports, ground rules specify what is allowed and not allowed, what is in bounds and out. To be sure, marriage is not a sport. Further, we don't want to invoke the image of competition by using the term *ground rules*. We just went to a lot of trouble in the last chapter to help you find ways to eliminate competitive attitudes. However, when things go downhill for couples, competition is a fact—competition over who will get his or her way. In our experience, these ground rules are powerful in helping couples stay on track and work as a team.

GROUND RULE NO. 1

When conflict is escalating, we will call a Time Out or Stop Action and either (a) try it again, using the Speaker-Listener Technique or (b) agree to talk about the issue later, at a specified time, using the Speaker-Listener Technique.

If we could get the attention of every couple and have them all agree to only one change in their relationship, we'd recommend following this ground rule. It's that important. This simple ground rule can protect and enhance relationships by counteracting the negative escalation that is so destructive to close relationships.

We suggest not only that you agree to this ground rule but also that you refer to it with a specific term such as Stop Action or Time Out, either term you like. That will help you interpret positively what you or your partner is doing. Otherwise, it becomes too easy to interpret what you're doing as avoidance. In fact, calling a Stop Action is one of the most positive things either of you can do for your relationship. You're recognizing old, negative behaviors and deciding to do something constructive instead.

We want you to approach this as something you are doing *together* for the good of your relationship. Sure, one of you may call Time Outs more often than the other, but if you both agree to the rule, you are really doing the Time Outs together.

It's important to know that you can call Stop Action if you realize that you, your partner, or both of you are getting out of control. Stop Action is called on the communication, not a person or relationship. Don't simply say "Stop Action" and leave the room—unilateral actions are usually counterproductive. Instead, say something like "This is getting hot. Let's stop the action and talk later, okay?" By including your partner in the decision, you're making the process mutual and, hence, de-escalating.

Another key to this ground rule is that you're agreeing to continue the argument—but productively—either right now or in the near future, after a cooling-off period. If you are a pursuing partner, this part of the ground rule addresses your concern that Time Outs could be used by an avoider to stop discussions about important issues. *This ground rule is designed to stop unproductive arguments, not all dialogue on an issue.* You do need to discuss important issues—just do it in a productive manner. In agreeing to use the Speaker-Listener Technique when you come back to talking about an issue, you're agreeing to deal more effectively with the issue that got out of hand.

The Stop Action itself can give the withdrawing partner confidence that the conflict won't get out of hand. Some withdrawing partners are even able to tolerate conflict better, because they know that they can stop it at any time. The Speaker-Listener Technique makes it still safer to deal with an issue by providing that all-important structure. This technique may work without using the Speaker-Listener Technique, but we're convinced that using it is more effective.

If you do decide to talk later, set a designated time immediately, if possible. Perhaps an hour later would be a good time to talk, or maybe the next day. If one of you was really angry when the Time Out was called, you may find that you can't talk when you come back to the discussion. That's okay. You can set a time after you both have calmed down. Next we'll give two examples, using couples who came to our PREP workshops, of this ground rule being used correctly.

Luke and Samantha had been married for only one year, but had already developed a pattern of frequent, intense arguments that ended with shouting and threats about the future of the relationship. Both came from homes where open, intense conflict was relatively common, so changing their pattern was not easy for them. As you will see, their arguments still escalate rather easily, but now they know how to stop when the argument gets going:

SAMANTHA: [*annoyed and showing it*] You forgot to get the trash out in time. The cans are already full.

LUKE: [*also annoyed, looking up from the paper*] It's no big deal. I'll just stuff it all down more.

SAMANTHA: Yeah, right. The trash will be overflowing all over the garage by next week.

LUKE: [irritated] Just leave it.

SAMANTHA: [very angry now, voice raised] You aren't getting a lot of the things done around here that you're supposed to.

LUKE: Let's call a Time Out—this isn't getting us anywhere.

SAMANTHA: Okay. When can we sit down and talk more about it? After "Home Improvement" tonight?

LUKE: Okay. As soon as the show is over.

There's nothing magic here. It's really very simple, but the effect is potentially powerful for your relationship. This couple used Time Out very effectively to stop an argument that wasn't going to be productive. Later, using the Speaker-Listener Technique, they sat down and talked about Samantha's concern that Luke wasn't meeting his responsibilities at home. They used the problem-solving techniques we presented in the last chapter to come up with some possible ways for the chores to get done.

In the next example, another couple used this ground rule to save an important evening from potential disaster. Both Byron and Alexandra were in their second marriage. They had been married to each other for six years and had no children. They wanted a family but had trouble conceiving, which added strain to their marriage. They had decided to take a weekend trip to a cottage in the mountains, to get away and spend a relaxing—perhaps romantic—few days together. They'd both been looking forward to this time together for months. This conversation took place on their first evening, as they got into bed together:

ALEXANDRA: [feeling romantic and snuggling up to Byron] It's so nice to get away. No distractions. This feels good.

BYRON: [likewise inclined, and beginning to caress her] Yeah, should've done this months ago. Maybe a relaxed setting can help you get pregnant.

ALEXANDRA: [bristling at the thought] Help you get pregnant? That sounds like you think it's my fault we're not getting pregnant. Why did you have to bring that up?

BYRON: [*anxious and annoyed at himself for spoiling the moment*] I don't think it's your fault. We've been through that. I just meant . . .

ALEXANDRA: [*angry*] You just meant to say that there is something wrong with me.

BYRON: Hold on. Stop the action. I'm sorry that I mentioned pregnancy. Do you want to talk this through now, or set a time for later?

ALEXANDRA: [*softening*] If we don't talk about it a little bit, I think the rest of the evening will be a drag.

BYRON: Okay, you have the floor. [*He picks up the remote control on the nightstand and hands it to her.*]

ALEXANDRA: (Speaker) I got all tense when you brought up pregnancy, and I felt like you were blaming me for our infertility.

BYRON: (Listener) So mentioning that subject raised unpleasant feelings, and more so because you felt blamed.

ALEXANDRA: (Speaker) Yes. That whole thing has been just awful for us, and I was hoping to get away from it for the weekend.

BYRON: (Listener) It's been really hard on you, and you wanted to just forget about it this weekend.

ALEXANDRA: (Speaker) I wanted us to focus on rediscovering how to be a little bit romantic, like it used to be.

BYRON: (Listener) Just you and me making love without a care.

ALEXANDRA: (Speaker) [*feeling really listened to and cared for*] Yes. Your turn.

FLOOR SWITCH.

BYRON: (Speaker) Boy, do I feel like a butthead. I didn't mean to mess up the moment, though I see how what I said affected you.

ALEXANDRA: (Listener) You feel bad that you said anything. You didn't mean to screw things up between us tonight.

BYRON: (Speaker) You got it. And I really don't think it's your fault we aren't pregnant. Whatever isn't working right in our bodies, I don't think of it as you or me screwing up. When I said what I said about you getting pregnant, I think of "us" getting pregnant, but really, it's you who will actually be pregnant. That's all I meant.

ALEXANDRA: (Listener) [*with a smile*] You didn't mean to be a butthead.

BYRON: (Speaker) [*chuckling back*] Yeah, that's what I'm saying. [*He hands her the floor.*] I think we should just avoid that whole topic for the weekend.

ALEXANDRA: (Listener) You think we should make infertility an off-limits topic this weekend.

BYRON: Yes!

Notice how effectively they used the Time Out to stop what could have turned into an awful fight. Alexandra was too hurt to just shelve the issue. She needed to talk right then, and Byron agreed. Doing so helped them defuse the tension and come back together, and it saved their special weekend.

GROUND RULE NO. 2

When we're having trouble communicating, we will use the Speaker-Listener Technique.

We hope you don't need much convincing about the wisdom of this ground rule. The key is to have a way to communicate safely and clearly when you really need to do it well. With this ground rule, you are agreeing to use more structure when you need it. The example above with Alexandra and Byron shows the value of this principle; however, often you don't need to call a Stop Action but still need to make the transition to a more effective mode of communication.

For example, suppose that you wanted to talk about a problem such as how money is being spent. You know from your history that these talks usually get difficult. You would be wise to follow this ground rule, raising the issue in this way: "Dear, I'm really concerned about money right now. Let's sit down and talk." Such a statement tells your partner that you are raising an important issue and that you want to talk it out using added structure. This is the most common use of this ground rule. You can learn to lower the control rods of your reactor before the problem escalates.

At other times, when the problem has already escalated, a Time Out might help, but it may be better to skip right to the Speaker-Listener Technique. In the next example, Allison and James used this ground rule to get back on track. They've been married for seven years, and before working on changing things, they had been locked into some unproductive communication and conflict patterns. They attended one of our workshops and later told us about this sequence of events. On this occasion, their new skills made a big difference.

One evening, they went out to dinner, and before they even ordered, they got into an argument in the middle of the restaurant:

ALLISON: [*matter of fact*] This reminds me. Dick and Barb asked us over for dinner next Saturday. I told them I thought we could do it.

JAMES: [*very angry*] What? How could you tell them we'd go without even asking? You know that I hate being around her.

ALLISON: [*angry, but speaking in a low, serious tone*] Lower your voice. People are turning to look at us.

JAMES: [*just as loud as before and just as angry*] So what? Let them stare. I'm sick and tired of you making decisions without talking to me first.

ALLISON: Don't talk to me like this.

JAMES: How 'bout I don't talk to you at all?

At that point, James got up and left the restaurant and went out to the car. He paced a bit, fuming and muttering about how difficult Allison could be at times. He then got into the car, intending to drive away and leave Allison at the restaurant. "Wouldn't that serve her right?" he thought. As he cooled off, however, he thought better of the idea. He got up, walked back into the restaurant, took his seat across from Allison, picked up a menu and handed it to her, and said, "Okay, you have the floor."

This might have been a good moment for a total Time Out, but instead, he decided that he wanted to talk this one out right now, productively. Allison went with it, and they proceeded to have an excellent discussion of the issue. As they passed the menu back and forth, the others in the restaurant must have thought they were having a terrible time making up their minds about what to order. Their transition to greater structure took them from what could have been a real meltdown to a victory for their relationship. Experiences like this serve to boost your confidence in your ability to work together and keep your relationship strong.

GROUND RULE NO. 3

When we're using the Speaker-Listener Technique, we will completely separate problem *discussion* from problem *solution*.

As we stated in the last chapter, it is critical to be clear at any given time about whether you are discussing or solving the problem. Too often, couples quickly agree to some solution, and the solution fails. A lot of added problems and hassles come from rushing to agreements without laying the proper foundation by communicating fully with each other.

Go back to Chapter Three and review the conversation between Tessie and Peter about Jeremy and preschool. Notice that they had a great discussion, but didn't seek a specific solution. They each expressed their concerns and then were ready to try problem solving on this issue. After they finished using the Speaker-Listener Technique, they continued this way:

TESSIE: I think we're ready for problem solving. What do you think?

PETER: I agree. I'm feeling like we had a good talk and got a lot out on the table. Now working on some solutions would be great.

With these simple comments, they have made the transition from problem discussion to problem solution and show that they've learned the value of separating the two. Discussion and solution are different processes, and each works better when you recognize this fact and act on it.

GROUND RULE NO. 4

We can bring up issues at any time, but the Listener can say: "This is not a good time." If the Listener doesn't want to talk at that time, he or she takes responsibility for setting up a time to talk in the near future.

This ground rule accomplishes one very important thing. It ensures that you won't have an important or difficult talk about an issue unless you both agree that the time is right. How often do you begin talking about a key issue in your relationship when your partner is just not ready for it? There's no point in having a discussion about anything important unless you're both ready to talk about it.

We emphasize this ground rule in appreciation of a fact of life: most couples talk about their most important issues at the worst times—over dinner, at bedtime, when you're getting the kids off for school, as soon as you walk in the door after work, when one of you is preoccupied with an important project or task—you get the picture. These are times when your spouse may be a captive audience, but you certainly don't have her or his attention. In fact, these are the most stressful times in the life of the average family.

This ground rule assumes two things: (1) that you each are responsible for knowing when you are capable of discussing something with appropriate attention to what your partner has to say and (2) that you can each respect the other when he or she says, "I can't deal with that right now." There simply is no point in trying to have a discussion if you're both not up for it.

You may ask, "Isn't this just a prescription for avoidance?" That's where the second part of the ground rule comes in. The person who isn't ready for a discussion takes responsibility for making it happen in the *near* future. This is critical. Your partner will have a much easier time putting off the conversation if he or she is confident that you really will follow through. We recommend that when you use this ground rule, you agree to set up a better time within twenty-four to

RAGNAR STORAASLI

forty-eight hours. This may not always be practical, but it works as a good rule of thumb. The following example shows how this works.

Martina and Alex are a couple with two children, a five-year-old girl and a two-year-old boy. As is typical of many couples with young children, they have little time in their marriage for sleeping, much less talking things out. As a result, they often are alone only at bedtime, after both kids are finally bathed and asleep. One night, they had this conversation:

ALEX: I can't believe how Mary wants to hear the same story ten times in a row. I thought she'd never get to sleep.

MARTINA: It's the same with naps. You'd think she'd be bored to death with those stories.

ALEX: I would. Speaking of boring things, we need to talk about those life insurance decisions. I know that agent will call back any day.

MARTINA: I know it's important, but I just can't focus right now. I think I could focus about ten minutes on David Letterman, and that's about it.

ALEX: Pretty wiped, eh? Me, too. Well, what would be a good time to talk about this?

MARTINA: No guarantee I'll be alive, but I think I might have the energy around lunchtime tomorrow. Could you come home? Maybe we'll get lucky and catch Matt in his nap.

ALEX: Sounds good. Let's watch Dave and crash.

It is now Martina's responsibility to bring the subject up again tomorrow and to make this talk happen. Because their agreement is rather specific, Alex should be able to show up at lunchtime for their talk. They may be too tired and busy for there ever to be a "perfect" time to talk this out, but some times are better than others.

As one variation of this ground rule, you may want to come to an agreement that certain times are never good for bringing up important things. For example, we have worked with many couples who have agreed that neither will bring up anything significant within thirty minutes of bedtime. These couples decided that they were just too tired at bedtime, and that it was more important to relax and wind down.

GROUND RULE NO. 5

We will have weekly "couple's meetings."

Most couples do not set aside a regular time for dealing with key issues and problems. The importance of doing so has been suggested by so many marriage experts over the years that it's almost a cliché. Nevertheless, we want to give you our view on this sage advice.

The advantages of having a weekly meeting time far outweigh any negatives. First, this is a tangible way to place a high priority on your marriage by carving out time for its upkeep. We know you're busy. We're all busy. But if you decide that this is important, you can find the time to make it work out.

Second, following this ground rule ensures that even if there's no other good time to deal with issues and problems in your marriage, you at least have this weekly meeting. You might be surprised at how much you can get done in thirty minutes or so of concentrated attention to an issue. During this meeting, you can talk about the relationship, discuss specific problems, or practice communication skills. That includes using all of the skills and techniques we've recommended in Part One of this book.

A third advantage of this ground rule is that having a weekly meeting time takes much of the day-to-day pressure off your relationship. This is especially true if you've gotten tangled up in the pursuer-withdrawer pattern. If something happens that brings up a gripe for you, it's much easier to delay bringing it up until another time if you know there will *be* another time. If you're the pursuing partner, you can relax; you'll have your chance to raise your issue. If you're the withdrawing partner, you're encouraged to bring up your concerns because you have a meeting set aside for just this purpose.

You may be thinking that this is a pretty good idea. But to put this good idea into action, *you must be consistent in taking the time to make the meetings happen.* We've heard repeatedly from couples that when they're getting along well, they have an urge to skip the meetings. Don't succumb to this urge.

Consider Roberto and Margaret. They'd set aside Wednesday nights at 9 P.M. as a time for their meeting, but if they were getting along well during the week, when Wednesday night rolled around, each of them would begin to think, "We don't need to meet tonight. No use stirring things up when we're getting along so well." Then one or the other would say, "Hey, dear, we're doing fine—let's just skip the meeting tonight."

What Roberto and Margaret came to realize is that they were having fewer conflicts partly because they were regularly having their meetings. After they canceled a few meetings, they noticed that more conflicts would come up during the week. They'd given up their time to deal with issues and reverted to the uncertainty of dealing with problems if and when they could. They decided that "if and when" was not placing the proper importance on their marriage and resumed their meetings.

If you actually do have little to deal with, fine. Have a short meeting, but have a meeting. Use these meetings to air gripes, discuss important issues, plan for key events coming up, or just take stock of how the relationship is going. When you're focusing on a specific problem, work through the steps for problem discussion and problem solution presented in the last chapter. When there's nothing more pressing, practice some of the skills presented in the program. Take the time and use it to keep your relationship strong.

GROUND RULE NO. 6

We will make time for the great things: fun, friendship, and sensuality. We will agree to protect these times from conflict and the need to deal with issues.

Just as it's important to set aside time to deal with issues in your relationship, it's also critical to protect key times from conflicts. You can't focus on issues all the time and have a truly great marriage. You need some time for relaxing together—having fun, talking as friends, making love—when conflict and problems are off limits. This is a key point that we'll discuss in the chapters on friendship, fun, and sensuality later in the book.

For now, we'll emphasize two points. First, make time for these great things. Second, when you're spending time together in one of these ways, don't bring up issues that you have to work on. And if an issue does come up, table it until later—for example until your couple's meeting.

Alexandra and Byron's discussion, which we presented earlier in this chapter, makes this point well. They were out to have a relaxing and romantic weekend, and this wasn't the time to focus on one of their key issues. Using Time Out and the Speaker-Listener Technique helped them to refocus on having fun. It's better still if you agree in the first place to keep such issues off-limits during positive times.

One essential benefit for your relationship is embedded in all these ground rules. When you use them properly, *you're agreeing to control the difficult issues in your marriage rather than allowing them to control you.* Instead of having arguments whenever issues come up, you're agreeing to deal with the issues when you're both able to do it well—and when you're both under control.

One of the most destructive things that can happen to your marriage is to have the growing sense that you're walking through a mine field. You know the feeling. You begin to wonder where the next explosion will come from, and you don't feel in control of where you're going. You no longer feel free to just "be" with your partner. You don't know when you're about to step on a mine, but you know right away when you do. It doesn't have to be this way. These ground rules do a lot toward getting you back on safe ground. They work. You can do it.

Following the next exercise, we'll turn our attention to deeper issues and more complex processes in relationships. Please continue to practice all of the skills we've presented thus far as we move ahead into the subjects of the next section: hidden issues, commitment, and forgiveness.

 ## Exercises

Your exercise for the end of this chapter is very straightforward. Discuss these ground rules and begin to try them out. You may want to modify one or more of them in some specific manner to make them work better for you. That's fine. The key is to review the rules and give them a chance to work in your relationship and, after you've given them a try, to talk about them again and agree on which ones you'll use regularly. We list the rules again here. You can note any changes you make to them in the space that follows each one.

SUGGESTED GROUND RULES FOR HANDLING ISSUES

1. When conflict is escalating, we will call a Time Out or Stop Action and either (a) try it again, using the Speaker-Listener Technique or (b) agree to talk about the issue later, at specified time, using the Speaker-Listener Technique.

2. When we're having trouble communicating, we will use the Speaker-Listener Technique.

3. When we're using the Speaker-Listener Technique, we will completely separate problem *discussion* from problem *solution*.

4. We can bring up issues at any time, but the Listener can say: "This is not a good time." If the Listener doesn't want to talk at that time, he or she takes responsibility for setting up a time to talk in the near future (you need to decide how "the near future" is defined).

5. We will have weekly "couple's meetings." (Schedule a time now.)

6. We will make time for the great things: fun, friendship, and sensuality. We will agree to protect these times from conflict and the need to deal with issues.

DEALING WITH CORE ISSUES

6

The Difference Between Issues and Events

S O FAR, we've focused on how you can manage conflict and disagreements in your marriage. Now we want to offer some help in dealing with everyday happenings and long-term arguments. All couples experience frustrating events and all couples confront difficult issues. In this chapter, we'll help you to understand how issues and events are connected and how important it is to deal with them separately. Then we'll discuss the deeper, often hidden issues that affect relationships.

The techniques and ground rules you've learned so far will be very valuable for handling both issues and events in a way that keeps you working together as a team. Read on and you'll see what we mean.

ISSUES VERSUS EVENTS

As we pointed out in Chapter Four, most married couples say that the three major issues that cause problems are money, sex, and communication. Other issues they commonly fight about are in-laws, children, recreation, alcohol and drugs, religion, sex, careers, and housework.

While these issues are important, we find that they're not what couples argue about most frequently. Instead, couples argue most often about the small, everyday happenings of life. We call them *events*. We want to help you separate out events from issues, and then to separate out the issues that are more apparent—like money, communication, and sex—from the deeper, often hidden, issues that affect your relationship. An example will help you see what we mean.

Ellen and Gregg are a couple who argue a lot about money. One day, Ellen came home from work and put the checkbook down on the kitchen counter as she went to the bedroom to change. Gregg looked at the checkbook and became livid when he saw an entry for $150 made out to a department store. When Ellen walked back into the kitchen, tired after a long day at work, she was expecting Gregg to hug her or ask, "How was your day?" Instead, the conversation went like this:

GREGG: What did you spend that $150 on?

ELLEN: [very defensive] None of your business.

GREGG: Of course it's my business. We just decided on a budget and here you go blowing it.

And they were off into a huge argument about money. But it happened in the context of an event—Gregg happening to look and see that Ellen spent $150. Events like this are common to all couples. In this case, Ellen had actually spent the $150 on a new sweater for Gregg because he had just received an offer for a new job. But that never even came up.

Issues and events work like the geysers in Yellowstone National Park. Underneath the park are caverns of hot water under pressure. The issues in your relationship are like those pressure points: the ones that give you more trouble contain the greatest amount of heat. The pressure keeps building up when you aren't talking about them in a constructive manner, then events trigger an eruption.

Yellowstone's Old Faithful can be spectacular and beautiful. However, the blast of negative energy in your relationship when an issue is triggered by an event isn't so pretty. And when it happens a lot, your issues are controlling you. You aren't controlling them. At Yellowstone, the eruptions release pressure for a while. In your relationship, the eruptions only add to the storehouse of negative energy connected to the issues.

Many couples, particularly those in unhappy relationships, only deal with important issues in the context of triggering events. For

RAGNAR STORAASLI

Ellen and Gregg, so much negative energy is stored up around the issue of money that it's easily triggered. They never sit down and talk about money in a constructive way; instead, they argue all the time as checks bounce, bills come in, or other money events happen. They never get anywhere on the big issue because they spend their energy just dealing with the crises caused by the events.

Another couple, Tom and Samantha, weren't discussing the issue of the intrusion of relatives on their time together. One evening, they went to a baseball game—the first time they'd been out for three or four weeks. On the way, Tom received a phone call from his mother on his mobile phone. When the phone call ended, Samantha confronted Tom:

SAMANTHA: Why do you always let her interfere with our relationship? This is our evening out.

TOM: [very hot under the collar] There you go again, blasting me when we're going out to have fun for a change.

SAMANTHA: [sounding indignant] Well, I didn't know we were planning on bringing your mother with us.

TOM: [his voice dripping with sarcasm] Ha, Ha. Real funny, Sam.

Their evening was now destroyed. They never even made it to the ballpark. They spent the night arguing about his mother calling and whether or not she was too involved in their lives.

As in this case, events tend to come up at inopportune times— you're ready to leave for work, you're coming home from work, you're going to bed, you're out trying to relax, the kids are around, friends have come over, and so forth. These are the worst times for dealing with issues.

We're suggesting that you edit out your desire to argue about an issue at the moment when an event triggers it. The key to this is saying to yourself, "I don't have to deal with this right now. This isn't the right time. We can talk later." Samantha could have said, "That phone call from your mother really set off an issue for me. We need to sit down and talk about it later." In this way, she would have acknowledged the event but left the issue for a time when they could deal with it more effectively. That's what we mean by separating issues from events.

Likewise, Tom could have said, "Listen, let's stop the action. I can see you're feeling hurt, but let's wait for a better time to talk about the issue. How about tomorrow after dinner?" If they'd been practicing the skills we've presented so far, this could have saved their evening by containing the event so that it didn't trigger the explosive unresolved issue of his mother and their time together.

They also could have tried to talk about the issue for a few minutes—agreeing to have a fuller discussion later. Tom might have said, "Let's talk about what just happened for a few moments and then try to move on and have a nice evening together." Couples can use the Speaker-Listener Technique if they want to make sure that both partners feel heard, then let the subject go until later.

One reason why people focus on events and let them turn into issue discussions is that they don't feel that "later" will happen, so why wait? And they jump in right away. Then they wind up in a marital mine field, with the issues being the explosives and the events being the triggers. We don't recommend that you try to talk out issues in the context of events. But if you really need to do it, make sure that you use the Speaker-Listener Technique.

Practicing the things we've been teaching will make it more likely that you'll handle events better and plan the time to deal with important issues. And you'll maintain a level of control as to where, when, and how the issues will be dealt with.

HIDDEN ISSUES

Most of the time people can recognize the issues that are triggered by events because they have almost the same content. With Ellen and Gregg, his looking at the checkbook started the event, and the issue was money. That's not hard to figure out. But you'll also find yourselves getting caught up in fights around events that don't seem to be attached to any particular issue. Or you may find that you aren't getting anywhere when you talk about particular problems; you're just spinning your wheels. These are signs that you aren't getting at the real issues. The real issue isn't about money or careers or housework or leaving the toilet seat up—it's deeper and more elusive.

Hidden issues often drive the really destructive arguments. For example, Samantha and Tom ended up arguing about his mother, but the real issue may be that Samantha felt that she wasn't important to Tom. When we say that issues are hidden, we mean that they're usually not being talked about openly or constructively. Instead, they're the key issues that often get lost in the flow of the argument. You may be very aware of feeling uncared for, but when certain events come up, that's not what's talked about. Just as Samantha may have been aware of feeling that Tom wasn't interested in her, that's not what they ended up fighting about. They were missing the forest (the hidden issues) for the trees (the events).

To summarize,

1. Events are everyday happenings such as dirty dishes or a bounced check.

2. Issues are the larger topics like money, sex, and in-laws that all couples must deal with.

3. Hidden issues are the deeper, fundamental issues that can come up with any issue or event.

We see several types of hidden issues in our work with couples—
issues of control and power, needing and caring, recognition, commitment, integrity, and acceptance. There are surely others, but these six
capture a lot of what goes on in relationships.

CONTROL AND POWER

With control issues, the question is who will have the status and
power. Who decides who does the chores? Are your needs and desires
just as important as your partner's, or is there an inequality? Is your
input important or are major decisions made without you? Who's in
charge? If you're encountering these kinds of issues, you may be dealing with the hidden issue of control.

Even if there are no ongoing struggles over control between you,
these issues can affect your relationship when you need to make decisions—even small ones. For example, what happens if one of you really wants to eat pizza and the other feels like having Chinese food. This
is an event without a lot of long-term significance. Nevertheless, if
either of you is unyielding in what you want, a lot of conflict can
develop over something as simple as cuisine. You may feel as if the
other person is trying to control you or as if you need to be in control.
A power struggle can result over just about anything.

Whatever the topic or disagreement, control issues are least likely to damage your relationship when you feel that you're a team, and that each partner's needs and desires are attended to in the decisions you make. That hasn't been the case for B. J. and Roslyn.

B. J. and Roslyn are like many couples where one keeps a closer eye on the budget and the other spends more freely. Roslyn goes through the roof every time she finds out that B. J. has bought something new for the stereo. Even though it's not in the budget, he buys new components all the time. Each partner feels the other one is controlling the money.

B. J. and Roslyn are locked in a power struggle that's being played out over money. Each of them wants control and feels as if the other one is taking something away. There's no concept of a team working together. After particularly bad events, as when B. J. bought the latest speakers, they didn't speak to each other for weeks. Of course, they rarely talk about power or control, just what's affordable and what's not. But that's what they really need to be talking about. B. J. is showing that he's in control by the way he spends money. "I'm not going to let her tell me what to do!" he thinks. He has the power to do what he wants—he thinks.

Often people are motivated to be in control because they're actually hypersensitive about being controlled by others, so control becomes a big issue. Usually these people have experienced a very controlling and powerful authority figure, often a parent, somewhere in the past. That's the case with B. J.

B. J. grew up in a family where his parents rarely let him make any decisions for himself. They were very controlling, and he made a vow never to be controlled by anyone again. He likes to buy stereo equipment, but his purchases also signify his great need for independence in relationships. The trouble is that he's acting independently even though he's married. It's not fair for him to blow the family budget. But unless he and Roslyn can learn to talk together about the underlying hidden issue of control, they'll never get anywhere with the budget.

This example shows why it's no accident that money is rated the number-one problem area in study after study. So many decisions in our lives revolve around money. If you have significant power or control problems in your marriage, it's likely that you struggle a lot with money as well as any number of other things. Money in and of itself isn't usually the deeper issue, but it's an issue that provides many events that can trigger the deeper issues.

Whenever you must make a decision together, an opportunity arises for control issues to be triggered. When you disagree, either one of you will get your way, or you'll compromise. But it's hard to compromise or let your spouse win an argument if it will make you feel controlled or powerless. It's best to keep such issues from being a problem in your marriage in the first place. Working together as a team is the best antidote to the hidden issue of control.

NEEDING AND CARING

A second major arena for hidden issues involves caring. Here, the main theme is the extent to which you feel loved. As we'll see, such issues are often felt as a concern that important emotional needs aren't being met.

Jill and Nelson are a couple who came to one of our workshops. They told us that they repeatedly fought over who should refill the orange juice container, but orange juice wasn't the real issue fueling their arguments. As it turned out, when Nelson's mother refilled the juice container, he thought of it as demonstrating her love and care for him. Since Jill wouldn't do it, he felt she didn't love him. Nelson was very aware of feeling uncared for, but in their arguments about orange juice he didn't talk about that feeling. Instead, he focused on what he saw as Jill's stubbornness and his felt need.

For her part, Jill was thinking, "Who is he to tell me to make the orange juice? Where does he get off saying I have to do it?" She felt that he was trying to control her by forcing her to live a certain way. That wasn't his motive, but she was very sensitive, since she'd previously been married to a domineering man. Nelson was acting the same way, not because of control issues but because he felt a need to be cared for in a certain way. For them, discussing this brought them closer, and orange juice no longer seemed especially important.

NELSON: (Speaker) So for me, it's really not about wanting to control you. I've been so primed by my upbringing to connect refilling the OJ with love that I've put this pressure on you to be sure that you love me.

JILL: (Listener) So for you, the key issue is wanting to know I care, not wanting to control me?

NELSON: (Speaker) [goes on to validate her, as well] Exactly, and I can see how you'd be feeling controlled without knowing that.

FLOOR SWITCH.

JILL: (Speaker) You're right. I've really felt you wanted to control me, and that's a real hot button given what I went through with Joe.

NELSON: (Listener) It really did seem to you that I just wanted to control you, and that's an especially sensitive area given what you went through with Joe.

JILL: (Speaker) You got it. I want to be your partner, not your servant.

NELSON: (Listener) Sounds like you want us to be a team.

JILL: (Speaker) Yep!

As you can see from the tail end of their conversation, learning to talk about the bigger concerns paved the way for greater connection instead of alienation over empty orange juice containers. This is another example where it would be pointless to solve the problem about the event—refilling the orange juice container—unless you were communicating well enough to get the hidden issues out in the open.

In our work with couples, we often see a particular trigger for issues of caring. Sometimes one partner is better about doing the exercises and practicing than the other. Sabrina and Jackson are one such couple. They participated in a workshop over several weeks. Both were in their second marriage, and they agreed that it was important to do things right this time. Nevertheless, Sabrina complained about it being hard to get Jackson to do the exercises. The events—his not doing all the work—led her to feel as if he didn't really care. This triggered arguments about the value of homework and about the cost of the program.

They finally were able to use their communication skills to talk about her feeling of being uncared for because of his avoidance. That's the key—to talk about these kinds of deeper issues rather than let them operate as hidden issues in arguments.

RECOGNITION

The third type of hidden issue involves recognition. Are your activities and accomplishments appreciated by your partner? While caring issues involve concerns about being cared for or loved, recognition issues are more about feeling valued by your partner for who you are and what you do.

Consider Burt and Chelsea, a couple who own a business together. Burt is president and treasurer of their corporation and Chelsea is vice president and secretary. Most of the time, they enjoy running their business together, but one day they were seated at a luncheon when someone asked Burt a question about the company. His quick response was, "I'm the only officer in this company." Chelsea, who was sitting right next to him, was furious and embarrassed.

We can only speculate about why Burt failed at times to recognize his wife's role in the company. Perhaps control issues were seeping out when he made this comment. Perhaps he thought, "I can do it all," and really did disregard her contributions to the company. Whatever his hidden motivations, such events will make Chelsea's involvement less and less rewarding. She may slowly pull away from him over time. If they want to prevent further damage to their relationship, they'd better talk openly about this key issue.

Such examples are common. For example, many men tell us that they don't feel like their wives place much value on the work they do to bring home income for the family. Likewise, we hear many women — whether or not they work outside the home—say that they don't feel as if their husbands appreciate what they do at home for the family. In either case, spouses may try hard for a while to get recognized, but they'll eventually burn out if no appreciation is expressed. It's okay to want your spouse to recognize and appreciate what you bring to the relationship. How long has it been since you told your partner how much you appreciate the things he or she does?

COMMITMENT

The focus of this fourth hidden issue is on the long-term security of the relationship, expressed by the question: "Are you going to stay with me?" One couple we worked with, Alice and Chuck, had huge arguments about their separate checking accounts. Whenever the bank statement arrived, Chuck would complain bitterly about Alice's having a separate account. This problem wasn't related to a money or hidden control issue. For Chuck, the hidden issue was commitment. He'd been married once before and his ex-wife had had a separate account. She decided to leave him after fifteen years of marriage, which was easier since she'd saved up several thousand dollars in her account.

Now, when the statement for Alice's account would arrive, he'd associate it with the thought that she could be planning to leave him. That was not her plan at all, but since Chuck rarely talked openly about his fear, she wasn't given the opportunity to alleviate his anxiety by affirming her commitment. The issue kept fueling explosions of conflict during these events.

Sometimes the issue of commitment is triggered by the success of one partner. Psychologist Stephen Beach and his colleagues have suggested that in distressed relationships, people are threatened by the success of their partners. In healthier relationships, partners tend to take pride in each other's accomplishments. Perhaps the commitment in distressed relationships is already threatened, and the success of one partner is seen by the other as providing more alternatives for leaving. Success can also trigger hidden recognition issues. If one partner is not feeling recognized and sees the other partner receiving a lot of recognition, this could intensify feelings of not being appreciated.

Do you worry about your partner's long-term commitment to you and the marriage? Have you talked about this openly or does this issue find indirect expression in the context of events in your relationship? In Chapters Eight and Nine, we'll focus in much more depth on how commitment issues affect relationships.

INTEGRITY

The fifth type of hidden issue deals with integrity. Have you ever noticed how upset you get when your partner questions your intent or motives? These events can spark great fury. With Stuart and Gladys, arguments frequently end up with each being certain they know what the other meant. Most often they're sure that what the other meant was negative. Both of them are therapists, so you'd think they'd know better, but they have a serious problem with making negative interpretations. Here's a typical example:

GLADYS: You forgot to pick up the dry cleaning.

STUART: [feeling a bit indignant] You didn't ask me to pick it up, you asked me if I was going by there. I told you I wasn't.

GLADYS: [really angry at what she sees as his lack of caring about what she needs] You did say you'd pick it up, but you just don't give a damn about me.

STUART: [feeling thoroughly insulted] I do care, and I resent you telling me I don't.

Gladys's caring issue is pretty much out in the open here even though they're not exactly having a constructive, healing talk about it. But Stuart's issue has more to do with integrity. It's not as evident, but it's there. He feels insulted that she's calling him an uncaring, inconsiderate husband who never thinks about her needs. Each partner winds up feeling invalidated.

As we pointed out earlier in this book, it's not wise to argue about what your partner really thinks, feels, or intends. Don't tell your spouse what's going on inside, unless it's about *your* insides! To do otherwise is guaranteed to trigger the issue of integrity. And anyone will defend his or her integrity when it's questioned.

ACCEPTANCE: THE MOTHER OF ALL HIDDEN ISSUES

There seems to be one primary issue that can underlie all the others listed here: the desire for acceptance. Sometimes this is felt more as a fear of rejection, but the fundamental issue is the same. At the deepest level, people are motivated to find acceptance and to avoid rejection in their relationships. This reflects the deep need everyone has to be both respected and connected.

You can see this issue come up in many ways. For example, some people are afraid that if they act in certain ways their partner is going to reject them. A lowered sense of self-worth would only make such fears more intense. People may ask for what they want indirectly rather than directly, for example, by saying "Wouldn't you like to make love tonight?" rather than "I'd like to make love with you tonight." Their real desires are filtered out because of a fear of rejection.

People act out hidden issues of acceptance and rejection in a number of other ways. Consider Hector and Louise's problem with Hector's yearly hunting trip. Hector and Louise have been married for five years, and things have gone remarkably well for them, especially considering that they've blended two families. They have four children, aged seven through fifteen, all from their first marriages. There are few problems they can't handle, largely because they took a course on stepfamilies when they were engaged. They talk regularly about the more important issues, which keeps things running pretty smoothly. However, there is one problem they've never really solved.

Once a year, every year, Hector goes hunting with his friends for two weeks. The men rent a cabin in the mountains and virtually disappear. The following argument was typical. It was late, and Hector was packing to leave at five in the morning:

LOUISE: I really hate it when you leave for this trip every year. You leave me to handle everything by myself.

HECTOR: [feeling a bit defensive] You knew when we got married that I did this every year. I don't know why you have to complain about it every time.

LOUISE: [going on the attack] I just don't think it's very responsible to leave your family alone for two weeks. The kids need you around more than that. They get very irritable while you're gone.

HECTOR: [He thinks, "Why do we have to do this every year? I hate this argument." Now he's getting angry.] I do a lot with them. You need to deal with this better.

LOUISE: [angrier herself] If you cared more about your family, you wouldn't have this need to get away from us for two weeks every year.

HECTOR: *[getting up to leave the room, feeling disgusted]* Yeah, you're right. You're always right, "my dear."

LOUISE: *[yelling after him as he walks out]* I hate it when you talk to me like that. You can't treat me like your dad treats your mom. I won't stand for it.

HECTOR: *[shouting from the other room]* I'm not like my father, and you aren't telling me what to do. I'm going, I'll keep going every year, and you might as well just get used to it.

What's really going on here? Getting ready for the trip is the event. They have this same nasty argument every year, usually the night before he leaves. It's as much a part of the tradition as the trip is. Neither of them likes it, but they haven't found a way to do it differently.

As Hector and Louise learned in our PREP classes, many hidden issues are being triggered. Deep down, Louise doesn't feel cared for when these trips come up. She feels lonely when Hector leaves and this is hard to handle since she sees him looking forward to being gone. She wonders if he's delighted to get away from her. She feels abandoned—reflecting some commitment issues that also get triggered. Her focus on the kids is a smokescreen for her real concerns.

Hector likes to be in control of his life, so that's one hidden issue being triggered here. This is reflected by his statement: "You aren't telling me what to do!" Also, as they argue unproductively, integrity comes up. He feels that she's calling into question his devotion as a husband and father. He sees himself as very dedicated to the family and just wants this two-week period each year to be with his friends. He doesn't think that's asking a lot.

Underneath it all, you can see acceptance as the most basic hidden issue driving the issues of power, caring, commitment, and integrity in their argument. Neither of them feels totally accepted by the other. This isn't a serious unresolved issue for them. After all, they do have a great relationship and generally feel good about each other. Yet the need for acceptance is so basic for all of us that it can become triggered by almost any event or issue—if we let it.

In this argument, Louise and Hector aren't talking about the hidden issues in any productive way. The deeper issues aren't totally hidden, but they aren't being dealt with directly and constructively, either. Let's discuss how to do this right.

RECOGNIZING THE SIGNS OF HIDDEN ISSUES

You can't handle hidden issues unless you can identify them. There are four key ways to tell when hidden issues may be affecting your relationship.

Wheel Spinning

One sign of hidden issues is when you find yourselves spinning your wheels as you talk about the same problem over and over again. When an argument starts with you thinking, "Here we go again," you should suspect hidden issues. You never really get anywhere on the problem because you aren't talking about what really matters—the hidden issue. Louise and Hector can and have argued in this manner for hours. It doesn't get them anywhere and they both know it. It's as if they're mired in mud; in fact they're slinging it.

Trivial Triggers

A second clue to hidden issues is that trivial issues are blown up out of all proportion. The argument between Jill and Nelson described earlier is a great example. Failing to fill the orange juice container seems like a trivial event but it triggers horrendous arguments driven by the issues of power and caring.

Another good example comes from one of our own relationships. Twelve years ago, when they were engaged, Scott Stanley and his fiancée, Nancy, had a major relationship blowout over a seemingly minor, irrelevant point. At the time, they were both graduate students living on different sides of Ohio. One Friday afternoon, Scott had just driven four hours to see Nancy, and the conversation went like this:

NANCY: What do you want for dinner tonight?

SCOTT: Why don't we just order pizza? It's raining so hard, I don't want to go out again.

NANCY: Okay, sounds good.

SCOTT: I'll call for delivery.

NANCY: Don't get on the phone right now. There's a thunderstorm, you could get struck by lightning.

SCOTT: That's ridiculous. You can't get struck by lightning on the phone during a thunderstorm. [*picking up the phone*]

NANCY: What do you mean, "You can't." I know you can. Put the phone down.

SCOTT: I'm calling now. Stand back if you're so worried. [*muttering*] I never heard anything so stupid.

NANCY: You can fry for all I care." [*stomping off*]

Once Scott got off the phone, they proceeded to get into a nasty argument about whether you could get struck by lightning while talking on the phone. The fight lasted into the evening and the next day. Late Saturday they stopped the argument, then were cool and distant the rest of the weekend. Because they couldn't get together very often, they wasted a valuable weekend talking about lightning and telephones.

You can't have a big argument about something that's meaningless unless there's a hidden issue. Something bigger was at stake. At the time, Scott and Nancy thought they were arguing about telephones and lightning. Nancy had good intentions when she said, "Don't get on the phone right now." She didn't want Scott blown across the room in ashes and cinders. That's pretty positive. But Scott experienced Nancy's statement as an attempt to control him, and that pushed his buttons. Then, when he started arguing with her about lightning and telephones, she got angry at him for not valuing her input. His response triggered recognition, caring, and control issues for her. So away they went.

By the way, Nancy was right. As a child she'd had a neighbor whose phone was blown across the room in flames when the house was hit by lightning. Even years later, when Scott was using this example on the Andrea Van Steenhouse call-in radio program in Denver, Nancy was tempted to call in and ask, "Who was right?" Perhaps there's still a bit of life in this event for Scott and Nancy.

Avoidance

A third sign of hidden issues is when one or both of you are avoiding certain topics or levels of intimacy. If walls have gone up between you, it often means that important, unexpressed issues are affecting the relationship. Perhaps it seems too risky to talk directly about feeling unloved or insecure. But the trouble is that these concerns have a way of coming up anyway.

Quite a few of the topics couples avoid reflect hidden issues in relationships. For example, we've talked with many couples from different cultural or religious backgrounds who strongly avoid talking about these differences. We think that this usually reflects concerns about acceptance. The deeper question is: "Will you accept me fully if we really talk about our different backgrounds?" Avoiding such topics not only allows hidden issues to remain hidden; it puts the relationship at greater risk since such differences can have a great impact on a marriage. Other common but taboo topics include sex, weight, money, politics, values, and religion. There are many such sensitive topics that people avoid dealing with in their relationships out of fear of rejection.

In addition to avoiding certain topics, many couples avoid certain kinds and levels of intimacy. Again, this can be a symptom of hidden issues. Consider the area of physical intimacy. We've heard many men complain that their wives just aren't as affectionate as they used to be. The wives often say the reason is that they don't feel valued and cared for in the marriage. As a result, they pull back from intimacy, especially sexual closeness.

The husbands notice this and sometimes press even more for physical affection to regain their connection. The wives pull back further, feeling that their husbands are just interested in sex. Unpleasant events begin to occur routinely in the bedroom.

One such couple, Jamal and Kayla, were stuck in this pattern. They'd been married for six years, with one child, Marvel, born in the first year of their marriage. This added the pressure of responsibility early on. Both worked outside the home and both felt that there was a lot more to do each day than time to do it in. The distance was growing daily in their relationship. Jamal avoided talking with Kayla about what was wrong; she avoided physical intimacy. It wasn't until they talked directly about the issues that they began to unhook themselves from the cycle. Jamal finally brought it up, and their talk went like this:

JAMAL: I've noticed that you don't seem too interested in touching or making love anymore.

KAYLA: You're right. I've been feeling like you're not interested in me except for sex.

JAMAL: That's not it. I feel like you aren't interested in me and that's one way I try to get close again. I don't want what we used to have to slip away.

KAYLA: [*a bit skeptically*] You mean to say that you're not just trying to use me?

JAMAL: I mean to say that I'm not trying to use you at all. I love you. I want to be close to you. When we make love and it's good, I feel that brings us back together. That's what I'm trying to do, bring us back together. I've been real sad about the wall between us.

KAYLA: That's a lot different from how I've been looking at it. I've been feeling that you don't care much and that you're only interested in sex.

JAMAL: [*listening nondefensively*] I hear that. I can even see how it might look that way, but that's really not it. I'm interested in everything about you and in getting us back on track.

KAYLA: It'd help me a lot to see that you were interested in other ways as well, like taking me out, or going for walks like we used to do. That kind of stuff lets me know you really love me.

JAMAL: That makes sense. We have gotten away from the things we used to really enjoy together.

KAYLA: Yes, we have. I do love you and want us to be closer again. I've been sad, too, about this distance. I was afraid it meant you weren't interested in me.

JAMAL: I'm relieved to hear you say that. I'm glad we're talking about it, finally.

Jamal finally really heard Kayla when she said that she felt he didn't love her. She finally heard—and was surprised—that he felt very sad about the growing distance and couldn't figure out how to get close again. This talk did more to bring them together than anything else could have done. In taking the risk to talk openly about their sadness and fear of rejection, each felt accepted and loved. With their love reaffirmed, they were free to reopen a number of avenues of intimacy that had been closed for some time—including the area of physical intimacy. The risk was worth it.

Scorekeeping

A fourth sign of hidden issues in your relationship is when one or both or you start keeping score. We'll talk more about the dangers of scorekeeping in Chapter Nine. For now, it's enough to know that scorekeeping reflects something wrong between you.

Scorekeeping could mean that you're not feeling recognized for what you put into the relationship. It could also mean that you're less committed, as we'll explain later. Or it could mean that you're feeling controlled and are keeping track of the times your partner has taken advantage of you. Whatever the issue, it can be a sign that important things are not being talked about—just documented.

As Louise senses Hector's hunting trip getting closer, she becomes focused on what looks like evidence of his distance from her. When he works a bit late or goes over to his brother's for a couple of hours, she begins to think that he's not paying enough attention—that maybe she's not as important to him as he is to her. She asks herself, "Why isn't he doing more for our relationship, the way I am?" Hector really does care and is interested. Most of the time Louise knows it, but she keeps score as this yearly event approaches because it raises important issues for her.

HANDLING HIDDEN ISSUES

What can you do when you realize that hidden issues are affecting your relationship? You can recognize when one may be operating and start talking about it constructively. This will be easier to do if you are cultivating an atmosphere of teamwork using the kinds of techniques we've presented thus far. We strongly recommend using the Speaker-

Listener Technique when you are trying to explore such issues.

If you're in an argument and suspect hidden agendas, call a Stop Action. Using the first ground rule in this way will help you shift the conversation to the level of the hidden issue—either right then or at an agreed-upon time in the near future. Later is usually better. You're not as likely to have the time or the ability to be very skillful in the context of some event.

Make sure to deal with the issue in terms of problem discussion, not problem solution. Be aware of any tendency to jump to solutions. In our opinion, the deeper the issue, the less likely it is that problem solving will be the answer. If you haven't been talking about the real issue, how could your problem solution address what's really at stake? What you need first and foremost is to hear and understand each other's feelings and concerns. Such validating discussions have the greatest impact on hidden issues. This alone can help to resolve a hidden agenda.

We believe that such talks have so much power because the most common root issue is the desire to know you're really accepted by one another. What better way to know that you're accepted than to feel that you're really being heard? Couples tell us that when they finally do talk about these issues, there's a tremendous sense of relief, as if a weight has been lifted. Even if something does need specific problem solving, you're better prepared by starting with discussion.

You also need to realize that just one talk usually won't resolve a hidden issue, because they often have many layers. It may be obvious that a hidden issue is operating, but this doesn't mean that the issue itself is obvious. Sometimes it's clear and sometimes it's pretty murky. You may not be able to identify the issue right away; you just know there's something uncomfortable that you need to keep talking about.

Hidden issues are like the monster under the bed. You don't want to look down to see what's there, but you know it's important and you know it's big. It will remain a monster in your mind until you actually look. Since dealing with these issues takes skill and effort, it's best if you're working as a team to discover, explore, and handle them. After all, if there was a monster under your bed, wouldn't you want your best friend along to help?

A DETAILED EXAMPLE: TV OR ME?

We round out this chapter with a story that shows how the really important issues will come out if you are communicating clearly and safely. Simon and Rachel are newlyweds who came to one of our workshops. Both were working long hours to make ends meet. When they did have time together, they'd frequently run into difficulties because Simon wanted to watch a lot of sports on TV and Rachel was very upset about this. Although many events concerned TV, much more important hidden issues were involved.

They could have argued forever at the level of the *events*—for example, who would control the TV—but they made much greater progress when they talked about the *issues* using the Speaker-Listener Technique. We hadn't told them to focus on hidden issues, but we can see how these issues emerged anyway. We find that this happens regularly when couples are doing a good job with the Speaker-Listener Technique. This was one of the first times Rachel and Simon used the technique, so their skills were a little rough around the edges, with some mind reading and less-than-ideal paraphrasing. However, they were communicating about the real issues better than they ever had before:

RACHEL: (Speaker) It seems as though you spend more time with the television than conversing with me. There are times when you can stay up late to watch television, but if it comes down to spending time with me, you're tired. You can go to bed and fall right to sleep.

SIMON: (Listener) So you are saying it's more comfortable for me to watch television than it is to be with you?

RACHEL: (Speaker) [*with a clear sigh of relief at being heard*] Yeah.

Rachel is not feeling accepted or cared for by Simon. This comes out clearly here, yet in the past when they'd argued about the TV, they never got to what was really going on—at least not in a way that drew them closer together. When Simon paraphrases Rachel's impression that he's more comfortable watching TV than being with her, he really hits home. That's exactly what it seems like to her. She can tell from the quality of his paraphrase that he's really listening to her. This does more to address her hidden issue of wanting him to care than all the problem solving in the world could do.

It's not clear whether he agrees that he's more comfortable watching TV, but it's clear that he heard her. If he's uncomfortable with her, it may be the result of how they've been mishandling the hidden issues around the TV events. They go on:

SIMON: (Listener) Can I have the floor?

SIMON: (Speaker) Before we were married, you never had any gripes about me watching sports.

RACHEL: (Listener) So what you're saying is that in the beginning I didn't mind the fact that you watched sports so much. We did spend a lot of time together, and that seemed to satisfy me.

SIMON: (Speaker) Right, and also, before we were married, even though we spent time together, you never really had the opportunity to see that I did watch football as much as possible.

RACHEL: (Listener) So what you're saying is that I didn't get to see this part of you—watching football—as much as I do now.

SIMON: (Speaker) Right. And you also didn't know about me playing sports, that I'm actively involved in other sports, too—not just football.

RACHEL: (Listener) So because you played sports in your previous time of knowing me, I should have known that you'd really be sports-oriented—I mean, watch sports all the time.

SIMON: (Speaker) Yes and no. I'm not saying that you should have known, but you saw that was a part of me, whether you want to accept it or not.

RACHEL: (Listener) Okay, so you say I saw this part of you being involved in sports—that this is something that I should have known was going to come out in the relationship. Is that what you're saying?

SIMON: (Speaker) More or less.

When Rachel complained about Simon's watching so much football, he felt she was attacking a core part of his identity. For him, the fundamental hidden issue revolves around acceptance of who he is and recognition of this part of him. He really gets this out in the open in his statement: "You saw that was a part of me, whether you want to accept it or not."

After more discussion on these deeper levels, Simon and Rachel went on to engage in some very effective problem solving about their time together and the time he spent watching TV. We don't believe that they could have done this without first dealing with the hidden issues.

Our goal in this chapter has been to give you a way to explore and understand some of the most frustrating occurrences in relationships. You can prevent a great deal of damage by learning to give events and issues the time and skill they require. The model presented here, along with all the skills and techniques described in the first section of the book, will help you do just that.

For all too many couples, the hidden issues never come out. Instead, they fester and produce levels of sadness and resentment that eventually destroy the marriage. It doesn't have to be that way. When you learn to discuss deeper issues openly and with emphasis on validating each other, the issues that generated the greatest conflict can actually draw you closer together.

Next, we turn to a chapter on expectations. So many hidden issues arise from deeply held expectations that we thought the topic deserved a chapter of its own. It also will help you understand what you expect from one another, and where those expectations come from.

Exercises

Think and write about these questions individually, on a separate piece of paper; then sit down and talk together about your impressions.

1. Think through the list of signs that hidden issues may be affecting your relationship. Do you notice that one or more of these signs come up a lot in your relationship? Here they are again. What do you notice?

    Wheel spinning

    Trivial triggers

    Avoidance

    Scorekeeping

2. Next, we'd like you to consider which hidden issues might operate most often in your relationship. Here's the list again. There may be some big issue you'd like to add to the list. Consider each issue and the degree to which it seems to affect your relationship negatively. Also, how deeply hidden are these issues in your relationship?

    Note whether certain events have triggered or keep triggering the issues. Make a list in the right-hand column, or on a separate piece of paper.

HIDDEN ISSUE	COMMON TRIGGERING EVENTS
Power and control	
Caring	

Recognition

Commitment

Integrity

Acceptance

3. Plan some time together to talk about your observations and thoughts. For most couples, certain hidden issues come up repeatedly. Identifying these issues can help you draw together as you each learn to handle them with care. Also, discussing these matters gives you an excellent opportunity to get in some more practice with the Speaker-Listener Technique. We recommend you set a regular couple's meeting to talk about hidden issues in the problem-discussion format. The emphasis needs to be on understanding your partner's point of view as fully and clearly as possible, not on resolving some immediate, concrete concern.

7

Unfulfilled Expectations and What to Do About Them

I N THE LAST CHAPTER, we explained how hidden issues can fuel conflict and distance between partners. Now we're ready to build on those concepts by focusing on expectations. We'll help you to explore your expectations for your marriage—what they are, where they come from, and whether or not they're reasonable. At the end of this chapter is a very important exercise with which you'll explore and share your expectations for your relationship. In fact, this chapter is primarily designed to prepare you for this exercise—it's that important.

Exploring your expectations will also help you to understand how issues—hidden or not—are triggered in your relationship. Exploring your expectations along with all the skills we've taught so far, will give you the best shot at preventing the kind of frustrating conflict we discussed in the last chapter.

HOW EXPECTATIONS AFFECT RELATIONSHIPS

Expectations exist for every aspect of a relationship. In the first part of the book we discussed how expectations can become powerful filters that distort your understanding of what happens in your relationship. The reason, we explained, is that people tend to see what they expect to see. In this chapter, we focus on your expectations of the way you think things are supposed to be in your relationship. For example, you may have specific expectations about such minor things as who will refill the orange juice container or who will balance the checkbook—the stuff events are made of. Or you may have expectations about common issues such as money, housework, in-laws, and sex. You may also have expectations about the deeper, often hidden, issues: how power will be shared or not shared, how caring will be demonstrated, or what the commitment is in your relationship. Expectations affect everything!

To a large degree, we are disappointed or satisfied in life depending on how well what is happening matches what we expect—what we think *should* happen. Therefore, expectations play a crucial role in determining our level of satisfaction in marriage. If we don't expect a lot, what actually happens may easily exceed our expectations. If we expect too much, it's likely that what happens will fall short of what we desire.

Consider Zoey and Maxwell. They've been married for only a year and things have gone pretty well. However, Maxwell is upset about Zoey's nights out with the girls. Like many young couples, they have a lot of expectations and issues to resolve about what's okay and what's not. Zoey goes out once or twice a week with her long-time girl-

friends, often to go shopping and sometimes to see a movie. This drives Maxwell nuts. Sometimes the event of her going out triggers huge arguments between them, like this one:

MAXWELL: [*feeling agitated*] I don't see why you have to go out again tonight. You've been out a lot lately.

ZOEY: [*obviously irritated, rolling her eyes*] How many times do we have to argue about this? I go out once a week and that's it. I don't see any problem with that.

MAXWELL: Well, I do. All of your girlfriends are single, and I know they keep their eyes open for guys.

ZOEY: So.

MAXWELL: So they're looking for guys and you're married.

ZOEY: [*angered, feeling attacked and accused of being loose*] We don't go out hunting for guys. I don't like it that you don't trust me.

MAXWELL: I just don't think a married woman needs to be out so often with her single friends. Guys notice a group of women, and you can't tell me your friends aren't interested.

ZOEY: [*turning away and walking toward the door*] You sound jealous. I'll be back by ten.

Zoey and Maxwell are arguing about an expectation. He didn't expect that she'd still go out with her girlfriends so often after they got married. He associates "going out" with being single, not married. Zoey expected to cut back on the time she spent with her friends, but not to stop seeing them altogether. These nights out mean a lot to her. She sees nothing wrong, except that Maxwell isn't handling it very well.

In this example, you couldn't really argue that either expectation is outrageous. What's much more important is that their expectations don't match, and this is fueling some conflict. You can easily imagine that hidden issues of caring and control are also at work. Maxwell could be wondering if Zoey really cares about being with him, since she still wants to go out regularly with her friends. Zoey could be feeling that Maxwell is trying to control her, a feeling she doesn't respond to warmly.

Studies show that it's more likely that relationships will develop problems when expectations are unreasonable. Do you think that Maxwell's or Zoey's expectations are unreasonable? Here's another example where the answer to that question is pretty obvious. Barb and Mike have been married for eleven years. He's a plumber and she does bookkeeping for several small businesses. Sex has become a huge issue over the years. If Mike had his way, they'd make love every night of the week, and some mornings, too. He not only has a strong sex drive; he also believes that there's something wrong with a marriage if a couple doesn't make love at least five times a week.

Since Barb only seems interested in making love once or twice a week, Mike believes that something is wrong with her, and he tells her so. Early in their marriage, she used to want to make love more often, and he expected they'd continue at that rate. If Barb shared Mike's expectation about lovemaking, there wouldn't be a problem, but because she doesn't, Mike's expectation is somewhat unreasonable. Unless they can negotiate some way out of this problem, there will be major conflict in the future.

EXPECTATIONS AND HIDDEN ISSUES

When hidden issues are triggered by events, it's usually because some expectation wasn't met. Underlying *power* issues are expectations about how decisions and control will be shared—or not shared. Underlying *caring* issues are expectations about how you are to be loved. Underlying *recognition* issues are expectations about how your partner should respond to who you are and what you do. Underlying *commitment* issues are expectations about how long the relationship should continue and, most important, about safety from abandonment. Underlying *integrity* issues are expectations about being trusted and respected. And underneath all of these expectation are core expectations about *acceptance* by your partner.

A hidden issue can't get triggered in the first place unless an expectation is violated. In the last chapter, we described the argument that took place when Scott told Nancy that it was ridiculous to worry about being struck by lightning. In doing this, he violated Nancy's expectation that she would be listened to and taken seriously. Conversely, when Nancy told Scott not to use the phone, she stepped on his expectation that she wouldn't tell him what to do. The clash of expectations about these most basic issues ignited the conflict that ruined their weekend. It takes a lot of skill and motivation to keep such conflicts from happening.

WHERE EXPECTATIONS COME FROM

Expectations build up over a lifetime of experiences. These expectations are based in the past but operate in the present. There are three primary sources for our expectations: our family of origin, our previous relationships, and the culture we live in.

FAMILY OF ORIGIN

We gain many expectations from our families as we grow up. Our family experiences lay down patterns—both good and bad—that become models for how we think things are supposed to work when we become adults. Expectations are transmitted both directly by what our parents say and indirectly by what we observe. Either way, we learn expectations in many areas of life. No one comes to marriage with a blank slate.

For example, if you observed your parents avoiding all manner of conflict, you may have developed the expectation that couples should seek peace at any price. If you now encounter disagreement and conflict, it may seem to you as if the world is going to end. If you observed your parents being very affectionate, you may have come to expect this to be true for your marriage. If your parents divorced, you may have some expectation in the back of your mind that marriages don't really last.

Often, two people come from such different families that they have a serious mismatch in some key expectations. One couple we worked with, Helen and Bill, came from very different families. In Helen's family, her father made virtually all the decisions—even down to what kind of toilet paper to buy. Bill's family was quite different. His mother left his father because he was a tyrant, and Bill went to live with his mother. She taught him by her actions and words never to treat his own wife as if she were a hired hand.

As you might imagine, Bill and Helen have had some trouble making decisions. Helen deferred to Bill for many decisions, and he found this disturbing. He told us that he felt pressured by all the responsibility. From his viewpoint, her letting him make all the decisions was not only the wrong thing to do; it also could lead to the marriage failing—as it did in his parents' case. So he'd try to get Helen to take more responsibility, while she tried to have him take charge. He saw himself as showing respect. She saw him as weak.

Because of their mismatched and unexpressed expectations, Helen and Bill experienced many conflicts in the context of decision-making events. Hidden issues were easily triggered. She would end up feeling that he didn't care enough to lead. Although in many ways she was giving him a lot of control, he felt pushed into this role and controlled by her. They were finally able to talk this through, using the Speaker-Listener Technique. This is just part of their talk; you can see how they were able to get the issues on the table:

HELEN: (Speaker) I've been expecting you to lead more, to make decisions, because that's what I grew up being used to.

BILL: (Listener) So you've expected this from me because that's what you grew up to expect.

HELEN: (Speaker)Exactly. I never really thought a lot about the expectation, but I can see now that I've had it and that it's been affecting us.

BILL: (Listener) So you're saying that while you've had this expectation, you haven't really thought a lot about it before. But you can see it's affected us negatively.

HELEN: (Speaker) Yes. That's just what I mean. Do you want the floor?

FLOOR SWITCH.

BILL: (Speaker) Yes, thanks. I can understand now why you've pushed me to make the decisions. I really want you to hear that it's not that I'm uncomfortable being responsible. But to me, sharing decisions is a way to show you respect.

HELEN: (Listener) So what looked to me like you pushing off responsibilities was really you wanting to share with me in making decisions.

BILL: (Speaker) Yes. That's it. Because of my own background, I've thought that our marriage would be hurt if I just went ahead and took all the control. I thought it meant you didn't care about us because you didn't share in making decisions with me.

HELEN: (Listener) So you've had an expectation that was a lot different from mine, and that led you to worry that we'd have trouble if we didn't share in making decisions.

BILL: (Speaker) And that's really been worrying me.

HELEN: (Listener) It's really worried you because you weren't sure I cared.

BILL: (Speaker) Right.

Helen and Bill had a much easier time dealing with decisions once they began to understand and talk openly about their expectations and to think about where they came from and the effects of their past on the relationship. Once they felt that they were being heard, they had a much better chance of negotiating the expectations they wanted to share in their relationship.

Another couple, Patricia and Willie, had constant fights about child rearing. Patricia came from a home where her mother and stepfather were extremely harsh in their discipline. Her stepfather in particular would chase the kids around the house when he was angry. If they were caught, they were hit wherever his hands happened to land. Almost worse was the way both parents yelled and screamed when the children would make the slightest mistake.

On the other hand, Willie came from a family where, in general, the kids could do whatever they wanted. There were limits, but they were pretty loose. Whenever their five-year-old son, Joey, acted up, Willie responded by raising his voice, but he actually did nothing to set limits on Joey's behavior. Joey had learned to all but ignore Willie's raised voice. There were no real consequences.

With her background, Patricia expected that when Willie raised his voice, someone was about to get hurt. Her expectation was based in the past but it still had real power. She'd even get sick to her stomach from the tension if she thought that someone was about to get in trouble. It was as if her stepfather was chasing her all over again.

At times, she saw Willie as being abusive even though he wasn't. Her expectations became powerful filters, distorting her perception of what was really going on. Actually, Willie, like his parents, was quite lenient. Sure, he could lose his temper and yell from time to time, but he was a softy.

As a consequence of their expectations, neither Willie nor Patricia provided consistent discipline for Joey, who suffered because of this lack of consistency. His teacher reported that he was one of the most difficult kids in the school; for his part, Joey didn't understand why the teacher was so insistent that he observe the class rules. What kind of expectations do you think he'll have when he grows up? Here, you can see how expectations may be handed down from generation to generation.

Conflicts caused by unexpressed expectations are very common. If we had the space, we could give literally thousands of examples. It's enough to say here that we each have many expectations based on our families of origin. Understanding this basic fact is the first step to dealing more effectively with those expectations and preventing increased conflict.

PREVIOUS RELATIONSHIPS

We also develop expectations from all the other relationships we've participated in—most importantly, from previous dating relationships or marriages. We have expectations about how to kiss, what is romantic, how to communicate about problems, how recreational time should be spent, who should take the first move to make up after a fight, and so on.

Suppose, for example, that in previous dating relationships, when you began to open up about painful childhood events, you were rejected. Logically, you may have developed the expectation that such a topic is off limits with certain people. On a deeper level, you may have the expectation that people can't be trusted with knowledge of the deepest parts of who you are. If so, you'll pull back and withhold intimacy in your present relationship.

Studies show that people who have come to expect that others can't be trusted have more difficulties in relationships. If you look at their entire life, this expectation will usually make sense; however, it can lead to trouble if the mistrust is so intense that they can't even allow someone they love to get close. This would be all the more reason to learn how to make a relationship safe for verbal intimacy.

Here's another example. Maybe you've been in relationships where your partner was creative in thinking up wonderful nights on the town. This person knew just how to plan an evening so that you both had a great time. You may now be with someone who isn't as creative, so you're disappointed. You've developed an expectation that your current partner isn't meeting to the same degree.

Many expectations are about such minor things that it's hard to imagine how they can become so important, but they can. It all depends on what meanings and issues are attached to these expectations. For example, one man, Phil, told us that his past girlfriend had drilled into him that she didn't want him opening doors for her. He thought, "Okay, no big deal." Now, with his wife, Susan, he was finding quite the opposite. She liked men to hold doors, and she'd get upset with him if he forgot. He had to work hard to unlearn the expectation he'd finally learned so well.

Door-opening events happen fairly often in life. For Phil and Susan, they triggered conflict because she'd interpret his trouble remembering as a sign that he didn't care about what was important to her. This is another example where negative interpretations cause more damage than the actual events. With his devotion challenged, Phil would get angry at her. This just confirmed what she already believed—that he didn't care.

Are you aware how many of the expectations you have for your partner are based on your experiences with others? It's worth thinking about, since your partner is a different person from those you knew, dated, or were married to in the past. It may not be realistic or fair to hold the same expectations for your partner that you had with someone else.

CULTURAL INFLUENCES

There are a variety of cultural factors that influence our expectations. Television, movies, religious teachings, and what we read can all have powerful effects on expectations. We'll focus a good deal on the religious issues in Chapter Fourteen.

What expectations would you develop about marriage from watching thousands of hours of television in America? For most of us, this is not a hypothetical question. We receive very powerful messages about what is acceptable from shows like "I Love Lucy" (women can best handle men by being silly), "The Honeymooners" (verbal abuse is okay), "The Brady Bunch" (it's easy to blend families), "The Cosby Show" (dual-career marriages cause no problems), and "Roseanne" (sarcasm is good for relationships). The daytime soap operas and talk shows also have their effect. What expectations do people learn from topics like "women who have affairs and the men who love them?" Affairs are no big deal?

One couple, Federico and Elena, had been married for three years. They approached us after a workshop and remarked that marriage was much harder than they'd expected. Like most of us, they had absorbed hours and hours of what television said about the way things should be. They each had developed the expectation that marriage should be blissful, and if it wasn't always that way, divorce was imminent.

Elena and Federico clearly loved each other and were committed to their marriage, which seemed to us to be much better than average. Yet here they were, feeling inferior, thinking that they weren't doing it right, because of some crazy expectations. They were greatly relieved when we were able to show them what marriages are really like. And the change in their expectations reduced some of the day-to-day pressure they'd been experiencing in their marriage.

HOW TO PUT EXPECTATIONS TO WORK FOR YOU

Expectations can lead either to massive disappointment and frustration or to deeper connection and intimacy between you and your partner. There are three keys to handling expectations well:

1. Being *aware* of what you expect

2. Being *reasonable* in what you expect

3. Being *clear* about what you expect

BEING AWARE OF WHAT YOU EXPECT

Whether you're aware of them or not, unmet expectations can lead to great disappointment and frustration in your relationship. You don't have to be fully aware of an expectation to have it affect your relationship.

Clifford Sager, a pioneer in this field, notes that people bring a host of expectations to marriage that are never made clear. These expectations form a contract for the marriage. The problem is that most people have little notion of what's in the contract when they get married. Sager further suggests that many expectations are unconscious, making it very hard to be aware of them. Not all expectations are deeply unconscious, but many become such a part of us that they function automatically. Like driving a car, much of what you do is so automatic that you don't even have to think about it.

At the end of this chapter, you'll have the opportunity to increase your awareness of your own expectations. One great clue to expectations is disappointment. When you're disappointed in your relationship, some expectation hasn't been met. It's a good habit to stop a minute when you're disappointed and ask yourself what you expected. Doing this can help you to become aware of the expectations that may be unconsciously affecting your relationship.

For example, Paul was sad everytime he'd ask his wife, Dawn, to go boating with him and she'd say, "That's okay, go ahead without me and have a great time." Dawn would rather stay home and garden, but

Paul worked very hard during the week as a repairman and boating was his greatest relaxation. Dawn didn't care for boating and wanted Paul to feel good about going without her.

Paul's sadness was a clue that some important expectation was at work. In thinking about it, he realized that he'd expected them to share this very important interest of his. If Dawn didn't want to, what did that mean? If nothing else, he felt torn between spending time with her and time on his boat.

Even though Dawn loved him dearly, his hope that she'd become interested in boating stirred deeper issues in him about feeling cared for. Once Paul was aware of his expectation and the reason for his sadness, he was able to express what boating with her meant to him. She'd had no idea how he felt. While Dawn still didn't love boating, she was glad to come more often once she knew that it meant so much to him.

After becoming aware of an expectation, the next step is to consider if it's reasonable.

BEING REASONABLE IN WHAT YOU EXPECT

As we noted earlier, many key expectations aren't either reasonable or realistic. Some unreasonable expectations are very specific. For example, is it reasonable to expect that your partner will never seriously disagree with you? Of course not. Yet you'd be surprised just how many people expect this. Is it reasonable to expect that once you're married, your partner will forsake all contact with old friends? Some people actually expect this to happen, but of course, that's not very realistic either.

Acting on unreasonable expectations is likely to lead to conflict. A specific example of this is the case of Sara and Randy. Both had high-pressure jobs in accounting, so it was critical that they learn how to handle conflict and free time.

In our program, Sara and Randy made tremendous progress using the techniques we presented in the first part of this book. They were handling what had been significant conflicts far better than they ever had before. Unfortunately, their progress was held back by Randy's expectation that using these techniques would prevent any more negative events from happening. That wasn't a reasonable expectation.

Meanwhile, Sara felt that all the efforts she'd made to change their relationship weren't being appreciated. Randy's unreasonable expectation colored everything, so that minor conflicts were seen as evidence that they hadn't made any progress at all. Not only did Randy expect that they'd no longer have conflicts, but this became a perceptual filter that caused him to miss all the great changes that were actually occurring.

We hope that couples who consistently apply our principles will have fewer, less intense negative events. But events will always happen, and issues will still erupt. There's a difference between not having any issues and handling issues well. Randy's expectation that there'd be no conflict was unreasonable and itself generated a lot of conflict until we pushed him to take a hard look at it. To overcome it, he had to become aware of his unrealistic expectation and challenge it within himself. It wasn't an expectation they had to meet as much as it was one for Randy to change—and he did.

BEING CLEAR ABOUT WHAT YOU EXPECT

A specific expectation may be perfectly reasonable but never clearly expressed. It's critical to express your expectations, and not just to be aware of them or evaluate their reasonableness. We all tend to assume that our model of the ideal marriage (made up of the sum total of our expectations) is the same as our partner's. Why should we have to tell our partner what we expect? We assume that he or she already knows.

This also is an unreasonable expectation. We assume that our partner knows what we want, so we don't bother to state clearly what we need. In fact, many partners feel that if they need to ask, something is wrong. Even worse, many think that if they ask and their partner responds, the outcome isn't meaningful. They say, "If I have to ask for a hug, it doesn't really mean much." We disagree! When you ask and your partner responds, that's evidence of your partner's love and commitment.

Unreasonable assumptions often occur in the sexual arena. How many people make the assumption that their partner should know just what is most pleasing sexually? We see this over and over again. One partner becomes angry because the other fails to meet a desire or expectation. But more often than not, the expectation has never been expressed. That's asking the partner to be good at mind reading.

Worse, when key expectations are not "read" by one partner, it's easy for hidden issues to be triggered. The one with the unmet expectation may feel that the partner doesn't care because he or she didn't figure out the expectation. We'll deal with the problems this causes sexually in Chapter Thirteen.

Here's another type of assumption: Martha and Ray had regular eruptions of conflict whenever they went to Ray's parents' house. Martha had the expectation that Ray would stay close by her. She didn't like being left alone in conversations with his mother, whom she perceived as prying into the secrets of their marriage. In contrast, Ray thought that he should give Martha as much opportunity as possible to get to know his parents. He sensed that Martha was distant after these visits, but he didn't understand why.

Martha's expectation that Ray would stay near her when visiting his parents was perfectly reasonable. Yet until she told him that was what she wanted, he was left to his own assumptions. He thought she'd be comfortable when he went off with his father, leaving her with his mother. Once she expressed her real expectation, however, he was able act on it and help her have a better time.

Unless you make your expectations clear, you'll have trouble working as a team. *You can't work from any kind of shared perspective if you don't share your perspective.*

You need to be aware of your expectations, be willing to evaluate them, and offer to discuss them. Otherwise, they'll have the power to trigger all the biggest issues in your relationship. And if you don't deal with them openly, you'll also miss an opportunity to define a mutual vision of how you want your marriage to be.

The exercises we're about to present are as important as any in this book. It takes time to do them well. It also takes considerable follow-up. We hope you can find the time and motivation to do the work. If you do, you'll improve your understanding of mutual expectations.

Combining that knowledge with the skills you are learning can have a major impact on the strength of your relationship—both now and in the future.

From the standpoint of giving you a lot to think about, we'd expect that this is one of the hardest chapters in this book. In addition to going through the exercises carefully, you might want to read the chapter a few more times. Again, think through what your key expectations are and how they affect your relationship. In the next chapter, we move on to the concept of commitment. This is a topic of great importance for relationships, and one in which people have quite a few expectations.

 Exercises

Use the exercise here to explore your expectations of your relationship. Spend some time thinking carefully about each area. Then write your thoughts down so that you can share them with your partner. Each of you should use a separate pad of paper. Each point below is meant to stimulate your own thinking. You may have expectations in many other areas. Please consider everything you can think of that seems significant to you. You won't get much out of this exercise unless you are able and willing to put some time into it. Many couples have found this type of exercise extremely beneficial for their relationship.

The goal is to consider your expectations concerning the way you want or expect the relationship to be, not how it is and not how you assume it will be in the future. Write down what you expect, whether or not you think the expectation is realistic. The expectation matters and will affect your relationship whether or not it's realistic. Consider each question in light of what you want for the future.

It's essential that you write down what you really think, not what sounds like the "correct" or least embarrassing answer. It also can be valuable to consider what you observed and learned in each of these areas in your family when you were growing up. This is probably where many of your beliefs about what you want or don't want come from.

1. Explore your expectations regarding:

    a. The longevity of this relationship. Is it "Till death do us part"?

    b. Sexual fidelity.

    c. Love. Do you expect to love each other always? Do you expect this to change over time?

    d. Your sexual relationship. What are the frequency, practices, and taboos of sex for you?

    e. Romance. What is romantic for you?

    f. Children. Do you want children? More children?

    g. Children from previous marriages. If you or your partner have children from a previous marriage, where do you

want them to live? How do you expect to share in their discipline? How do they fit into your new marriage and
lifestyle?

h. Work, careers, and provision of income. Who will work in
   the future? Whose career or job is more important? If
   there are or will be children, will either partner reduce
   work time out of the home to take care of them?

i. The degree of each partner's emotional dependency on
   the other. Do you want to be taken care of? How? How
   much do you expect to rely on each other to get through
   the tough times?

j. Basic approach to life. As a team? As two independent
   individuals?

k. Loyalty. What does that mean to you?

l. Communication about problems in the relationship. Do
   you want to talk these out? If so, how?

m. Power and control. Who do you expect will have more power and in what kinds of decisions? For example, who will control the money? Discipline the kids? What happens when you disagree in a key area? Who has the power now, and how do you feel about that?

n. Household tasks. Who do you expect will do what? How much household work will each of you do in the future? If you live together now, how does the current breakdown match up with what you expect in the future?

o. Religious beliefs and observances. Be specific about where, when, or what rituals you'd expect to observe. If you have no kids, but plan to, how will you bring them up? You will be asked to explore such expectations in much more detail at the end of Chapter Fourteen.

p. Time together. How much time do you want to spend together? Alone? With friends or family, at work, and so on?

q. Sharing feelings. How much of what you are each feeling do you expect should be shared?

r. Friendship with your partner. What is a friend? What would it mean to maintain or have a friendship with your partner?

s. The little things in life. Where do you squeeze the toothpaste? Is the toilet seat left up or down? Who sends greeting cards? Think carefully about the little things that might irritate you (or might be going really well). What do you want or expect in each area?

t. Forgiveness. How important is forgiveness in your relationship? How should forgiveness affect your relationship?

u. Now, with your mind primed from the work you've just done, consider again the hidden issues we described in the last chapter. Do you see any other ways that they may influence or be influenced by your expectations? What do you expect in the areas of power, caring, recognition, commitment, integrity, and acceptance?

v. List any other expectations about how you want things to be that you feel are important, and that are not already listed above .

2. Now go back to each area just listed and rate each expectation on a scale of 1 to 10 according to how reasonable you think the expectation is. On this scale, 10 means "Completely reasonable. I really think it's okay to expect this in this type of relationship" and 1 means "Completely unreasonable. I can honestly say that even though I expect or want this, it's not a reasonable expectation in this type of relationship." For example, suppose that you grew up in a family where problems were not discussed, and you're aware that you honestly expect or prefer to avoid such discussions. You might now rate that expectation as not very reasonable, after all.

   Now, place a big checkmark by each expectation that you believe you haven't ever clearly discussed with your partner.

3. After you and your partner have had the opportunity to work on the exercise individually, plan to spend time together discussing these expectations. Please don't do this all at once. You should plan on a number of discussions, each covering only one or two expectations. Discuss the degree to which you each felt that the expectation being discussed was shared in the past. Use the Speaker-Listener Technique, if necessary, to keep these discussions clear and safe for real sharing. The goal of these discussions is to develop a full and clear understanding of each partner's expectations and beliefs.

4. Talk about the degree to which you both feel the expectations are reasonable or unreasonable, and discuss what you want to agree to do about them.

5. Talk about what your overall, long-term vision is for the relationship. What expectations do you share about your future together?

8

Understanding Commitment

COUPLES WHO HAVE REMAINED happily married for years usually attribute their success to such factors as commitment, communication, and friendship. We believe that commitment is such an important topic that we'll devote two chapters to it. In the language of the last chapter, commitment is a critical issue in relationships—one that relates to the way you deal with conflict and also to your expectations for your relationship.

Early on, commitment wasn't even a part of the PREP approach. However, exciting new findings from Scott Stanley's research fueled our interest in making commitment a central part of PREP. In our seminars, we actually introduce Scott—who has gained national recognition for his work on commitment—as Doctor Commitment!

The model we present in this chapter will help you to think about how commitment affects your relationship. You'll use the exercises at the end of this chapter to evaluate your commitment to that relationship. And, in the next chapter, we'll discuss the key implications of commitment for the health of the relationship.

Most married couples consider commitment the glue that holds their relationship together. The kind and depth of your commitment has a lot to do with your chances of staying together and being happy. But it has been difficult for researchers to study commitment because people have such different ideas about what it is.

WHAT IS COMMITMENT?

What comes to your mind when you think of commitment? When we ask couples in our workshops, here's what they say most often:

Trust	Covenant
Love	Devotion
Loyalty	Dedication
Obligation	Follow-through
Determination	Stick-to-it-iveness
Hanging in there	Priority
Till death do us part	Sacrifice
Teamwork	Fidelity
Trapped	Glue
Seeing a future	

Obviously, people have a lot on their minds when the topic of commitment is brought up. That's why we need a framework for understanding commitment that ties these concepts together. To do this, we'll discuss two couples in some detail. Both marriages reflect commitment, but the type of commitment is very different. Notice what's similar and what's different as you consider these marriages.

BOB AND MARY ANDERSON: FEELING TRAPPED IN THEIR RELATIONSHIP

Bob and Mary are a couple in their early thirties who married eight years ago. They have a four-year-old son and a seven-year-old daughter. Bob manages the meat section in a large grocery store and Mary is a secretary in a doctor's office. Like most couples, Bob and Mary started out very much in love but have gone through some tough times. Raising two kids has proved more stressful than either expected. This, combined with the stress of major job changes for both of them, has left them feeling tired and distant.

Mary has considered divorce on more than a few occasions and frequently thinks about leaving Bob. Bob also feels unhappy with the marriage, but he hasn't considered divorce to be much of an option. He also hasn't thought of any ways to improve the marriage. He hopes for more but hasn't told Mary this, and he believes that trying to get closer just doesn't work. When he does try to do something positive, he feels shut out by Mary. He's become anxious over the thought that she might leave, but he senses that any energy put into the marriage at this point might be wasted effort. "Maybe things will get better when the kids leave home," he thinks. "I've just got to stick with it and hope for the best."

Mary and Bob both work with people they find attractive. Larry is a single, good-looking man at Mary's office who's made it clear that he's interested in Mary. She's been seriously contemplating an affair and finds herself thinking about it more and more. Mary is very much aware of the changes she's gone through over the years and is afraid that Bob will never be the kind of lifelong partner that she hoped for. Furthermore, she feels that she's putting a lot more into the marriage than Bob is, with little return for her time and effort. She's resentful that he doesn't seem to appreciate and accept all she's done for him. Like Bob, she's thinking that it's just not worth the effort to try harder.

As Mary thinks about leaving Bob, difficult questions plague her. First, she wonders how the kids would respond to divorce. Would it hurt them? Would Bob want custody? Would it be hard to get a divorce? Would Bob try to stop her? How could they afford lawyers? She also wonders how she could support herself on her income alone. Who would get the house? Could either of them afford to keep the house separate from the other? Would Bob pay child support? If she married again, would another man accept her children?

As Mary considers these questions, she decides that maybe the costs of getting a divorce are greater than she wants to bear, at least for now. Sure, she's in pain, but she balances this against the pain and stress a divorce could bring. A feeling of despair hangs over her. Feeling trapped, she decides that staying is better than leaving, but staying isn't great.

DEIDRE AND ERIC SEMPLETON:
A DEEPER COMMITMENT

Deidre and Eric were married fifteen years ago. They have three children, a seven-year-old boy, an eleven-year-old boy, and a thirteen-year-old girl. Although they've had their stressful times, both Deidre and Eric have few regrets about marrying one another. They met when they both worked for a large insurance company. He was working in sales and she had worked her way up to being manager of the claims department.

Their kids present some real challenges. The middle boy has a serious learning disability and requires attention and support. Their oldest daughter is beginning to show signs of rebellion, which also is a cause of concern. Despite this, Deidre and Eric usually feel the other's support in facing the tasks of life. Eric does occasionally become aware of an attraction to women he meets in his work. However, because of his commitment to Deidre, he's decided not to dwell on "what if?" possibilities. He's happy with Deidre and he doesn't want to consider being with anyone else.

Everyone has regrets at times in marriage, but for Deidre and Eric these times are few. They genuinely respect and like each other, do things for each other, and talk fairly openly about what they want out of life and marriage. Because of their moral beliefs about divorce, they resist thinking about splitting up, even when they're not getting along very well. Each is willing to help the other attain what is desired in life. Simply put, they feel like a team.

As you can see, these two couples have very different marriages. The Andersons are miserable, while the Sempletons are enjoying life. Both marriages are likely to continue for the time being, which in itself reflects some kind of commitment. But it's not just the level of happiness that separates these two marriages. The Sempletons have a much different, *deeper* kind of commitment. To understand the difference, we need a broad model of commitment.

DEFINING COMMITMENT

Michael Johnson, a colleague of ours at Pennsylvania State University, points to a useful distinction in how we use the word *commitment*. The sentence "John certainly is committed to his career" conveys one meaning. Used in this way, John's *dedication* to his work is expressed. The second way we commonly use the word is seen in a statement such as "Mary made a commitment to organize this project, and she can't back out now." In this use, *commitment* conveys a sense of obligation or what we call *constraint*. Mary isn't free to quit the project. On the basis of this distinction, we've found the definitions below helpful in understanding the kinds of commitment people have in their relationships.

A commitment characterized by what we call *personal dedication* refers to an individual's desire to maintain or improve the quality of the relationship for the joint benefit of both partners. Personal dedication is reflected in an intrinsic desire (and associated behaviors) not only to continue in the relationship but also to improve it, sacrifice for it, invest in it, link personal goals to it, and seek the partner's welfare, not simply one's own.

In contrast, a commitment characterized by *constraint* refers to forces that keep individuals in relationships whether or not they're dedicated. Sometimes people stay in marriages in which they are unhappy—or even abused—because of constraint commitment. For other couples, constraint commitment is perceived positively; it adds a level of stability to the relationship. Constraint commitment may arise from either external or internal pressures; in general, constraints make the ending of a relationship more economically, socially, personally, or psychologically costly.

Bob and Mary Anderson have a commitment characterized by constraint. Mary, in particular, is feeling a great deal of constraint and little dedication. She feels compelled to remain in a marriage that is dissatisfying for a host of reasons—children, money, family pressure, and so on. Bob also has high constraint commitment and little dedication, although he's less intensely dissatisfied with their day-to-day life.

Like Mary and Bob, Deidre and Eric Sempleton have a good deal of constraint commitment, but they also have an abiding sense of dedication to one another. Any thriving marriage will produce a significant level of constraint over time. In fact, happier, more dedicated couples are just as likely to have considerable constraints as less satisfied, less dedicated couples at similar points in their lives. Happier couples simply don't think a lot about constraints, and when they do, they often draw comfort from them. Together, the forces of constraint and dedication produce a glue that takes couples through thick and thin. This glue gives couples like the Sempletons a comfortable sense of being rooted together in the complexity of life.

Take a moment and reflect on the list that came to mind when you thought about commitment. Terms such as *loyalty, trust, devotion, sacrifice,* and *priority* relate to what we are calling *personal dedication.* Terms such as *obligation, till death do us part, covenant,* and *trapped* relate to what we are calling *constraint commitment.*

Notice that terms such as *glue, stick-to-it-iveness, follow-through, seeing a future,* and *hanging in there* cut across both categories. These terms reflect the overall effect of a broad-based commitment characterized by both dedication and constraint—what we call having a long-term view.

Let's look in more detail at how constraint and dedication operate in relationships.

THE COMMITMENT OF CONSTRAINT

Theorists and researchers have only recently identified the factors that are characteristic of commitment in relationships. These dimensions are starting to be described in the research literature, especially in the work of Michael Johnson at Pennsylvania State University and Caryl Rusbult at the University of North Carolina, as well as in our own studies at the University of Denver.

As we discuss these factors, consider the kind and level of commitment that you have in your relationship. At the end of the chapter, you'll have the opportunity to assess your own level of commitment. Keep in mind that many of the dimensions we'll focus on could also be understood as areas where people have important expectations as to how things should be. As we said in Chapter Seven, differences in expectations that are not handled well can lead to many problems.

There are two broad kinds of constraint to consider: moral and pragmatic. We'll describe the dimensions of these specific types as follows.

MORAL CONSTRAINTS

Some constraints have a moral flavor. We'll focus on these to start.

Immorality of divorce refers to the belief that divorce is, in general, morally wrong. Some believe this; others don't. Married people who believe in this are more likely to stay in their marriages. Research shows that those with stronger, more traditional religious beliefs are much more likely to believe that divorce is wrong. Those who have previously been divorced are less likely to believe this than those who've never been divorced.

Because of their upbringing, neither Bob nor Mary has a strong moral objection to divorce per se. Other factors play a much greater role in their level of constraint. In contrast, Eric and Deidre both believe that divorce is generally unacceptable. In this sense, they have a greater level of constraint commitment than Bob and Mary.

Metacommitment is another type of moral constraint that relates to the belief that you should finish what you start. *Meta*commitment, means commitment to commitment. We've heard people say that they remain committed partly because they don't want to be "quitters." This kind of belief could serve as an element of constraint when you feel that you must keep on trying. One couple who took our workshop told us that they were on their third marriage. They said they'd rather die than have this one fail. Needless to say, they did seem very motivated about what we have to say in PREP.

This dimension relates less to religious standards and more to the individual's value system. Bob Anderson isn't particularly religious, but he has a strong sense of duty. He doesn't want to give up, but, unfortunately, he doesn't seem to know what to do that would be more constructive, either.

Concern for children's welfare is another key dimension with a moral flavor. Many people stay married because they believe that it's best for their children. This seems to be one of the greatest concerns for Mary Anderson in considering divorce. She's especially worried about custody, living arrangements, and standard of living in thinking about the effects on the children. Deidre and Eric Sempleton would be just as concerned about the impact of divorce on their children—if they were thinking about it. In effect, they'd be just as constrained, but because they're not unhappy, there's no focus on this dimension.

Concern for partner's welfare can be another constraint. As with concern for children, the emphasis here is on the desire to avoid causing harm to others. We've talked with many couples where this was a key constraint and all that was holding the relationship together. One man told us, "I'd really like to leave Sally. I don't feel happy with her, but I care about her too much to devastate her with a divorce." His heart was not really in the marriage, but he didn't want to cause his wife—and himself—the pain that a divorce would bring.

All of the types of constraint mentioned above come from a sense of compassion, guilt, or duty, often in combination. We'll now describe other constraint dimensions that have more of a pragmatic than a moral flavor.

PRAGMATIC CONSTRAINTS

These constraints relate to your perception of what would be gained or lost if you ended your relationship.

Irretrievable investments are the cause of one kind of constraint. The key here is the perception of investments that would be lost if the relationship ended. These investments might be in the form of physical possessions or less tangible factors.

Some couples decide to stay together because they can't bear to divide up key possessions. For instance, many people are very attached to their house; they realize that if they divorce neither of them will be able to stay in the house on one income, so they stay together. We know couples who've tried to divorce and remain in the same house. It didn't work. A couple of years ago, this was tried by the couple in the movie *The War of the Roses.* The Roses divided up their home into "red" areas (his) and "green" areas (hers), with "shared time allotments" for use of the kitchen. Mr. Rose actually felt that he won with this arrangement, bragging to his attorney, "I've got more square footage." What a commitment—to the house!

Less tangible investments relate to a person's comfort level with predictable patterns. You may feel that you've invested great energy in getting your partner "broken in," and you don't want the hassle of having a new partner squeeze the toothpaste in the wrong place. Or you may derive comfort from knowing that your spouse understands a lot about you because of all the time you've invested in sharing. The key here is that you've put a lot of time and energy into this relationship and this investment would be lost if it all ended. This is a motivation to stay.

Bob derives a good deal of comfort from the routine of his life with Mary. Perhaps they've lost something, but he's not interested in starting over with someone else. Although he's begun to wonder if it's worth it to invest any more energy in the marriage, he isn't ready to give up what he's put into the relationship so far. Deidre and Eric have also invested a lot in each other, and this adds to their constraint commitment. Neither would want to lose what they have. For them, the investment is simply further evidence of their ongoing dedication.

Social pressure refers to the forces that third parties exert on couples to maintain relationships. Social pressure will be greatest when you know many people as a couple who want to see your relationship continue. A woman we met at a workshop remarked privately to us, "If I ever left Fred, my parents would kill me. Sometimes I think they like him more than me." She was not actively thinking about divorce, but when the thought did occur, she was very aware of how displeased her parents would be if she left Fred.

This is an area of great similarity between the Sempletons and the Andersons. Both couples have been together a long time, have children, and have many friends and family members who would be shocked if they split up. In both cases, their friends and families would ask a lot of questions about the advisability of ending the marriage.

Most couples believe that their friends and families want their relationship to continue. This is usually the case unless a marriage is clearly very harmful in some way, as in the case of abuse or infidelity. Couples also sense greater social pressure the longer they've been together. The time they've spent together and changes such as having children raise the stakes. The effects of social pressure may explain why so many couples end up making monsters of each other to their friends and family during a separation or divorce. Statements about how terrible their partner is serve to reduce the pressure to "work it out." Some people really have been terrible to their spouses; in other cases, these complaints are exaggerated to reduce social pressure.

When people who have trashed their spouse later try to make their marriage work, they're likely to get flak about going back. One couple we worked with had done so much damage to each other's reputation that their friends and families virtually disowned them for trying to make their marriage work later on. Each had described the other as a monstrous abuser to their families, but when their conflict settled down, neither of them still saw the other in this light. Unless you're definitely contemplating divorce, be careful what you say to your friends and family during periods of serious conflict.

Termination procedures refer to the immediate steps needed to end a particular relationship. Here, the focus is not on the long-term consequences of leaving as much as on the difficulty of the specific steps required to end the relationship. Ending a casual relationship may be no more difficult than not making another date, but ending a marriage requires legal negotiations, changed residences, and detailed financial untangling. The greater these hassles are, the more likely it is that couples will stay in their relationships.

Mary Anderson is very focused on the "hassle factor." She has considered the legal steps required and the likelihood that Bob would make it difficult to obtain a divorce. This is an unknown factor for her, but she suspects that these steps would be difficult, and she isn't prepared to take them. The steps would be just as difficult for Deidre and Eric if they had the desire to divorce, but they don't.

The quality of the alternatives is a very important dimension in considering constraint commitment. In fact, one way to think about commitment is as a choice of one alternative over others. In general, the poorer the alternatives, the greater the constraint. This dimension represents the degree to which people would be unhappy about any or all of the broad range of possible life changes that would occur if their relationship ended: residence, economic status, friendships, and so on.

You can't really weigh the alternatives in a vacuum. When people think about them, they weigh them in contrast to their current quality of life. Two key dimensions related to the alternative life-style are the economic and social dimensions. We'll focus on these separately.

Economic dependence is a key constraint that falls within the general category of the quality of alternatives. Some people stay in relationships because they can't afford—or don't want to afford—living without their partners. Although the current situation may be unpleasant, the alternatives look worse—adding to the constraint. For both the Sempletons and the Andersons, ending the marriage would lead to a reduced standard of living. In economic terms, women tend to lose more than men in a divorce and are far more likely to end up living close to the edge of poverty. In fact, divorce and the complications of child-support disputes are a leading cause of poverty for mothers and children.

Research shows that a woman's standard of living is likely to go down 74 percent following divorce, whereas a man's is likely to go up. Not surprisingly, as women have made financial gains in our culture, they have become more likely to leave husbands than in the past. Mary is especially aware of the relevance of this constraint to her life. She has a decent job with a good income, but one income can't support the same standard of living as two. The choice between financial security and living on the edge is clear-cut to many people.

Unavailability of partners refers to the social constraint resulting from the perception that if you left your present partner, no one else would be available. All things being equal, you are more likely to stay in your present relationship when you perceive your alternatives to be poor—assuming that you want a relationship, of course. As people grow older, they are somewhat more likely to believe that other partners are less available. This probably affects women more than men, since there are fewer men relative to women in older age groups. This statistic may be offset by the fact that women are somewhat less likely than men to want another spouse after a divorce or death. Nevertheless, if you want to be in a relationship but perceive your other options to be poor, you're more likely to stay.

Perception is more important than reality here. Whatever the reality, Mary is factoring this consideration into her thinking. Bob isn't considering leaving, so he hasn't thought much about the availability of other women. And because the Sempletons are fairly happy with one another, the availability of other partners doesn't even come into play.

Thus, both the Sempletons and the Andersons have a good deal of constraint commitment. This gives the Sempletons a feeling of stability, while the Andersons feel trapped. There's a huge difference in their levels of satisfaction. But that's not all; there's also a great difference in their levels of dedicated commitment. Now we'll explore just what that means.

THE COMMITMENT OF PERSONAL DEDICATION

As with constraints, we want to help you to understand dedication by describing ingredients that are consistent with fully developed dedication in relationships.

Desiring the long term refers to wanting the relationship to continue into the future. Do you want to grow old with your partner? Wanting to be with your partner in the future is a core part of dedication in our model. There's both an expectation and a desire for the relationship to have a future. As we'll discuss in detail in the next chapter, the long-term expectation that a relationship will continue plays a critical role in the day-to-day quality of that relationship.

Mary Anderson isn't thrilled by the idea of her marriage continuing. It's likely to continue for now, but she doesn't really want it to. Bob is unhappy, too, but he does want the marriage to continue. Both of the Sempletons want their marriage to continue. In fact, they talk a lot about "their" future together, reflecting their dedication to one another. When couples have strong dedication, they talk about their plans for their future.

The priority of the relationship refers to the importance that you give your relationship relative to everything else. When people are more dedicated to their partners and relationships, they live and behave in ways that show it. Many people are so involved in work, hobbies, or children that the relationship takes a backseat. To some degree, this can reflect a problem with overinvolvement elsewhere as much as a lack of dedication.

At some point, we all have to accept that how we live reflects what's most important to us. Unfortunately, the Andersons have allowed their marriage to become a lower priority, and they're suffering for this. Their marriage isn't bad as much as it's neglected. They no longer think it worthwhile to work at it. If couples are going to make it, they have to turn this pattern around.

The Sempletons have the attitude that each of them is truly important to the other. There are times when Eric is angry about what he sees as Deidre's overinvolvement in her work, but he doesn't seriously doubt that he matters to her. Likewise, Deidre sometimes thinks that Eric is too involved in sports with "the boys," but she recognizes his dedication to her and the family all the same.

"We-ness" refers to the degree to which couples participate in their relationship as a team, rather than as two separate individuals who focus mostly on what's best for themselves. This has been called "we-ness," because *we* transcends *I* in thinking about the relationship. It's crucial to have a sense of an identity together if a relationship is to grow and be satisfying. Without this sense of being a team, conflict is more likely as problems pit one against the other instead of "us" against the problem.

In Chapter Six, we described a couple who were both executives in their business. Yet, in describing the organization to others, the husband stated that he was the only officer of the corporation, which wasn't true. His description of their business showed that he didn't think of them as a team. This kind of event no doubt triggered significant hidden issues of recognition, commitment, and acceptance in their relationship.

Whether couples see themselves as a team is often reflected in how they handle their finances. For example, couples who pool their finances are somewhat less likely to break up. One couple in a second marriage told us of their endless arguments about "my money" and "your money." Like many other couples, they tried to keep two separate budgets. But as we all know, what one partner does financially will affect the other, as with every other aspect of marriage.

We're not saying that your marriage is in trouble if you keep your finances separate, but there may be trouble ahead if you have a pervasive sense of "mine" versus "yours." This attitude can fuel conflict and competition, since when there's no clear sense of being part of a team, deeper issues such as caring, recognition, and control are easily triggered.

We aren't suggesting that you merge your identity with your partner's. Rather, we are saying that it is healthy to have a clear sense of yourselves as two individuals coming together to form a team, and that the team's goals are important. What a difference this makes in how you view life!

There's a big difference between the Sempletons' marriage and the Andersons' on this dimension. Bob and Mary each feel quite alone; they have no abiding sense that they're a team working through the ups and downs of life. In contrast, the Sempletons draw comfort from their history of working together.

Satisfaction with sacrifice is the degree to which people feel a sense of satisfaction in doing things that are largely or solely for their partner's benefit. The point is not to find pleasure in martyrdom, but to give of yourself for your partner's benefit. We'll have more on martyrdom in the next chapter.

Satisfaction with sacrifice is one of the few dimensions in our studies where we've found relatively large differences between men and women: women reported less satisfaction in sacrificing than their partners. We believe that this is a result of cultural factors. It's expected that women will place a higher priority on relationships, and, therefore, will sacrifice more for their partners, so they get less recognition for the sacrifices they do make. When a man sacrifices, it may be more noticeable to both himself and his partner because it's not as expected. Men get more recognition, and as a result, they may get more pleasure from making sacrifices.

Nevertheless, relationships are generally stronger if *both* partners are willing to make sacrifices, as Deidre and Eric are. This may be an old-fashioned idea, but research suggests that some degree of sacrifice is a normal, healthy aspect of a solid relationship. In the absence of an attitude of sacrifice, what do you have? You have a relationship in which at least one of you is in it mostly for what you can get. That's not a recipe for satisfaction or growth.

Bob and Mary have stopped giving to each other. Bob doesn't think he'll get anything back if he gives more, and Mary already feels that she's giving more than her share. Neither of them feels like sacrificing anything at this point. They both believe that they're giving up a lot just by being there.

Looking for new partners refers to a notion discussed by several commitment theorists. In our research, we have specifically focused on monitoring potential, alternative partners. The more one is attracted to or attuned to other potential partners, the less personal dedication there is to the current partner. Do you find yourself *seriously* thinking about being with people other than your spouse? We must emphasize "seriously," because almost everyone is attracted to other people from time to time. Dedication is in jeopardy if this attraction to others has become intense, especially if you have a particular person in mind. One study showed that people who are highly dedicated actually mentally devalue attractive, potential partners.

Eric has been tempted a time or two by women he's worked with over the years. At one point, he worked with a woman named Nancy whom he found very attractive. He was aware of this attraction and considered it a threat to his marriage. As a matter of will, he decided not to dwell on Nancy and what he liked about her. At times, he'd think about what wasn't so great about her compared to Deidre. It's not that Nancy wasn't a great woman—she seemed to be—but he couldn't see any percentage in thinking about her, because of his commitment to Deidre. The point is that when you're tempted, you can choose to look less and think less about attractive alternatives. This amounts to focusing on why the grass isn't greener on the other side of the fence.

In the field of mental health and marriage counseling, professionals often tell people that fantasizing (sexually or otherwise) is harmless. You may or may not agree with this. However, the above research suggests that regularly fantasizing about *real, available,* alternative partners could be dangerous for your marriage. Some people have suggested that this amounts to thought control, and that we're telling you what to think about. Far from it. We have no interest in controlling what you do or think, but we do want you to know what happier couples tend to do. Finding yourself thinking a lot about being with someone else is a red flag. It's your choice how much mental energy you'll devote to thinking about "what if?" and how much you'll put into making your present relationship all it can be.

Quite often, when Mary Anderson notices Larry at her office, she thinks about being with him. She spends more and more time wondering "what if?" She has even wondered about having an affair as a way of "testing" that relationship. Bob, too, has considered other women. The key difference between them on this dimension is that no one is tempting to Bob right now. If Mary and Bob are to regain a deeply satisfied marriage, they both need to devote their mental energies to improving their relationship, not to "what if?" fantasies.

Are you seriously thinking about being with someone else? If your relationship is about to end or if your partner is leaving you, it would be perfectly logical for you to wonder "what if?" If you're planning on keeping your marriage strong, maintain your focus on tending to your own lawn rather than yearning for the grass on the other side of the fence.

HOW DOES COMMITMENT DEVELOP? HOW DOES DEDICATION DIE?

Dedication is believed to develop in relationships mainly from the couple's initial attraction and satisfaction. Think back on the beginning of your relationship. Because you liked being together, you began to be more dedicated to staying together. As your dedication became more apparent, you may have noticed that you became more relaxed about the relationship. In most relationships, there's an awkward period where the desire to be together is great but the commitment is unclear. That produces anxiety about whether or not you'll stay together. As your mutual dedication became clearer, it seemed safer to invest in the relationship.

Because of your dedication, you did things that increased constraint. Essentially, *today's dedication becomes tomorrow's constraint.* For example, as dedication grows, a couple will decide to go from a dating relationship to an engaged relationship. As dedication grows further, they decide to become married, then perhaps to have children. Each of these steps, taken as a reflection of dedication, adds to the constraint. You may have taken some of these steps in your relationship.

Research shows that couples at these different developmental points have predictable differences in their levels of constraint on most of the dimensions mentioned above. That's why we say that it's natural for levels of constraint to grow in marriage. Like the Sempletons, couples who are more dedicated tend to be much more satisfied with their marriage. The relationship between satisfaction and dedication is reciprocal. Greater dedication will usually lead to greater satisfaction, and dedication grows out of satisfaction in the first place. Also, when they're truly dedicated, people are more likely to behave in ways that protect their marriage and please their partner, so the effect on satisfaction is positive. It's very nice to see that your partner really cares about you and protects the relationship from all the other alternatives in life.

Studies show that most couples have high levels of dedication early on, when they're engaged or early in their marriage. What happens to kill this dedication for some couples over time? For one thing, if conflict isn't handled well, satisfaction with the marriage will go down steadily. Since satisfaction partly fuels the dedication, the dedication begins to erode along with the satisfaction. With dedication in jeopardy, giving to one another is eroded further, and satisfaction is likely to decline rapidly.

But that's not the whole story. Dedication isn't just about happiness. It's also based on personal choices, values, and confidence. Some people may find it easier than others to sustain the kind of commitment reflected in the dimensions of dedication discussed here. Perhaps even more important, we think that dedication erodes when people begin to feel that their effort doesn't make any difference. This is another way in which poorly handled conflict kills a marriage. The partners begin to believe that no amount of dedication matters, and it gets hard to keep trying. When this happens, they're well on the road to a high-constraint, low-dedication, low-satisfaction marriage—if not divorce. That's not where most of us want to be.

The secret to satisfying commitment is to maintain not just constraint but high levels of dedication. Although constraint commitment can add a positive, stabilizing dimension to your marriage, it can't give you a great relationship. Dedication, on the other hand, is the side of commitment that's associated with healthy, satisfying, and growing relationships. In fact, dedicated couples not only report more satisfaction with their relationships; they also report less conflict about their problems and greater levels of self-disclosure. Are you just existing in your relationship, or are you making it what you hoped it would be?

How to make your marriage a high priority is your choice. It's your choice to sacrifice more at times for your partner. It's your choice how to protect your relationship from attractive alternatives. Fundamentally, these are matters of the will. We recognize that in some relationships, increasing your dedication to your partner will not make much appreciable difference. Nevertheless, far more often, your partner will respond very positively—and in kind—to evidence of your dedication.

In the next chapter we'll discuss important implications of commitment and show what you can do to build a stronger marriage. But before we move on, we want to give you the opportunity to assess your commitment to your relationship.

 Exercises

On the basis of what you've read so far, you should have some idea of your levels of dedication and constraint. The following exercises will help you to refine your impressions.

In our research, we ask couples a large number of questions to help us assess their commitment. You can get a good idea of how you're doing with your commitment by answering the questions below. *We don't recommend that you write your answers in this book, and we suggest that you keep your answers to yourself. These exercises are best done individually, for your own reflection. Only in the priorities exercise are you asked to compare notes.*

ASSESSING CONSTRAINT COMMITMENT

Answer each item by circling one number to indicate how true the statement seems to you. Use the following scale for your answers: 1 = Strongly disagree, 4 = Neither agree nor disagree, and 7 = Strongly agree.

1 2 3 4 5 6 7   The steps I would need to take to end this relationship would require a great deal of time and effort.

1 2 3 4 5 6 7   A marriage is a sacred bond between two people that should not be broken.

1 2 3 4 5 6 7   I would have trouble finding a suitable partner if this relationship ended.

1 2 3 4 5 6 7   My friends or family really want this relationship to work.

1 2 3 4 5 6 7   I would lose valuable possessions if I left my partner.

1 2 3 4 5 6 7   My partner would be emotionally devastated if I left, so even if I wanted to leave I might not.

1 2 3 4 5 6 7   I couldn't make it financially if we broke up or divorced.

1 2 3 4 5 6 7   My life-style would be worse in many ways if I left my partner.

1 2 3 4 5 6 7   I feel trapped in this relationship.

1 2 3 4 5 6 7   It is important to finish what you've started, no matter what.

Your answers to these few questions can tell you a lot. We can't give you an average score on these items since we don't use them in quite that way in our research. But it's obvious that the higher the score, the greater the level of constraint. In any case, we want you to use your responses for reflection. Are you aware of constraints? How great do they seem to be? What kind of constraint seems the greatest?

Most important, do you feel trapped? Almost everyone does from time to time and this is normal. You might be more concerned if you frequently feel trapped. Having a good deal of constraint but not feeling trapped is normal in a healthy marriage. The best marriages have two partners who are both dedicated to one another and who feel comfortable with the stability implied by constraint.

ASSESSING DEDICATED COMMITMENT

The following items will help you to gauge your level of dedication. Use the following scale for your answers: 1 = Strongly disagree, 4 = Neither agree nor disagree, and 7 = Strongly agree.

1 2 3 4 5 6 7   My relationship with my partner is more important to me than almost anything else in my life.

1 2 3 4 5 6 7   I want this relationship to stay strong no matter what rough times we may encounter.

1 2 3 4 5 6 7   It makes me feel good to sacrifice for my partner.

1 2 3 4 5 6 7   I like to think of myself and my partner more in terms of "us" and "we" than "me" and "him" or "her."

1 2 3 4 5 6 7   I am not seriously attracted to anyone other than my partner.

1 2 3 4 5 6 7   My relationship with my partner is clearly part of my future life plans.

1 2 3 4 5 6 7   When push comes to shove, my relationship with my partner comes first.

1 2 3 4 5 6 7   I tend to think about how things affect us as a couple more than how things affect me as an individual.

1 2 3 4 5 6 7   I do not often find myself thinking about what it would be like to be in a relationship with someone else.

1 2 3 4 5 6 7   I want to grow old with my partner.

We can give you an idea of what your score means on these dedication items. To obtain your score, simply add up the numbers you circled. In our research—with a sample of people who were mostly happy and dedicated in their relationships (including everyone from those who had been dating for a few months to those married for over thirty years), the average person scores about 58 on the items on this scale. If you scored at or above 58, we'd bet you are pretty highly dedicated in your relationship. By contrast, dedication may be quite low if you scored below 45. However you scored, consider what it may mean for the future of your relationship.

CONSIDERING PRIORITIES

A key way to look at dedication is to consider what your priorities are. How do you actually live your life, and what does this say about your commitment? The following form will help you to consider your priorities. You'll not only rate what you think yours are, but also what you think your partner will say about yours and what you think your partner's are. Two copies of the

form are included. You should each complete your form separately, then compare notes. Don't be defensive. Consider the
impact on your relationship of the answers each of you has
given.

If you see a need to make your relationship a greater priority,
talk together about the specific steps you can take to bring
this about. You might find the problem-solving model from
Chapter Four helpful for this. We'll also have many specific
suggestions that can help in the last part of this book.

PRIORITIES EXPLORATION FORM

In column 1 on the next page, please list what you consider
your top five priorities in life, from greater to lesser importance. In column 2, please list what you think your partner
would say are your top five priorities. For example, if you think
your partner would say that work is your top priority, put
that first in column 2. In column 3, list what you believe are
your partner's top five priorities. Below the columns is a list of
possible priorities for you to consider. This list is given merely
to aid you in considering your priorities. Feel free to use your
own words, and be as specific as possible.

Your rating of your priorities	Your guess of your partner's rating of your priorities	Your rating of what you believe are your partner's priorities
1. _____	1._____	1. _____
2._____	2. _____	2._____
3._____	3. _____	3._____
4._____	4. _____	4._____
5._____	5. _____	5._____

SOME POSSIBLE PRIORITY AREAS

Work and career	House and home	Possessions	Friends
Children	Sports	Hobbies	Pets
Your partner	Future goals	Relatives	Television
Religion	Education	Co-workers	Car

Your rating of your priorities	Your guess of your partner's rating of your priorities	Your rating of what you believe are your partner's priorities
1. _____	1. _____	1. _____
2. _____	2. _____	2. _____
3. _____	3. _____	3. _____
4. _____	4. _____	4. _____
5. _____	5. _____	5. _____

SOME POSSIBLE PRIORITY AREAS

Work and career	House and home	Possessions	Friends
Children	Sports	Hobbies	Pets
Your partner	Future goals	Relatives	Television
Religion	Education	Co-workers	Car

9

The Power of Commitment

IN THE LAST CHAPTER, our goal was to understand the commitment in your relationship. In this chapter, we'll go deeper by focusing on ways to apply some of the major implications of commitment to maintaining healthy and long-lasting marriages.

If you have a solid commitment with dedication, we want to help you prevent it from eroding. If you have lost some dedication over the years, we want to help you get it back. We'll focus on two key themes. First, we'll discuss the benefits of a long-term view in marriage. Second, we'll discuss self-centeredness and its effects in relationships.

THE IMPORTANCE OF A LONG-TERM VIEW

When people are committed, they have a long-term outlook on their relationship. In a healthy relationship, dedication and constraint combine to produce a sense of permanence. This is crucial for one simple reason: *no relationship is consistently satisfying.* What gets couples through tougher times is the long-term view that commitment brings. They have the expectation that the relationship will make it through thick and thin. One study actually showed that couples with greater commitment spend more of their money on things like appliances—

reflecting a belief in a future together. You don't buy a washer with someone you aren't planning to stay with!

We want to be very clear about one thing before we go on. Sometimes it's wise to bring a relationship to an end. We're not saying that everybody should always devote a herculean effort to save a relationships, no matter how abusive or destructive it is. For the great number of couples who genuinely love each other and want to make their marriage work, however, a long-term perspective is essential for encouraging each partner to take risks, disclose his or her inner self, and trust that the other person will be there when it really counts.

In the absence of a long-term view, we're prone to focus on the immediate payoff. This is only natural. If the long-term benefit is uncertain, we naturally concentrate on what we're getting in the present. Essentially, the short-term view says: "Give it to me now and give it to me quick. There's no certainty in any future here."

The hidden issue of commitment, which we discussed in Chapter Six, is easily triggered when the future of the relationship is uncertain. When the commitment is unclear, there's pressure to perform, as opposed to being accepted—a core issue for everyone. One partner may subtly convey to the other, "You'd better produce or I'll look for

RAGNAR STORAASLI

someone who can." Most of us resent feeling we could be abandoned by the person from whom we most expect to find security and acceptance. Not surprisingly, people usually won't invest in a relationship with an uncertain future and rewards. If you know that your effort won't pay off now and you have no hope for the future, why invest at all?

We focused on the Sempletons and the Andersons in the last chapter. The Andersons are held together mostly by constraint. While some sense of stability comes from constraint, they don't have the full sense of a future together that comes from a combination of dedication and constraint. As a result, each withholds any more effort, waiting for the other to somehow make it better. It seems too risky to do anything else.

In contrast, the Sempletons don't have the perfect marriage (who does?), but they have a strong expectation of a future rooted in balanced commitment. Their belief in their future is reflected in frequent talks about the life they're planning together. They've maintained their commitment, and especially their dedication. They do things for each other, show respect, and protect their marriage in terms of priorities and alternatives.

The Sempletons' long-term view allows each of them to "give the other some slack," leading to greater acceptance of each other's weaknesses and failings over time. Whereas the Andersons experience anxiety or resentment over the core issue of acceptance, the Sempletons feel the warmth of a secure commitment, in which each conveys the powerful message: "I will be here for you." That's the essence of commitment.

MARRIAGE AND THE STOCK MARKET

We have found that financial metaphors can help to explain why a long-term perspective is so vital. In our seminars, we call them the "Dean Witter" portion of our presentation. Experts consistently report that over the long haul, the stock market generally outperforms all other kinds of investments. They also say that most people for whom retirement is many years away should consider investing in stocks, usually through mutual funds.

In stock-oriented mutual funds, investors do best when they don't worry about day-to-day swings in performance and maintain a long-term view. Investors tend to do poorly when they look in the newspaper each day, see if their fund is doing as well as others, and constantly move their investments from one fund to another. Such people tend to panic. They transfer their money so often that long-term growth is compromised.

Think of your marriage as a long-term investment. The ups and downs in the stock market and the value of a good mutual fund are like the ups and downs in satisfaction in marriage. They're inevitable—and normal. Good marriages may have long periods of time when satisfaction is down, only to rebound later to mutual joy, just like the stock market. If you wait for market conditions to be just right, you never get started. If you become too focused on the down cycles, you can bail out too quickly and lose much of what you've invested.

Isaac and Lana are a younger couple with two children under the age of five. Like many young couples, they've experienced a good deal of stress and frustration while rearing their young children. The children bring them great joy, but also a lot of work. After one of our workshop talks on commitment, Isaac came up and stated: "I had no idea that it was normal for couples to go up and down in their level of happiness over the course of a marriage. I thought there was something wrong with us!"

Isaac had an expectation that marriage was supposed to be blissfully happy and romantic throughout a lifetime. If he hadn't realized the problem with this expectation, he and Lana would have had big trouble down the road. It could have led him to bail out during a period of stress because the marriage wasn't performing according to his original, unrealistic expectation.

Unending bliss is just not what marriage is like for most people. It's wonderful at times and very hard at other times. Sometimes it's wonderfully hard. That's why it takes commitment—and a long-term view.

Are You Hedging Your Bets?

People with short-term views scrutinize the costs and benefits of their relationship on a day-to-day basis, just like the investor who checks the paper every day in search of a better deal. These people are likely to move their investments around so much—in affairs or involvements in outside activities, for example—that the marriage is weakened. They're hedging their bets. Their energies are so divided that there isn't enough left over for the marriage. So even though they may say "marriage and family" when they're asked what the most important thing is in their life, that's not how they're living. They're at risk of losing what they say they value most. Unfortunately, many people don't recognize this risk until it's too late.

Why does this happen? Sometimes, energy is invested in activities that have a more appealing short-term payoff at the expense of a long-term return in the relationship. Many people throw themselves into their work when they're dissatisfied at home. There's nothing wrong with loving your work, but when the time and effort needed in the marriage is sacrificed for other things, the marriage will suffer for it.

One of the most dramatic examples of moving your investment around is having an affair. Statistically, most affairs come at times when the present relationship is dying or dead. Current satisfaction is so low and the long-term commitment is so uncertain that one person begins investing in another relationship. This can blossom into a full-blown affair. Affairs don't have to lead to divorce, but there are few more destructive ways to hedge your bets.

Now, you might be thinking, "Don't investment experts also tell you to diversify?" Yes. But the healthy way to diversify in marriage is through the multiple avenues of intimacy available in marriage. If you strengthen your marriage in many areas, such as through friendship and fun, sensual or spiritual connection, or just better communication, you are diversifying your ability to connect—but diversifying *within* the marriage.

Investing for the Long Haul

Unless you're planning to end your present relationship, nothing is gained and much is lost by waiting around for the right time to invest positively. Regular investment in the marriage is critical if you want to prevent problems in the first place or to begin turning things around.

Because investors with short-term views tend to get burned in the stock market, financial experts often advocate a strategy called "dollar cost averaging." In this strategy, you choose a good mutual fund and you stick with it. You are advised to invest a set amount in the fund in regular intervals (say, $50 a month) over the long haul. Unless one is good at "timing the market," this strategy is considered very effective for beating inflation and saving something for the future. Whether the market is up or down, you send in the investment.

We believe that marriages work much the same way. It is best if both partners are regularly investing in the marriage whether the market—their satisfaction level—is currently up or down.

You make investments when, among other things, you communicate well and validate each other, handle conflict well, do fun things together, put self-interest aside and do something that helps your partner, preserve friendship, forgive your partner, and are able to resolve problems that have been bothering you. These are the very things we're showing you how to do in this book. You can think of the PREP approach as investment guidance for the most important relationship in your life.

Sometimes we abuse the value of the long-term view by taking advantage of our partners. In the rush of life we fail to put all we should into the marriage because we take for granted that our partner will be there and can wait for our attention. This is one negative consequence of commitment. We don't take advantage of people this way when we're dating. Don't take your partner for granted. Keep investing regularly!

Risk and Reward

Like the stock market, marriage is risky. We tried to convince you of that early in this book with depressing statistics about divorce. But, as with stocks, the corresponding payoff can be great. Why else would so many people seek a relationship that has such high risks?

Unfortunately, we often act as if we can get something for nothing—as if we can have a deeply rewarding relationship without the effort. We all fall for the allure of "something for nothing" from time to time, but let's face it—it never really works out that way. If you want something worthwhile, you have to invest yourself and your resources to get it.

If you're in a good relationship with a balanced commitment, the risk of investing won't seem very great. If, on the other hand, you're in a relationship where the long-term view is compromised for some reason, there's a lot of risk, and steady investment may seem like the height of stupidity. The problem is that pulling back will simply hasten the erosion of what little satisfaction and commitment is left. Is that what you want to have happen?

Financial experts don't advocate putting your money somewhere and then paying no attention to what happens to it. Neither do we. It makes sense to reflect now and then on how things are going. If the long-term growth in your relationship has been pretty dismal and you're unhappy, you have to confront the situation constructively. Don't ignore it. In fact, constructive confrontation is another form of investment in the relationship. It takes dedication.

For example, Bonnie and Archibald have been married for twenty-five years. Like many couples, they've had serious ups and downs. Unfortunately, the downs have greatly outweighed the ups over the past five years. Bonnie's bitter about Archibald's devotion to his work in computers. He's never home, or at least that's the way it seems to her. She truly believes that he doesn't care. He's angry with her about her lack of interest in his hobbies, ballooning and biking, interpreting this as a lack of interest in him.

Neither Archibald nor Bonnie try very much anymore, and divorce has been openly discussed. Although they're rightly concerned about the prospect of throwing "good money after bad," they have no shot at a good marriage if they don't both take dedication to heart and invest wholeheartedly in the relationship. If one or, better yet, both of them start to make an effort, each may respond to the other more than they think possible.

There are no guarantees for Bonnie and Archibald, and there may be a significant risk in putting in the effort to invest in the relationship again. But unless one of them clearly wants out, there's also a certain risk in not investing the effort, the risk that their marriage will die. We hope that you're not at such a point; and we believe that you can keep from getting there by regular, steady investment in your marriage.

SCOREKEEPING

One manifestation of low commitment and the short-term view is scorekeeping. This is the tendency to monitor what you're getting out of the relationship relative to what you're putting in. People who are experiencing the erosion of dedication tend to be more attuned to the day-to-day, short-term payoff of the relationship. They ask, "Am I getting what I deserve for what I'm putting into this?" They're keeping score. When the future is uncertain, the score today is all that matters.

You don't have to be married a long time to be a scorekeeper. We all do it from time to time. Forest and Margie are a young couple we saw in one of our University of Denver research projects. Though they'd been married only six months, they'd both had become very unhappy since they said "I do." It seemed to each of them that the dominant message now was "I won't." They both had a variety of expectations that were not being fulfilled in the marriage, and they were already feeling ripped off.

Margie had begun counting the amount of time Forest spent at home each week and asking herself, "Why does he have to be out two nights a week with his pals?" Forest had begun noting how seldom Margie pursued lovemaking. He felt that he was the one always showing interest, and he didn't like it one bit. He asked, "Why do I always have to initiate things?" Although they had some legitimate gripes with one another—and some unrealistic expectations—the greater damage was being done by all the scorekeeping.

Why is scorekeeping so destructive? Why not tune in to what you're getting and expect to get back what you're putting in? Obviously, it's only fair for both partners to pull their weight in a marriage. The problem occurs because scorekeeping is fundamentally and hopelessly biased in favor of the one keeping score and therefore can hurt even healthy relationships.

Why is scorekeeping biased? You're with yourself all the time, right? (That was not a trick question.) Are you with your partner all the time? No. Of all the positive things you and your partner each do for the relationship, who do you most often see doing something for the relationship? Yourself, of course. You are a continual observer of your own behavior, not your partner's.

Here's the bottom line. Even if there were some way to judge and things were equal, scorekeeping would lead you to conclude that you were doing more for the relationship than your partner. This attitude is just a hop, skip, and a jump from serious resentment and bitterness, because you'll think that things are unfair even when they're not. Are you keeping score? If so, you may be heading for trouble.

There are three keys to combating scorekeeping. First, you must be alert to the unfairness of your scorecard. We all keep score from time to time, but recognizing that the score isn't objective goes a long way toward preventing resentment from building up. Second, counter the bias directly by looking for specific things your partner does that you appreciate or that are good for you. Third, concentrate on what *you* can do that's good for your relationship, not on what you think your partner isn't doing. It helps if your partner is willing to do this too. But even if that doesn't happen, remember that you can only control what you do, not what your partner does.

TRUST AND COMMITMENT

We are often asked in our workshops about the association between trust and commitment. The answer also relates to the importance of the long-term view. *Webster's New World Dictionary* defines *trust* as: "firm belief in the honesty, reliability, etc. of another; faith . . . confident expectation, hope." In a relationship, trust means being able to count on your partner to be there for you. The relationship between trust and commitment is best described with another financial metaphor.

In the past few years, the only topic that has been bigger financial news in the United States than the deficit has been the catastrophe in the savings and loan industry. One of the more notable failures nationwide was the collapse of Silverado Savings and Loan in Colorado. Silverado is now out of business, although we'll all be paying for some time for its failure.

Suppose that you're looking for a new savings and loan so you can start a savings account. You notice that one opens up on the corner near your home, and a sign goes up that says, "Silverado Savings and Loan: We're Back to Serve *You.*" Are you going to run right down and deposit your money? Not likely. You probably have doubts about the long-term stability of the institution and wouldn't trust them to be there for you in the future.

Marriage works the same way. Without the long-term view, who's going to trust enough to invest in a marriage? If you don't trust your partner, you're less likely to invest, period. However, if you don't show your dedication by investing, how is your partner supposed to trust you and invest back? Forest and Margie, whom we discussed a few pages back, will need to stop scorekeeping and show each other that they are both willing to invest for the long term. If each of them can see the other making the effort, they can really turn things around.

Trust and commitment depend on one another. You'll commit more when you trust more, and you'll trust more when you see your spouse providing commitment, and especially dedication. If you both can learn to maintain and display your dedication, you help each other to trust.

If you want your partner to trust you, show that you're dedicated and planning to be there. What other part of the equation can you directly control besides your own level of dedication? In the next chapter, on forgiveness, we'll talk about regaining trust that's been lost.

TRASHING THE LONG-TERM VIEW

As we stated in the first chapter, commitment may become a weapon in a fight. Although Bob and Mary Anderson, whom we met in the last chapter, aren't going to get a divorce any time soon, the topic sometimes comes up during bad arguments. Consider the following conversation and its effects on trust, power, and commitment:

BOB: Why does this house always look like a pigpen? You're never here to get things done.

MARY: I'm out doing so many things because we have kids, and kids need a lot of attention.

BOB: I end up having to clean up all the time and I'm tired of it.

MARY: Oh, and I don't clean up? When you're here, you disappear into your shop. I don't see you doing all that much cleaning up. I do most of it—not you.

BOB: Yeah, yeah, I disappear all the time. You just don't give a damn about this marriage. I don't even know why we stay together.

MARY: Me neither. Maybe you should move out.

BOB: Not a terrible idea. I'll think about it.

What just happened in this argument? At the end of the fight they both seemed to be trying to convince each other that they weren't committed. You can't get much more short-term than to suggest divorce. When you do this, you might as well slap a sign on your forehead that says, "Silverado: Come Invest with Us." Fat chance! The free toaster doesn't overcome the kind of mistrust bred in such arguments. This is an adult form of the kind of arguments children have all the time:

LITTLE BOBBY: I'm not sure I can make it to your birthday party. I have a baseball game.

LITTLE MARY: Well, I wasn't sure I really wanted you to come, anyway.

LITTLE BOBBY: Oh, yeah? I wouldn't come to your crummy birthday party if you paid me.

LITTLE MARY: Oh, yeah? See if I care.

Different age, same story. Such statements reflect the massive frustration each of them is feeling. They also reflect a desire to gain control or power by trashing commitment. They're both trying to say, "I can live without you just fine" and "You can't control me because I don't care what happens to us."

If you can convince someone who's hurt you that you don't care and aren't really committed, you gain some power and control. The reason is simple. People who are more committed may give in when there are disagreements because they have a greater stake in making the relationship work. This amounts to a very destructive expression of power and control issues, which usually takes place in the context of events. Questioning commitment during moments of extreme frustration fosters anxiety and competition—anxiety about whether or not the relationship is going forward and competition about who will be hurt less. In fact, both partners are likely to be hurt a great deal.

If you are trying to make your marriage work, it's important not to bring up the topic of divorce, period. Likewise, don't threaten to have affairs. Such statements go counter to the long-term view. They erode trust and reinforce the perception that it's risky to invest. If you've made such comments from time to time, ask yourself whether having your partner give up is what you want to accomplish

If you sense problems in the balance of commitment or power, or if you're uncertain of the long-term view, discuss these issues head-on in a constructive manner. As we discussed in Chapter Six, it's critical that you deal with the big issues *as issues*. They're powerful and should be handled with special care—for example, using the structure of the Speaker-Listener Technique. It isn't wise to address big issues in moments of frustration over the events in your relationship.

If you see yourself as less committed than your partner, ask yourself why this is the case. Is it a way to gain power in the relationship? Does it reflect a lack of trust on your part? Is it a way to be in control and protect yourself? The most satisfying, healthy marriages show balanced levels of commitment over time. We emphasize *balanced* and *over time!* Trust takes time to develop or regain. Your commitment says that you have the time for this to happen.

Now we turn to another important set of implications of commitment in a discussion of selfishness and self-centeredness.

SELFISHNESS

Our culture encourages devotion to self. Notions of sacrifice, teamwork, and placing a high priority on the partner and on a dedicated relationship have not enjoyed much positive press lately. In fact, our society seems to glorify the individual and vilify whatever gets in the way. And we all pay for these attitudes.

In contrast, we suggest that dedication is fundamental to healthy relationships and that selfishness is fundamentally destructive. Selfishness may sell, but it doesn't bring lifelong happy unions. Do you want to get your way all the time or have a great relationship?

BEING TEAM-CENTERED

Dedication is more about being team-centered or other-centered than being self-centered. To be team-centered is to be sensitive to your partner, to take your partner's perspective, to seek to build your partner up, and to protect your partner in healthy ways, *because you're a team.*

It means making your partner's health and happiness as much a priority as your own health and happiness. It means doing what you know is good for your relationship—like listening to your partner—even when you don't particularly want to. It means protecting your commitment from alternative attractions. If you want to prevent breakdown in your relationship, cultivate attitudes and behavior that reflect dedication to the team.

To be selfish and self-centered is to be insensitive to your partner, to see things only your way; to seek your own good above all else, and to protect yourself first and foremost. It's always surprising to us when people we work with who live this way are disappointed that their great marriage never materializes.

One of the best things about the early stages of most relationships is the relative lack of self-centeredness. When they are courting, people think up ways to put their partners first and spend a lot of time listening. But such a focus on the partner's needs often doesn't last.

One couple who came to a PREP workshop, Martin and Jennifer, had a serious problem with selfishness. Jennifer described to us her frustration with Martin during a break. She said that things had gone pretty well until they had a baby four years into the marriage. While Jennifer was caring for the baby, Martin disappeared into his basement to work on his hobbies. Jennifer asked him to be more involved with their little girl, but he didn't seem interested. She'd been very clear about her expectation, but he hadn't responded.

Martin loved spending time on his projects. It seemed he liked having the baby primarily because Jennifer spent so much time with her that he felt free to disappear. While we can't know all of his motives, it did seem that Martin was being pretty selfish. He left Jennifer to do most of the child rearing and focused intensely on what he wanted to do, not on what his wife and baby girl needed.

Selfish attitudes and behavior can and will kill a relationship. Such attitudes aren't compatible with dedication. Whereas dedication reflects "we-ness" and, at times, sacrifice, our culture asserts individual rights and the need to protect ourselves from all insult and criticism. But in our view, you can't have a great marriage when each partner is primarily focused on what's best for himself or herself. In a culture that reinforces the self, it's hard to ask, "What can I do to make this better?" It's a lot easier to ask, "What can my partner do to make me happier?"

We are *not* advocating martyrdom. In the way the term is commonly used, a martyr does things for you not out of concern for what is best for you, but because she or he wants to put you in debt. This is not dedication; it's usually insecurity and selfishness masquerading as doing good.

The key is not only what you do for your partner, but also why you do it. Do you do things with an attitude that says, "You'd better appreciate what I'm doing"? Do you often feel that your partner owes you? There's nothing wrong with doing positive things and wanting to be appreciated, but there is something wrong with believing that you're owed, as if your positive behavior is building up a debt for your partner.

It's probably no coincidence that the "me" attitude of the seventies and eighties was also associated with some of the highest divorce rates of all times. Good marriages and other long-term relationships are not about rampant self-centeredness, but about caring for and building up one another. The kind of deeply intimate, caring, and lasting marriages most people seek are built and maintained on dedication to one another expressed in the kinds of constructive behavior we advocate throughout this book.

CODEPENDENCY OR COMMITMENT?

Codependency has come to mean all things to all people. The term has virtually no meaning anymore because people use it for everything bad in relationships—and some things that are good. We address the topic briefly here so as not to be misunderstood.

The original idea of codependence came out of work with alcoholism. Professionals noticed that often significant others in the life of the alcoholic would "help" the alcoholic in ways that actually promoted the problem—for example, "enabling" the alcoholic by covering his or her failure to be a responsible person.

Counselors began to realize that some people need to reinforce the alcoholic's dependency. This often reflects a need to be a caretaker—and in control. The central idea of codependency is that people sometimes "help" or give to others in ways that are destructive to both parties because of deeper insecurities and issues of control. Such behavior can look like dedication, but it's not.

The problem in our culture is that people have been labeled codependent for giving of themselves in truly constructive ways. In simplistic thinking, sacrifice is now considered codependent, as is being other-centered or team-centered. Try, however, to have a really great marriage without giving of yourself—at times sacrificially.

Sure, you *can* give too much in ways that harm the relationship and yourself. Does it really show dedication to tolerate a spouse's demanding or impolite behavior? No. This is not dedication. Does it show dedication not to confront the alcoholism in a partner's life? No. It shows far more dedication to constructively confront the behavior that threatens to destroy you, your partner, or the marriage. Having acknowledged the dangers of codependency, we still suggest that too many people are too self-centered too much of the time to truly experience the kind of relationship they deeply desire.

HOW CAN YOU INCREASE COMMITMENT?

Instead of asking, "What have you done for me lately?" ask yourself what you're doing to improve and strengthen your relationship. You have the greatest control over your own dedication and behavior, not your partner's. In most relationships, positive behavior is reciprocated, so do your best to encourage your partner to behave positively by behaving more positively yourself. *It's your choice!*

You can decide to make the relationship better by refusing to succumb to the competitive mode. Show that you value the relationship and want to build it up. Try to do things that will foster teamwork. Keep at it and don't keep score. One couple, Elizabeth and Frank, told us how they reinvigorated their marriage at the seven-year point. They'd been so busy building a home and family that they both were feeling distant in their relationship. Their long-term view was still intact but they'd lost something they'd had at first. They decided to talk it out and, in a way, each was relieved to hear the concerns the other was feeling. They risked by sharing and listening to the hurt— an act that in itself is evidence of dedication:

ELIZABETH: [*catching Frank after dinner one night, while the kids played outside*] You know, I've been thinking.

FRANK: What about?

ELIZABETH: I think we've been doing pretty well, but I don't think we're putting enough into our relationship.

FRANK: I see that, too. It's like we put so much time into the house, the kids, and work that there's not a lot left for us.

ELIZABETH: It's been painful for me when I have the time to think about it. I never thought it'd happen to us.

FRANK: [*moving closer, looking at Elizabeth*] It's really been worrying you, hasn't it?

ELIZABETH: Yeah. This isn't the way it was supposed to go for us.

FRANK: I know what you mean. I've felt sad about us losing something, but it's hard to put my finger on it. I just know something's been missing.

ELIZABETH: I'm glad to hear you say that. I was afraid that you hadn't noticed.

FRANK: [*putting his arms around her*] I have. I'm glad you brought it up. We have too much going for us to let the distance grow any further. Let's sit down and talk about what we can do about it.

ELIZABETH: I'll get some decaf.

This talk ignited a positive chain reaction in their marriage. Frank and Elizabeth renewed their dedication to one another in several ways. They made time together a greater priority and followed through. Each of them began to look for ways to do more special things for the other. They doubled up on their efforts to handle conflicts and disagreements with respect. They also talked more openly about plans for the future, developing a greater sense of the long term and being a team again. Essentially, they each decided to recapture the strength of their dedication. It's not so hard when you both really want to do it.

To repeat, *it's your choice*. You can't make your partner do anything. But, assuming that you both want to make your marriage work for the long haul, you'll be most successful by reflecting on how *you* can boost or maintain *your* dedication. As with Elizabeth and Frank, the bottom line was action. If your dedication is strong, keep it that way—and act on it.

HELP! ALL WE HAVE IS CONSTRAINT COMMITMENT

This section is for those of you whose marriage is in serious trouble. If that's not you, you might skip to the end of this section. Unfortunately, many couples are like Bob and Mary Anderson, whom we focused on in the last chapter. As you recall, all they have is constraint, with little of the rewarding relationship they both want. Our primary focus in this book is to prevent marriages from getting to that point. However, we also work with marriages that are held together only by constraint. We don't think couples have to stay in their rut. If that's where you are, it's not too late to turn things around, as long as you both want to do the work.

Because you are reading this book, we assume that you want to make your marriage work. So what can you do if you find yourself in a marriage characterized by constraint without dedication? The key question is how you can redevelop dedication. First, you need to believe that this is possible. Despite our success in predicting how groups of couples will do, we cannot predict the future of *your* relationship, but we find that many (although certainly not all) couples are able to repair and strengthen the most lifeless, frustrating marriages. Second, you must really want to do this, because it will take *sustained* work, and you will have to work against some tendencies that now exist in the relationship. If you want to breathe life into your marriage, here's one approach you can try.

I. *Sit down together and talk about the state of your marriage.* It's important that you both face up to the problems in your marriage. Probably neither of you is feeling good about it. Rather than becoming defensive or arguing, this is where you both should try, and try hard, to validate each other and show empathy for the pain.

This is pain you probably can both identify with. In listening carefully to each other you begin the process of drawing closer together. Paradoxically, one of the most powerful things you may share is a similar feeling of loss and sadness about your relationship. We've observed that, in the strongest marriages, the couples seem to be able to share their pain about the marriage as another form of intimacy. After all, is there anything about which you feel more strongly?

2. *Remember what you used to have together.* Spend some time reminiscing together about the good old days. What were things like when you first met? What attracted you to each other? What did you do on your first date? What kinds of things did you used to do for fun? Do you still do any of these things? What were some reasons you decided you wanted to marry in the first place?

Most couples find this kind of reminiscing enjoyable and enlightening. It can be fun to remember the good old days. It reminds you that at one time you had some pretty great feelings for one another. Beware of the tendency to rewrite history and see experiences that were truly positive at the time as negative now.

It's nearly impossible to recapture the euphoria many couples felt early on, but you can recapture some of the good feelings that once characterized your relationship. There was a spark there, a delight in getting to know each other. In some ways, this step is an attempt to regain an appetite or desire for the relationship.

3. *Decide to turn things around.* Although you can try to repair your marriage without your partner's active participation, making a commitment to do it together is far better. Look at it this way. Since you're staying together because of constraints that mean a lot to you, why not agree together to make the marriage enjoyable and not merely endurable? This is a rational attitude. You probably both have some deeper longing for this to occur anyway or you wouldn't care about following these steps.

This is fundamentally a decision of your will. We believe most people, if they want something badly enough, have enough control over their own lives to make a decision about it and stick to it.

4. *Do the things you did at first.* The point is simple but the potential impact is profound. Early in a relationship, couples talk more as friends (see Chapter Eleven), do more fun things together (see

Chapter Twelve), are more forgiving (see Chapter Ten), are more likely to look for the good and not the bad in each other (see Chapters One through Three), and usually do a better job of controlling conflict (see Chapters One through Six).

Be committed to becoming less self-centered and more other-centered. Where you've been selfish, admit it to yourself and turn the pattern around. The things you can do to restore dedication in your marriage are the same things that couples do to prevent marital distress and divorce in the first place. These are the strategies of PREP.

The reason these strategies work is that they reinforce the original feelings that motivated dedication to grow early in the relationship. As we pointed out in the last chapter, commitment theorists believe that dedication develops out of satisfaction in a relationship. And dedication leads to constraint. You've developed plenty of constraint. Now you need to come full circle by allowing this level of constraint to motivate you to rediscover satisfaction and dedication. We believe that you can do this if you're both committed to the task. As part of your efforts, it's critical that you control conflict. Poorly handled conflict is incredibly damaging to everything else that's good in a relationship.

5. *Stay at this process.* Keep working at these steps, especially step 4. Expect progress, not an instant miracle. Expect ups and downs. Recognize that your efforts can and will pay off if you both stick to it. What does this require? A long-term view and applied dedication.

We hope we've given you a feel for how powerful commitment can be in a relationship. Where you think the relationship is heading (long-term view) and what you are putting into it (dedication) are critical issues. You could take many specific actions based on these ideas, but you're the best judge of what needs to be done. Only you know to what degree a short-term view, scorekeeping, or selfishness are placing your marriage at risk. In the next chapter, we turn to the topic of forgiveness. We'll focus on how to keep resentment and bitterness from accumulating in ways that can destroy what you've built in your relationship.

John F. Kennedy once captured the essence of commitment by saying, "Ask not what your country can do for you; ask what you can do for your country." We'd paraphrase the sentiment this way: "Ask not what you can get from your partner, ask what you can give!" We can think of no better advice for preventing relational breakdown, or for recovering what you once had.

What did that NIKE ad say? Just do it.

 Exercises

To get the most out of this chapter, reflect on the questions below. We recommend that you think about your answers individually, then meet and talk about your reflections. You'll notice that we ask you to reflect more on your own behavior and perspectives than on your partner's. What is *your* point of view and what are *you* doing in this relationship?

1. What is your outlook on this relationship? Do you have a long-term view? Why or why not? If you have a long-term view, are you comforted by it or do you feel trapped?

2. To what degree do you engage in scorekeeping? Do you notice the positive efforts your partner makes for you and the relationship? Can you try to notice the positive efforts more? Do you think that some things are unfair and feel the need to confront your partner about them? Will you do that constructively?

3. Does your basic orientation in your marriage reflect more selfishness or team-centered sensitivity? What kinds of things do you do that express selfishness? What things do you do that demonstrate a desire to meet your partner's needs?

4. Has the dedication between the two of you eroded to dangerously low levels? What do you want to do about this?

5. If your relationship is going well, what do you think is the most important factor in keeping it that way?

Now schedule some time to talk. These talks should be handled carefully. We suggest that you use the Speaker-Listener Technique to share some of your most important impressions. Take this as an opportunity to come together, rather than an excuse to get defensive and angry. Talk openly about what you want and how you're going to get there.

10

Forgiveness and the Restoration of Intimacy

WE ROUND OUT THIS PART of the book with the often-misunderstood topic of forgiveness. Unless you and your partner are perfect, you'll need forgiveness to keep your relationship vibrant and growing. In terms of keeping a relationship strong and happy, this topic is as important as any we present in PREP. It's also crucial for recovering from difficult times in your marriage.

In the early versions of PREP, we assumed that forgiveness would happen naturally, so we didn't focus on it. But our experiences with couples told us that help was sometimes needed in this important area. We've been saying all along that conflict is inevitable. So too are mistakes. When mistakes and conflict are not handled well, resentment can build, adding to a reservoir of bitterness that fuels hidden issues and furthers conflict. Threats to intimacy result. Focusing regularly and constructively on forgiveness can help you keep resentment in check and enable you to stay emotionally connected over time. A willingness to forgive is a powerful expression of dedication. In this chapter, we want to build on your commitment of dedication by giving you a powerful model for making forgiveness happen.

A key goal we have is to help you to keep moving forward in your relationship rather than backward. All too often, when an annoying event happens, partners bring up the past and become mired in marital quicksand. This is often evidence of a lack of forgiveness. We want to give you a way to get out and stay out of the quagmires of marriage. First, we'll focus on the need for forgiveness, what it is, and what it is not. This will set the foundation for specific steps you can take when forgiveness is needed.

THE NEED FOR FORGIVENESS

We all tend to look to marriage as a safe haven, but there is a risk of getting hurt from time to time in any relationship. Unless you've been dating only a few weeks, the chances are that you've been hurt deeply by your partner. Many things can cause minor or major hurts, including put-downs, avoidance, negative interpretations, abusive comments, forgetting something important, making decisions without regard for the needs of the partner, affairs, addictions, and impoliteness.

Unless you have very unrealistic expectations, you know that both of you will commit sins of omission and commission over the course of your marriage. Minor infractions are normal, and it's important to expect them to happen. It's far more valuable to learn how to move on at these times than to expect them not to happen at all. For some couples, more major sins will happen as well. When that's the case, greater effort is needed to put the events in the past. The more significant the issues or events that caused harm, the more likely it is that you'll need some of the specific steps we'll recommend later in this chapter.

Let's look at two different couples in need of making forgiveness happen. Both examples demonstrate the importance of forgiveness, but the infractions are very different—one minor and one major—and they have very different implications.

OOPS, I FORGOT: THE DOMICOS

Mary and Tony Domico met each other in a Parents Without Partners support group and later married. Each had been married once before and each had primary custody of the children from the first marriage. They found they that had much in common, including a desire to marry again. Nothing has been remarkable about their marriage and blended family except that they've done a great job of it. They've handled the myriad stresses of bringing two sets of children together, and they've become a family. They have their ups and downs, but they handle the problems that come up with respect and skill.

Tony, who is an engineer with a construction firm, recently saved the company from financial disaster by noticing a critical design flaw in the company's plans for a high-rise office building. For this and other reasons, he was chosen to be honored as Employee of the Year at a yearly luncheon for the company. He was happy about the award and happier still to receive a substantial bonus for his "heads-up" work.

Tony asked Mary to attend the luncheon and she said she'd be glad to come. He was proud to be honored, and wanted Mary to share this moment with him. Because the company is very family-oriented, most of the employees—male and female—brought their spouses and significant others to the function. Tony told his fellow workers and his boss that Mary would be coming. A place was kept for her at the front table, right beside Tony.

Mary became distracted on the big day and completely forgot about the luncheon. While she was out picking up groceries, he was at the party feeling very embarrassed. Here were his peers, honoring him, and his wife failed to show up, without any explanation. He was also a little worried, since it was unlike Mary to miss anything. So he fumed and made the best of the situation, telling his co-workers that she'd probably been held up at the doctor's office with one of the kids.

As soon as Tony walked in the door that evening, Mary remembered what she had forgotten:

MARY: [distressed] Oh no! Tony, I just remembered . . .

TONY: [cutting her off] Where were you? I have never been so embarrassed. I really wanted you there.

MARY: I know, I know. I'm so sorry. I wanted to be there with you.

TONY: So where were you? I tried calling.

MARY: I was at Safeway. I completely spaced out about your lunch—I feel terrible.

TONY: So do I. I didn't know what to tell people, so I made some-

thing up about you maybe being at the doctor's office with
one of the kids.

MARY: Please forgive me, dear.

Should he? Of course. What does it mean for him to forgive in this
context? Now consider a very different example, one in which the
same questions have much more complicated answers.

MAYBE THE GRASS IS GREENER: THE SWENSONS

Johann and Megan Swenson have been together for fourteen years.
They met in college where they both majored in business. They married shortly after they graduated and then moved to the Midwest.
Johann took a job as a buyer in a retail chain and Megan became the
business manager of a firm that makes windows and frames for home
construction. After three years they had their first child, a delightful
girl named Marjorie. Two years later they had another girl, Lisa, who
is serious, very bright, and a real handful at times.

Everything sailed along just fine until about the eighth year of their
marriage, when Megan began to notice that Johann was gone more
and more. His job demanded a lot of overtime, but did he really need
to be gone that much? She became suspicious. Without much time or
open communication together, it was hard to know what was going
on. She began to feel as if she didn't know Johann anymore, and she
suspected that he was having an affair. She'd been attracted to other
men, so why couldn't it happen to him? She'd make phone calls to the
office when he was supposed to be working late, but he was rarely
there. When she asked him about this, he'd say that he must've been
down the hall, in the copy room, or talking with a colleague. That
didn't wash with her.

Megan got sick and tired of being suspicious. One night she told
Johann she was going to see a friend and left. They had arranged for a
baby-sitter to watch the kids so he could go in to work. Borrowing her
friend's car, Megan followed him as he left the neighborhood. She followed him to an apartment complex, noting the door where he went
in. She sat, and sat, for three hours; then she got out to look at the
name on the mailbox—Sally something-or-other.

"Not good, this is not good," she said to herself. It felt as if gravity was pulling her stomach down through her intestines. Now what? Megan's not a woman who likes to wait to find things out. She decided to knock on the door. After fifteen minutes, Sally came to the door in her bathrobe.

SALLY: [*seeming quite tense*] Can I help you?

MEGAN: [*calm but falling apart on the inside*] Yes. Please tell Johann I'm out here in the car and I'd like to talk to him.

SALLY: [*gaining composure*] Johann? Who's Johann? I'm alone. Perhaps you have the wrong address.

MEGAN: [*sarcastically*] Perhaps I could take a look.

SALLY: I don't think so. Look, you have the wrong address, whatever your problem is. Good-bye!

MEGAN: [*yelling out as Sally closes the door*] Tell Johann I'll be at home—if he remembers where that is.

Johann rolled in an hour later. He denied everything for about three days, but Megan was quite sure of herself and wasn't about to back down. She told Johann to get out: "An affair is bad enough, but if you can't even admit it, there's nothing left for us to talk about." Johann fell apart. He began drinking and disappeared for days at a time. Megan felt even more alone and betrayed. Although she still loved Johann, her rage and resentment grew. She said: "I thought I could trust him. I can't believe he'd leave me for someone else!"

As his denial crumbled, Johann's sense of shame was so great that he was afraid to deal with Megan head-on. He just stayed away from home. "She told me to get out, anyway," he told himself. Yet it really bothered him that Megan was being so tough. He asked himself, "Is it really over?" In a way, he found new respect for her. No begging or pleading for Megan, just toughness. He liked Sally, but he didn't want to spend his life with her. It became clearer to him that it was Megan he wanted to be with.

Of course, Megan didn't feel tough at all. She was in agony. But she was very clear about what she'd seen. There was no chance that she'd go on with Johann unless he dealt with her honestly, and she wasn't sure whether she wanted to stay or leave. Then she came home one night to find Johann sitting at the kitchen table with a terrible look of pain on his face.

JOHANN: [*desperately*] Please forgive me, Megan. I don't know . . . I'll get help. I don't know . . . I'm not sure what happened.

MEGAN: [*cool outside, raging inside*] I'm not sure what happened either, but I think you know a lot more than I do.

JOHANN: [*looking up from the table*] I guess I do. What do you want to know?

MEGAN: [*icily, controlling her rage*] I'd like to know what's been going on, without all the B.S.

JOHANN: [*tears welling up*] I've been having an affair. I met Sally at work, we got close, and things sort of spun out of control.

MEGAN: I guess they did. How long?

JOHANN: What?

MEGAN: [*voice raised, anger coming out*] How long have you been sleeping with her?

JOHANN: Five months. Since the New Year's party. Look, I couldn't handle things here at home. There's been so much distance between us . . .

MEGAN: [*enraged*] So what! What if I couldn't handle it? I didn't go looking for someone else. I don't want you here right now. Just go. [*turning away, heading into the next room*]

JOHANN: If that's what you want, I'll go.

MEGAN: [*as she walks away*] Right now, that's what I want. Please leave me alone. Just let me know where you'll be for the kids' sake.

JOHANN: [*despondent*] I'll go to my parents'. That's where I've been lately.

MEGAN: [*sarcastically*] Oh, thanks for telling me.

JOHANN: I'll leave. Please forgive me, Megan, please.

MEGAN: I don't know if I can. [*goes upstairs as Johann slips out the back door*]

At this point, Megan had some big decisions to make. Should she forgive Johann? Could she forgive him? She'd already decided that she might never trust him again, not fully. He clearly wanted to come back, but how could she know that he wouldn't do this again the next time they had trouble together?

What do you think? Should she forgive Johann, and what does it mean for her to forgive him?

WHAT IS FORGIVENESS?

Forgiveness is a decision to give up your perceived or actual right to get even with, or hold in debt, someone who has wronged you. *Webster's New World Dictionary* says it this way: "1. to give up resentment against or the desire to punish; . . . 2. to give up all claim to punish; . . . 3. to cancel or remit (a debt)." The picture of forgiveness is a canceled debt. *Forgive* is a verb; it's active; it's something you must decide to do! When

one of you fails to forgive, you can't function as a team because one of you is kept "one down" by being indebted to the other.

Because of this, a lack of forgiveness is the ultimate in scorekeeping, with the message being "You are way behind on my scorecard, and I don't know if you can catch up." In that context, resentment builds, conflict increases, and, ultimately, hopelessness sets in. The real message is "Maybe you can't do enough to make this up." People often walk away from debts they see no hope of paying off.

As we have seen, infractions can be small or large, with the accompanying sense of debt being small or large as well. Mary has a much smaller debt to Tony than Johann has to Megan. Either way, the opposite of forgiveness is expressed in statements such as:

"I'm going to make you pay for what you did."

"You are never going to live this down."

"You owe me. I'm going to get even with you."

"I'll hold this against you for the rest of your life."

"I'll get you for this."

These statements may sound harsh, but the sentiments are quite relevant to marriage. When you fail to forgive, you act out these kinds of statements, or even state them openly. We'll focus on some of the most important issues people have raised when we talk about forgiveness in our public presentation. These issues usually have more to do with what forgiveness isn't than what it is.

WHAT FORGIVENESS ISN'T

Maxine, a fifty-five-year-old woman in her second marriage, had been brought up to believe that to forgive meant to forget. She said to us, "It seems so hard to forgive and forget, how can you really do this?" We said nothing about forgetting in defining forgiveness. You hear the phrase "forgive and forget" so often that they become get equated even though they have nothing to do with one another. This is one of the greatest myths about forgiveness. Can you remember a very painful wrong that was done to you for which you feel you've forgiven the other person? We bet you can. We can, too. This proves the point.

Just because you have forgiven another person—and given up a desire to harm that person in return—doesn't mean you have forgotten that the event ever happened. Fortunately, when people say "forgive and forget," they usually mean that it's necessary to put the infraction in the past. There's value in that, but forgiveness should not be measured in this way. If putting the incident in the past means that you've given up holding it over your partner's head, that's right on. Another misconception related to "forgive and forget" is the belief that if a person still feels pain about what happened, he or she hasn't really forgiven the one who caused the pain. You can still feel pain about being hurt in some way, yet have fully forgiven the one who harmed you.

Megan Swenson may come to the point of completely forgiving Johann, as defined above. She may work through and eliminate her rage and desire to hurt him back. However, in the best of circumstances, what happened will leave her with a wound and a grief that will remain for many years. In the case of the Domicos, the way in which Mary hurt Tony was far less severe, with fewer lasting consequences. As it turned out, he did forgive her. He didn't dwell on it and he didn't need to grieve about it. However, when he is reminded of it, for example, at company events, he remembers and feels a twinge of the humiliation he felt on that day. This doesn't mean that he's holding it over Mary or trying to get even. He has forgiven her. The incident is just a painful memory along the road of their marriage.

George, a newlywed in his mid twenties, asked us about responsibility at one of our workshops. He was afraid that forgiving meant ignoring responsibility. He asked, "But, in forgiving, aren't we are saying that the one who did wrong isn't responsible for what was done?" This is the second big misunderstanding about forgiveness. When you forgive, you're saying nothing about the responsibility of the one who did wrong. The one who did wrong is responsible for the wrong, period. Forgiving someone does not absolve that person of responsibility for her or his actions. It does take the relationship out of the mode where one punishes the other, but it shouldn't diminish the responsibility for the wrong that was done.

In this light, it's important to distinguish between punishment and consequences. You can be forgiven from the standpoint of your partner not seeking to hurt or punish you, but you can still accept and act on the consequences of your behavior.

Let's summarize so far. If you have been wronged by your partner, it's up to you to forgive or not. Your partner can't do this for you. It's your choice. If you've wronged your partner in some way, it's your job to take responsibility for your actions and, if needed, to take steps to see that it doesn't happen again. This assumes that the infraction is clear and you're both humble and mature enough to take responsibility. If you want your relationship to move forward, you need to have a plan for forgiving. Even if you don't want to forgive—perhaps because of your own sense of justice—you may still need to do so for the good of your marriage.

The Domicos followed this model in the ideal sense. Mary took complete responsibility for missing the luncheon by apologizing and asking Tony to forgive her. He readily forgave her, and had no intention of holding it against her. Their relationship was even strengthened by the way they handled this event. Tony gained respect for Mary's total acceptance of responsibility, and Mary gained respect for Tony's loving and clear desire to forgive and move on. We've seen many couples for whom events like Mary and Tony's blew the relationship out of the water. Neither accepted any responsibility and neither forgave the other. The event simply added to their storehouse of resentment and further fueled the ongoing conflict.

Before we move on to specific steps you can take to keep forgiveness going, we want to discuss the crucial distinction between forgiveness and restoration in a relationship. What do you do if one partner can't or won't take responsibility? How can you move forward then?

WHAT IF YOU'VE BEEN WRONGED BUT YOUR PARTNER WON'T TAKE RESPONSIBILITY?

Forgiveness and restoration usually go hand in hand in a relationship, as they did with Tony and Mary. Intimacy and openness in their relationship was quickly restored because no barriers were placed in the way. They both handled their own responsibility without complication. When this happens, restoration, in which the relationship is repaired for intimacy and connection, will naturally follow.

But what do you do if you've been wronged in some way and your partner takes no responsibility? Do you allow the relationship to continue as it was? For one thing, you must be open to examining the possibility that your partner really didn't intend to do anything wrong, even though you were hurt by what happened. There can be a sincere difference in the interpretation of what happened and why. Thelma and Charles Barker, for example, had such an event. They'd been married eleven years and the relationship was generally satisfying. Although they weren't handling conflict that well, their dedication remained strong. On one occasion, Charles was cleaning out the garage and threw out all sorts of old boxes. He thought he was doing a great job, too. The garage hadn't looked so good in years.

At the time, Thelma was away for a few days. When she returned, she was very pleased, just as Charles had thought she'd be. The problem was that he'd thrown out a box containing mementos from her days as a track star in high school. It was an accident. He'd even noticed the box and thought he'd put it aside to protect it. Perhaps his daughter, who was helping him, put it with the other boxes by mistake. Anyway, it was gone—for good.

When Thelma realized that the box was gone, she went into orbit. She was enraged. She accused Charles of being "stupid, insensitive, and domineering." She felt that he didn't care, and that throwing out her stuff was just another sign that he needed to control everything.

What happened was unfortunate. Thelma had every right to be upset; the mementos meant a lot to her. But it really had been a mistake. With her control issue triggered, Thelma was being unfair in accusing Charles of intentionally hurting her. This was a very negative interpretation. In fact, he was trying to do something he knew she'd like.

When you're harmed in this way, it's okay to expect an apology—not because your partner *intended* to hurt you, but because a mistake *did* hurt you. Charles can apologize to Thelma, but she has a long wait ahead if she needs to hear him say, "You're right. I threw out your things because I'm a control freak and I think I can do whatever I want with anything in our house. I'll work on it." Not likely.

Whether or not you both agree on the nature of the infraction or mistake, you can still move ahead and forgive. It may be hard, but if you don't, you and the relationship will suffer added damage. In fact, there's good reason to believe that when you hang on to resentment and bitterness, you put yourself at risk for psychological and physical problems such as depression, ulcers, high blood pressure, and rage. That's no way to live.

Now for the really difficult case. Suppose it's very clear to you that your partner did something wrong and isn't going to take any responsibility, as in Johann and Megan's situation. No one is going to deny that Johann has done something wrong. He must be responsible for his own behavior if the marriage is to have any chance of moving forward. Sure, they're both responsible for letting their marriage slip. They'd grown very distant and neither is more to blame than the other for that. However, in response to this, it was his decision to have the affair. He's responsible for that action, not Megan.

When Johann showed up in the kitchen asking for forgiveness, the worst thing Megan could have done would be to go on as if everything had returned to normal. It hadn't. You can't sweep things like this under the carpet. Megan could have decided then to forgive him, but that's a separate decision from whether or not she should have allowed a full restoration of the relationship. Here's what we mean.

When Johann came back to the house that night, Megan didn't know what level of responsibility he was taking for the affair. She asked, "What if deep down he really blames me for it? What if he thinks it's my fault for not being more affectionate?" If she thought that he felt justified or wasn't serious about changing, why should she allow restoration of the relationship? It would be a great risk to take him back. Still, she can forgive him. Either way, it'll take time.

Here's what actually happened. For a few days, they had some very nasty talks on the phone. With so much tension in the air, it was easy for arguments to escalate, yet Johann persistently stated his desire to rebuild the marriage. He wanted to come back. One night, Megan asked Johann to come to the house for a talk. She arranged for the children to be with her parents for the evening, then met with Johann and poured out her anguish, pain, and anger. He listened. She focused on how his behavior had affected her, not on his motives and weaknesses. He took responsibility to the point of offering a sincere apology and saying that he didn't blame her for the affair. Now she thought there was a chance that they could get through this. Their talk concluded this way:

JOHANN: I've had a lot of time to think. I believe I made a very bad choice that hurt you deeply. It was wrong of me to begin the relationship with Sally.

MEGAN: I appreciate the apology. I needed to hear it. I love you but I can't pick up where we left off. I need to know that you'll get to the root of this problem.

JOHANN: What do you want me to do?

MEGAN: I don't want to say. I don't know. I've got so many questions that I don't know which way is up. I just know that I needed to hear you say you'd done something very wrong.

JOHANN: Megan, I did do something wrong. I know it. It's also very clear to me—clearer than it's been in a few years—that I want this marriage to work. I want you, not someone else.

MEGAN: I'd like to make it work, but I'm not sure I can learn to trust you again.

JOHANN: I know I hurt you very deeply. I wish I could undo it.

MEGAN: That's what I want. I suppose I can forgive you, but I also need some way to believe that it won't happen again.

JOHANN: Megan, I'd like to come back home.

MEGAN: That's okay with me, but I need to know we'll go and get help to get through this.

JOHANN: Like a therapist.

MEGAN: Yes, like a therapist. I'm not sure what to do next, and I don't want to screw this up. If you'll agree to that, I can handle having you come back home.

JOHANN: That makes sense.

MEGAN: Don't expect me to go on as if nothing's happened. I'm very, very angry with you right now.

JOHANN: I know, and I won't pressure you to act like nothing happened.

MEGAN: Okay.

As you can see, Megan really opened up and Johann validated her pain and anger. He didn't get defensive. If he had, she was prepared to work on forgiveness but end the marriage. She gained hope from this talk. Megan knew she could forgive—she's a very forgiving person. She also knew it would take some time—she's no fool. And she knew they needed help. The future looked uncertain and there was a lot to work through if they were going to restore their relationship.

Johann did the best he could under the circumstances. The next day, he began calling around to find the best therapist. He wanted a professional who knew what they needed to do to move forward. This showed Megan that he was serious about repairing their marriage and provided evidence of long-unseen dedication.

The relationship couldn't be restored until they got to work. It took time, but they did the work. Megan remembers—she's not going to be able to forget—but the ache in her heart gets weaker all the time as they've moved forward through forgiveness and on to restoration of their relationship.

WHAT ABOUT REGAINING TRUST?

We're often asked how to regain trust when an incident has seriously damaged it. The question is not as important for minor matters of forgiveness; for example, there's no loss of trust between the Domicos. But the Swensons have a great loss of trust. Whatever the incident, suppose that forgiveness proceeds smoothly and you both want restoration. How do you regain trust? It's not easy. We'll make four key points about rebuilding trust.

I. *Trust builds slowly over time.* As we said in the last chapter, trust builds as you gain confidence in someone being there for you. While research shows that people vary in their general trust of others, deep trust only comes from seeing that your partner is there for you over time. Megan can only regain her trust in Johann slowly. The best thing that can happen is for a considerable amount of time to go by without a serious breach of trust. That takes commitment and new ways of living together. They can't afford to let the same kind of distance build up again. And if Johann has another affair, it will probably be impossible for Megan to trust him again.

2. *Trust has the greatest chance of being rebuilt when each partner takes appropriate responsibility.* The best thing Johann can do to regain Megan's trust is to take full responsibility for his actions. If Megan sees Johann doing all he can do to bring about serious change without her prodding and demanding, her trust will grow and she'll gain confidence that things can get better—not perfect, but better. As we said in the last chapter, it's easier to trust when you can clearly see your partner's dedication to you.

Megan can also help to rebuild Johann's trust. For one thing, he'll need to see that she doesn't plan to hold the affair over his head forever. Can she really forgive him? If she reminds him about the affair, especially during arguments, he won't be able to trust her statement that she wants them to draw closer and move ahead.

3. *If you've lost trust, recognize that you can do more today to further damage it than to regain it.* It takes a long time to regain trust but only a moment or two to crush it. If Johann comes home tonight to be with Megan, still trying, she'll gain a little more trust. On the other hand, if he comes home two hours late without a good excuse, Megan's trust will take a big step backward. Mistakes are going to happen, but the commitment to change must remain clear. The commitment says that you have the time and the motivation to rebuild trust.

4. *Surveillance doesn't increase trust.* You can't gain trust by following your partner around every moment of the day to make sure he or she doesn't do anything wrong. It won't add to Megan's trust to follow Johann wherever he goes or to call up friends and ask what he's been up to. Sure, if he has an affair again, she might find it out sooner. Otherwise, all she'll know for sure is that Johann doesn't get off track when he knows she's watching his every move.

The exception to this is when you both agree that some checking up is okay. Megan and Johann could agree that for a time, he'll call frequently or she'll call him to touch base more often than usual. But long term, Megan will have to come to trust

Johann again for both of them to relax in their relationship. Let's hope that her trust will not be misplaced. To trust again is a risk. Your partner could let you down again and there's no way to be sure that this won't happen. That's why they call it trust. As with forgiveness, it involves letting go.

STEPS TO MAKE FORGIVENESS AND RESTORATION HAPPEN

So far, we've focused on the meaning of forgiveness and what it takes to make it come about. We now want to give you a more specific and structured approach for making forgiveness happen. In suggesting specific steps, we don't mean to imply that forgiveness is easy. But we do want you to use these steps to get through the toughest times. The steps are similar to those in the problem-solving process we suggested in Chapter Four. They can work very well to help you reach forgiveness when you have a specific event or recurring issue to deal with. We can't guarantee to give you the motivation or humility required, but we can help you to set the conditions that make forgiveness happen.

Each step has some key pointers. We'll use the example of Thelma and Charles, given earlier in this chapter, to highlight the points. This will summarize many of the points made in this chapter, as well as providing a road map for handling forgiveness. As with other strategies we've presented, our goal here is to provide specific steps that can help couples handle difficult issues well.

I. *Schedule a couple's meeting to discuss the specific issue related to forgiveness.* If an issue is important enough to focus on in this way, do it right. Set aside the time without distractions. Prepare yourselves to deal with the issue openly, honestly, and with respect. As we said in Chapter Five in discussing ground rules, setting aside specific times for dealing with issues makes it more likely that you'll actually follow through and do it well.

After their initial rush of anger, Thelma and Charles agreed to work through the incident of the discarded box. They set aside time on an evening when the kids were at a school function.

2. *Set the agenda to work on the issue in question.* Identify the problem or harmful event. You must both agree that you're ready to discuss it in this format at this time. If not, wait for a better time.

When Thelma and Charles met, the agenda was pretty clear: how to forgive and move on from what happened to her box of mementos. They agreed that this was the focus of their meeting and that they were ready to handle it.

3. *Fully explore the pain and concerns related to this issue for both of you.* The goal in this step is to have an open, validating talk about what has happened that harmed one or both of you. You shouldn't try this unless each of you is motivated to hear and show respect for your partner's viewpoint. The foundation for forgiveness is best laid through such a talk or series of talks. Validating discussions go a long way toward dealing with the painful issues in ways that bring you closer together. This would be a great place to use the Speaker-Listener Technique. If there's ever a time to have a safe and clear talk, this is it.

Using the Speaker-Listener Technique, Thelma and Charles talked for about thirty minutes. Charles listened carefully to her anguish about losing the things that meant a lot to her. She edited out her prior belief that he'd somehow thrown them out on purpose. She'd calmed down by now and could see that blaming him in this way didn't make sense. She listened to how badly he felt for her loss. She also validated his statement that he had specifically tried not to throw out her things. They felt closer than they had in quite a while.

4. *The offender asks for forgiveness.* If you've offended your partner in some way, an outward appeal for forgiveness is not only appropriate but very healing. A sincere apology would be a powerful addition to a request for forgiveness by validating your partner's pain. Saying, "I'm sorry, I was wrong—please forgive me" is one of the most healing things that can happen between two people. Apologizing and asking for forgiveness is a big part of taking responsibility for having hurt your partner. This doesn't mean that you sit around and beat yourself up for what you did. You have to forgive yourself, too!

But what if you don't think you've done anything wrong? You can still ask your partner to forgive you. Remember, forgiveness is a separate issue from why the infraction or mistake occurred. So even if you don't agree that you did anything wrong, your partner can choose to forgive. It's harder, but it's doable. Listen carefully to your partner's pain and concern. Even if you feel that you haven't done anything wrong, you may find something in what is said that can lead to a change on your part to make the relationship better.

Charles couldn't say that he'd done something wrong on purpose. It was a mistake. Nevertheless, he openly asked Thelma to forgive him and he apologized for not being more careful. He also learned that she felt at times as if he did whatever he wanted with everyone else's belongings in the house. He agreed to give that some thought.

5. *The offended agrees to forgive.* Ideally, the one needing to forgive clearly and openly acknowledges his or her desire to forgive. This may be unnecessary for minor infractions, but for anything of significance, this step is important. It makes it more real and memorable and increases the accountability between you to find the healing you're seeking.

This step has several specific implications. In forgiving, you are attempting to commit the event to the past and agreeing that you won't bring it up in the middle of future arguments or conflicts. You both recognize that this commitment to forgive doesn't mean that the offended will feel no pain or effects from what happened. But you're moving on. You're working to restore the relationship and repair the damage.

Thelma agreed not to bring up in moments of anger the fact that Charles had thrown out her box. In forgiving him, she committed to letting go of any notion that he was indebted to her for what happened. There would be no pay back. At the same time, Thelma wasn't going to get her things back. She'd be sad whenever she thought about it. That wouldn't be often, but there would be times when she'd wish that she could look at the things in the box. Charles would have to accept that she'd feel this pain from time to time.

6. *If it's applicable, the offender makes a positive commitment to change recurrent patterns or attitudes that give offense.* Again, this step depends on your agreement that there's a specific problem with the way one of you behaved. It also assumes that what happened is part of a pattern, not just a one-time event. For the Domicos and the Barkers, this step isn't very relevant. For the Swensons, it's critical.

   If you have hurt your partner, it also helps to make amends. This is not the same as committing to make important changes. When you make amends, you make a peace offering of a sort— not because you "owe" your partner, but because you want to demonstrate your desire to get back on track. It's a gesture of goodwill. One way to make amends is by doing unexpected positive acts. This shows your investment and ongoing desire to keep building your relationship.

   In Thelma and Charles's case, he scheduled a dinner for just the two of them at her favorite restaurant, going out of his way to show her that she was special to him. She'd already forgiven him, but this gesture took them further along the path of healing. Besides, it was fun. Their friendship was strengthened.

7. *Expect it to take time.* These steps are potent for getting you on track as a couple. They begin a process; they don't sum it up. These steps can move the process along, but you may each be working on your side of the equation for some time to come. Even when painful events come between you, relationships can be healed. It's your choice.

We hope that you're encouraged by the possibility of forgiveness and reconciliation in your relationship. If you've been together for only a short time, this may seem like more of an academic discussion than a set of ideas that are crucial for your relationship. If you've been together for some time, you understand the need for forgiveness. We hope that this will happen naturally in your relationship. If it does, keep at it. Do the work of prevention. The rewards are great. If you need to initiate forgiveness and barriers of resentment have built up, begin tearing them down. You can do it. These steps will help you get started.

In Part Three, we turn to the sublime. The direction shifts to how you can enhance all the most wonderful aspects of marriage: fun, friendship, spirituality, and sensuality. We have literally saved the best for last. If you've been working on what we've presented thus far, you're now ready to experience the wonders of marriage.

🐦 Exercises

There are two parts to this assignment, one to do individually and one to do together. Use a separate pad of paper to write down your thoughts.

1. First, spend some time in reflection about areas where you may harbor resentment, bitterness, and lack of forgiveness in your relationship. Write these things down. How old are these feelings? Are there patterns of behavior that continue to offend you? Do you hold things against your partner? Do you bring up past events in arguments? Are you willing to push yourself to forgive?

   Second, spend some time reflecting on situations where you may have really hurt your partner. Have you taken responsibility? Did you apologize? Have you taken steps to change any recurrent patterns that give offense? Just as you may be holding onto some grudges, you may be standing in the way of reconciliation on some issues if you've never taken responsibility for your end.

2. As with everything else we've presented, practice is important for really putting positive patterns in place. Therefore, we recommend that you plan to sit down at least a couple of times and work through some issues with the model presented in this chapter. To start, pick less significant events or issues, just to get the feel of things. This helps you to build confidence and teamwork.

   If you've identified more significant hurts that haven't been fully dealt with, take the time to sit down and tackle these meatier issues. It's risky, but if you do it well, the resulting growth in your relationship and in your capacity for intimacy will be well worth it. It's your choice.

PART THREE

ENHANCEMENT

11

Preserving and Protecting Friendship

IN THIS LAST PART OF THE BOOK, we want to help you preserve and enhance the really great things in your relationship. Like flowers without sunlight and water, many marriages wither and die from a lack of attention to the best parts of the relationship. We want to help you prevent that from happening. To start, we'll focus on friendship.

As we've discussed, partners bring a whole array of expectations to their relationships, and one of the most positive is that they'll be good friends. Having a strong friendship is one of the best ways to enjoy your relationship and to protect it for the future. Let's look at some important principles for keeping friendship alive and well in your marriage, or for rebuilding it if it's decayed from lack of attention.

THE IMPORTANCE OF PRESERVING FRIENDSHIP

Several years ago we conducted a study on the goals that partners had for their relationships. We asked couples in all stages of a relationship, from those who were planning marriage to couples in long-standing marriages of twenty years or more, to rank a list of possible goals such as financial security, satisfying sex, and raising a family. What do you think that most people—both men and women—told us? It turned out that the single most important goal for marriage was to have a friend.

WHAT IS A FRIEND?

How would you answer this question? When we've asked people, they've said that a friend is someone who supports you, is there for you to talk with, and is a companion in life. In short, friends are people we relax with, open up to, and count on. We talk and do fun things with friends. In this chapter, we'll focus on the talking side of friendship, and in the next chapter, we'll focus on the role of fun in building and maintaining your relationship and your friendship.

Unfortunately, many couples who start out as friends don't stay that way. The friendship—one of the best aspects of the relationship—isn't preserved and protected. Falling short of the expectation of being friends can lead to strong feelings of disappointment and sadness. To get an idea what can happen over time to friendship in marriage, let's look at some common barriers.

BARRIERS TO FRIENDSHIP

Despite our high hopes and best intentions, barriers to friendship in marriage inevitably appear. Here are some reasons why.

There's No Time

We all lead busy lives. Between work, the needs of the children, the upkeep of the home, the PTA, and the town council, who's got time for friendship? Friendship, the very core of a relationship, often takes a back seat to all these competing interests.

For example, Evelyn and Herman are a dual-career couple who've been together about five years. They had a two-year-old girl named Linda at the time we met them. While they were happy with their marriage and life together, they felt as if something was slipping away:

HERMAN: We used to sit around for hours just talking about things. You know, like politics or the meaning of life. We just don't seem to have the time for that anymore.

EVELYN: You're right. It used to be so much fun just being together, listening to how we each thought about things.

HERMAN: Those talks really brought us together. Why don't we do that anymore?

EVELYN: We don't take that kind of time like we used to. Now, we've got Linda, the house—not to mention that we both bring too much work home.

HERMAN: It seems like we're letting something slip away. What can we do about that?

Herman asks a great question—"Why don't we do that anymore?" —and Evelyn has an answer that many of us can relate to. All too often, couples fail to take the time just to talk as friends. The other needs and cares of life crowd out this time to relax and talk. But that's not the only reason friendship weakens over time.

We've Lost That Friendship Feeling

Many people have told us that they were friends with their spouses to begin with, but not now—they're *just married*. It's as if once you're married, you can't be friends anymore. You can be one or the other, but not both. Well, that's a mistaken belief.

The strongest marriages we've seen have maintained a solid friendship over the years. Take Geena and Pierre, who've been happily married for over forty years. While they were at one of our workshops, we asked them what their secret was. They said that it was commitment and friendship. They started out with a great friendship and never let it go. They've maintained a deep respect for one another as friends who freely share thoughts and feelings about all sorts of things, in an atmosphere of deep acceptance. That's kept their bond strong and alive.

Don't buy into an expectation that says that because you're married—or planning to be—you can't stay friends. You can!

We Don't Talk Like Friends Anymore

Think for a moment about a friendship you enjoy with someone other than your partner. How often do you have to talk with that person about problems between the two of you? Not often, we'd bet. Friends aren't people with whom we argue a lot. In fact, one of the nicest things about friendships is that we don't usually have to work out a lot of issues. Instead, we're able to focus on mutual interests in a way that's fun for both of us.

Friends talk about sports, religion, politics, philosophy of life, guys, women, sex, love, fun things they've done or will do, dreams about the future, and thoughts about what each of them is going through at this point in life. Friends talk about points of view and points of interest. In contrast, what do couples talk about most after they've been together for years? Let's list some of the common things: problems with the kids, problems with money and budgets, problems with getting the car fixed, concerns about who's got time to finish some project around the home, concerns about in-laws, problems with the neighbor's dog, concerns about each other's health—the list goes on and on.

If couples aren't careful, most of their talks end up being about problems and concerns—not points of view and points of interest. Problems and concerns are part of married life, and they must be dealt with, but too many couples let these issues crowd out the other, more relaxed talks they once shared and enjoyed. And since problems and concerns can easily become events that trigger issues, there's much more potential for conflict in talking with a spouse than a friend. That brings us to the next barrier.

We Have Conflicts That Erode Our Friendship

One of the key reasons couples have trouble staying friends is that friendship-building activities and discussions are disrupted when issues arise in the relationship. For example, when you're angry with your partner about something that's happened, you're not going to feel much like being friends right then. Or worse, when you do have the time to be friends, conflicts come up that take you right out of that relaxed mode of being together. We believe that this is the chief reason that some couples talk less and less like friends over the years.

One couple, Claudia and Kevin, were having real trouble preserving friendship in their relationship. They'd been married for fifteen years, had three children, and were rarely able to get away just to be together. They bred dogs together but hadn't been away to a dog show since they first had children. On one occasion, they'd gotten away to a show and had left the kids with Kevin's parents. It was their first chance to be away alone in years.

They were sitting in the hot tub in the hotel, enjoying talking together about their dogs and the show, when a conflict came up that ended their enjoyable time together:

CLAUDIA: [*very relaxed*] This is such a nice setting for the dog show.

KEVIN: [*equally relaxed, holding Claudia's hand*] Yeah. This is great. I can't believe the size of that shepherd.

CLAUDIA: Me either. I don't think I ever saw a German shepherd that big. This reminds me. If we're going to breed Sasha again this year, we'd better fix that pen.

KEVIN: [*tensing up a bit*] But I told you how big a job that was. We'd have to tear out that fence along the property line, build up the side of the hill, and pour concrete for the perimeter of the fence.

CLAUDIA: [*sensing his tension and now her own*] Would we really have to do all that? I know we have to get the pen fixed, but I don't think we'd have to make that big a deal out of getting it done.

KEVIN: [*growing angry*] There you go, coming up with things for me to do. I hate having all these projects lined up. That's a really big job if we're going to do it right.

CLAUDIA: [*getting ticked off, too*] You always make such a big production out of these projects. We don't have to do the job that well to make the pen usable again. We could do it on a Saturday.

KEVIN: [*turning away*] Maybe you could. But I don't want to do it unless we do it right, and we can't afford to fix that fence the right way right now.

CLAUDIA: [*looking right at Kevin, with growing contempt*] Heck, if you watched how you spent money for a couple of months, we could pay someone else to do the whole thing right, if that's so important to you.

KEVIN: [*angry and getting out of the tub*) You spend just as much as I do on stuff. I'm going up to the room.

Notice what happened here. There they were, relaxed, spending some time together, being friends. But their talk turned into a conflict about issues. As Claudia raised the issue of breeding their dog, Sasha, they got into an argument in which many issues were triggered—projects around the home, their different styles of getting things done, and money. Perhaps some hidden issues were triggered as well. What had been a great talk as friends turned into a nasty argument as spouses.

When couples aren't doing a good job of keeping issues from erupting into their more relaxed times together, it becomes hard to keep such positive times going in the relationship. The worst thing that can happen is that time to talk as friends becomes something to avoid. As we said earlier in the book, the growing perception is that talking leads to fighting—including talking as friends. So the baby gets thrown out with the bathwater. This is one of the chief reasons some couples lose touch with friendship over time. But as we'll see, you can prevent that from happening.

I Already Know My Partner Very Well

It's too easy for people to assume that their partner doesn't change much over time. Couples begin to assume that it's not going to be interesting to talk as friends. They think that they already know how their partner thinks about just about everything. But is this really true? We don't think so. Everyone goes through changes all the time. New events happen, new ideas replace old, and we're touched by many of the things that happen to us.

For example, Sam has been married to Lucy for eleven years, yet they each recognize that there are always new things they can talk about as friends. For instance, Sam was reading a recent issue of *Newsweek* magazine that contained a chilling article on how slavery still exists in various forms around the world. What really got to Sam was a picture of a little boy, no more than three years old, lifting two heavy bricks in a factory in a Far Eastern country. This little boy and his family were enslaved because of family debts that hadn't been paid.

Sam was torn up looking at this picture, because their son Kyle was the same age as the boy in the picture. Thinking about the contrast brought up many emotions in Sam, but there was no way that Lucy could know about his reactions unless he shared them. This was something Sam had just experienced. He shared his reactions to the article and Lucy was able to appreciate his feelings and talk about her own reaction as well.

Sharing such reactions to life as you live it can be a very rewarding part of your friendship together. You can't know what new thoughts and ideas your spouse is having unless you're able to talk as friends.

We're Victims of the Boomerang Effect

One of the major barriers to friendship in marriage occurs when thoughts shared at tender and intimate moments are used later as weapons in fights. When that happens, it's incredibly destructive to friendship.

George and Harriet had been married for three years and just had their first child. Harriet had been feeling overwhelmed by the demands of her career and their new baby, so she'd begun talking with a therapist. After one particularly emotional but productive session, she shared with George her feeling of being vulnerable and not very confident about her parenting ability.

Later that week, they got into a fight over who should get up with the baby in the middle of the night. As the fight escalated, Harriet accused George of feigning sleep so she'd have to get up all the time. George got defensive and said, "Why are you accusing me of not holding up my end? You admitted yourself that you aren't handling motherhood very well. Why don't you deal with your own problems before you start blaming me for things?"

This devastated Harriet, and she left the room crying, saying that she'd never tell him anything personal again. Unfortunately, events like this happen all too often in relationships. Through positive, intimate experiences as friends, we learn things about our partners that, if we aren't careful, can be used later when we feel more like enemies. But the corrosive effect of using shared intimacies as weapons is great. Who's going to share personal and revealing information if it might be used later in a fight?

We Were Never Friends

What if friendship wasn't there in the beginning? If that sounds like you, you may not be sure how to be friends now. It's rare for couples not to develop friendship early on since there are few arranged marriages anymore. Most couples start out with a big emphasis on friendship. Yet some couples do miss this important stage of development in the relationship.

Mark and Karen were one such couple. They'd been dating for less than five months when they found out that Karen was pregnant. Although they were still just getting to know each other, they felt a sense of love and caring for each other and decided to get married. Four years later, they had three children in diapers and still didn't really know each other. If that sounds like you, remember that it's just as important to build a friendship as it is to maintain one you already have.

Now that we've covered some of the common barriers to keeping friendship alive, we want to share some tips to help you protect this vital part of your relationship. The ideas we'll now suggest can work for building, rebuilding, or maintaining friendship in marriage. That's because they capture what couples do to nurture friendship in the first place.

PROTECTING FRIENDSHIP IN YOUR RELATIONSHIP

In our work with couples, we've found some core principles that help us to protect and enhance friendship. If you have a good friendship going, these principles will help prevent your friendship from weakening over time. If you've lost something in terms of being friends, use these ideas to regain what you've been missing.

MAKE THE TIME

While it's great to be friends no matter what you're doing, we think that you can benefit by setting time apart specifically to talk as friends. For that to happen, you must make the time. Otherwise, all the busy stuff of life will keep you occupied with problems and concerns. We mentioned how Geena and Pierre had preserved and deepened their friendship over the forty years they'd been married. One of the things they did to keep friendship alive was to plan time to be alone together. They'd take long walks together and talk as they walked. They'd go out to dinner. They'd take weekend vacations from time to time, without the kids. They made the time and it's been paying off for over forty years.

If couples are really serious when they tell us that friendship is important, they need to plan time to be together as friends. That means putting a priority on this aspect of intimacy. This is one of the key investments you can make in your relationship. Some of you may need to give yourself permission to spend time as friends. Often, people say, "Where's the time?" We understand. One of our friends summed up the time pressure by saying, "Time is the commodity of the nineties." Despite the pressures, you need to realize that you'll be better parents and do better in your work if your marriage is doing better. This means putting some boundaries around all the other things you have to do in life—and carving out time for friendship. But that's not all you need to do to protect friendship.

PROTECTING FRIENDSHIP FROM CONFLICT

In Part One of this book, we focused on skills and techniques you can use to handle conflicts well, such as the Speaker-Listener Technique, good problem-solving skills, and ground rules. In Part Two, we added to this theme by presenting the issues-and-events model as well as concepts on forgiveness. These strategies are powerful tools for dealing with conflict, but you didn't become a couple only to handle conflict well; it's something you have to do if you want to protect the more wonderful aspects of intimacy from the damage of mishandled conflict. So one key to keeping friendship alive is being sure that you're handling conflict well and protecting your friendship times from conflict.

Marsha and Kevin, an engaged couple, told us about a fight that broke out during what had been a relaxing dinner at their favorite restaurant. One of their major issues was religion—Marsha was Jewish and Kevin was a Methodist. They met while playing on a coed softball team at work and became friends first, before starting to date. They viewed each other as best friends and proudly talked about how their friendship was the cornerstone of their relationship.

On this night their dinner conversation was flowing well when Marsha started talking about her feelings about a meeting taking place in Washington between Yitzhak Rabin and Yasur Arafat. It went like this:

MARSHA: I think it's wonderful that Rabin and Arafat are talking about peace in the Middle East. It's as if . . .

KEVIN: [*excitedly interrupting*] There's no way. How could these two groups who've hated each other for years ever work together? I don't think it can happen.

MARSHA: [*quiet, feeling hurt at being interrupted*]

KEVIN: [*He senses her pulling back but doesn't want to deal with it for fear of starting a fight. He tries to change the subject.*] You know, they say this place might be bought by someone else. I wonder how they'd change the menu?

MARSHA: [*She now feels more hurt because he's changing the subject. She took this to mean that he doesn't care about her views on the Middle East and, more important, her concerns about being Jewish.*] I wish you cared more about what I think and feel about being Jewish. It's really important to me.

KEVIN: [*not sure where she's coming from, but feeling attacked*] I never said anything about that.

MARSHA: You changed the subject. You do that whenever I bring up being Jewish.

KEVIN: [*angry now*] You didn't bring up being Jewish. You brought up Arafat and Rabin. If you're so sensitive about being Jewish maybe we shouldn't even be together.

MARSHA: [*feeling very hurt and angry*] You know, you might be right.

Marsha and Kevin's conversation illustrates how friendship talks can quickly turn into discussions about relationship issues, just as events can turn into issues. Such patterns continue and intensify for many people to the point where their foundation of friendship is eroded. After all, who wants to talk about topics if they frequently turn into unpleasant arguments?

We were able to teach Martha and Kevin the importance of protecting their friendship by using the skills covered earlier in this book. The key for them was to learn to maintain their ability to talk in ways that promoted intimacy rather than conflict. In teaching them our approach, we asked them to return to the conversation they'd had in the restaurant—to "rewind the tape," so to speak—to the point where Kevin brought up the question of compatibility. Here's how they handled the same conversation differently and got back on track:

KEVIN: Hold it, stop the action—I really don't mean that. I'm committed to our relationship. But I get so frustrated when you bring up the religion issue.

MARSHA: I know, I do tend to bring up that issue a lot, perhaps at times when it's not relevant. But I do value our ability to talk about world events and to disagree at times.

KEVIN: So do I. Let's talk about the religion issue in our next couple's meeting. For now, let's get back to talking about what's ahead for the Middle East.

MARSHA: Great. We do need to talk about our religious differences, but let's focus on just talking as friends right now.

Although this was role playing, it's exactly what they need to be able to do when such issues get triggered by events in real life. Notice carefully what they did. First, they separated out the event (talking about Israel and the Palestinians) from the issue (their religious differences and compatibility). Second, they agreed to talk later about the very important issue of religious differences. In doing this, they weren't avoiding the issue but were planning to give it the attention it deserved.

Third, in taking control of where the conversation was heading, they showed appreciation for the fact that they were out to spend time together as friends and not deal with issues right then. When you're spending time together as friends, it's not appropriate to discuss critical issues—not if you plan to both protect your friendship and successfully deal with important issues. Separate out the times when you deal with issues from the times when you relax and talk as friends.

One last point about protecting your friendship from conflict. *Never use thoughts shared in moments of intimacy as weapons in a fight.* Nothing adds fuel to the fire like betraying a trust in this way. As we said earlier, this is incredibly destructive and creates huge barriers to future intimacy. If you're getting so mad that you're tempted to do this, you probably aren't handling issues effectively enough in your relationship. This means that you may need to work harder—and together—on all of the principles and techniques we emphasized in Part One. It takes a lot of skill and practice to get to the point where you can handle conflicts with respect and mastery, but it's worth the work.

HOW TO TALK LIKE FRIENDS

Now let's move on to discuss how you can talk like good friends. We want to highlight some points about the way friends talk that can help you to protect and enhance your relationship.

Listen Like a Friend

Good friends listen with little defensiveness. You don't have to worry as much about hurting friends' feelings or offending them. That's

because friends care about what you think and feel, and relationship issues are rarely at stake. We heard one person sum it up this way: "A friend is glad to see you and doesn't have any immediate plans for your improvement." When you're talking as friends and neither of you is trying to change anything about the other, you can relax and just enjoy the conversation. Even when you let your hair down and talk about something really serious, you don't want a friend to tell you what to do. You just want someone to listen. It feels good to know that someone cares. Friends often provide that kind of support, and you can do this for each other in your relationship.

If you really want to push your listening skills, try using the Speaker-Listener Technique. While we mostly think of the structure as benefiting couples when they have difficult issues to talk about, the emphasis on good listening can be a plus when you're talking as friends. Either way, paraphrasing key points your partner makes can boost the intimacy of friendship talks. That's because good listening skills tend to open people up. Active listening invites the speaker to go on, to say more, to be vulnerable or silly or whatever. It feels great to have a friend who really wants to know more about you. Listening in this way is a gift you can give to your partner.

Friends Aren't Focused on Solving Problems

Most of the time, when you're with a friend, you don't have to solve a problem. There may be a limited amount of time, but there's no pressure to get something done. As we said in Chapter Four, when you feel pressed to solve a problem, you cut off discussions that can bring you closer together. That's why it's so important not to talk about relationship issues when you're planning time to be together as friends; there's too much temptation to solve problems and give advice.

Even when you're talking about problems that have nothing to do with your relationship together, giving too much advice can throw a wet blanket on the conversation. It can appear as if you're saying, "If only you'd see the wisdom of what I'm telling you to do, we could move on and talk about something more interesting." People don't usually want advice from a friend as much as they want to know that someone cares. Don't give in to the temptation to give advice or solve problems in your time together as friends. Try to keep the avenues of discussion open so that you can learn more about each other.

Try It

We recommend that you set aside times to talk as friends. Let's summarize the keys for making this happen:

1. Ban problem issues and relationship conflicts from these times.

2. Find some time when you can get away from the pressures of life. Don't answer the phone. For example, go out to dinner and leave the kids with a babysitter.

3. Focus on topics of personal or mutual interest.

4. Listen to each other in ways that deepen the sharing between you.

You might think that this sounds contrived. We've heard that concern before, but it's not our goal to contrive friendship. We want couples to know how to preserve and protect it—and to follow through. As we said at the start of this chapter, friendship is a core expectation people have for marriage. If you set the basic conditions for it to happen, it will blossom and continue to build throughout your marriage. If you aren't careful, it can slip away.

If your friendship is strong and you want to prevent it from eroding, these suggestions can help you to do that. If you've been together for a while and have lost something in terms of friendship, it's time to work on getting it back. The ideas above can help you do that, too.

Like much else you've learned about in this book, friendship is a skill. To keep your friendship strong, you may have to work on it a bit, but we can't think of anything of greater importance for the long-term health of your marriage than to stay friends. In this chapter, we've tried to outline some of the strategies that really make friendships work, especially those that help you communicate. As we move to the next chapter, we'll change the focus to fun. This is another key area of intimacy and friendship in marriage that's often taken for granted. As with friendship, most people want to have fun with their partners. We hope you do, too, because we have some specific ideas about how you can preserve enjoyment in your relationship.

 ## Exercises

1. Plan a quiet, uninterrupted time. Take turns picking topics that are of interest to each of you. Ban relationship conflicts and problem solving. Then consider some of the following topics.

   a. Some aspect of your family of origin that you've been thinking about.

   b. Personal goals, dreams, or aspirations.

   c. A recent book or movie. Pretend that you're professional critics, if you like.

   d. Current events, such as sports or politics, for example.

2. Take turns pretending to be your favorite television interviewers, and interview your partner about his or her life story. This can be a lot of fun, and it's very much in the spirit of listening as a friend. The best interviewers on TV are experts at listening and drawing their guests out of themselves. Try to draw one another out in sharing together as friends.

3. Talk together about how you can build time for friendship into your weekly routine. If you both believe that it should be a priority, how do you want to demonstrate that?

12

Increasing Your Fun Together

I N THE LAST CHAPTER, we talked about the importance of being friends with your partner. Now we'll build further on the theme of enhancing your relationship by focusing on how to preserve and increase fun in your relationship. You'll notice many similarities between this chapter and the last. In fact, it'll seem as though you've read many of the key points before. Nevertheless, fun is such an important aspect of your connection together that we think it deserves its own chapter. Fun is important!

Couples are often surprised that we include a focus on fun in our workshops and ask, "Why is fun so important?" In general, fun experiences provide couples with another key way to connect and achieve intimacy. Here, we'll discuss the value of fun and also offer you some key ways for keeping it alive in your relationship.

THE IMPORTANCE OF PRESERVING FUN

Fun plays a vital role in the health of family relationships. In the early versions of PREP, it was a very small part of the program. However, as a result of a study we conducted in Denver several years ago, we learned that we weren't paying enough attention to the role of fun in marriage. It always had seemed like common sense to believe that fun was important, but this research highlighted that fact.

RESEARCH ON FUN

Howard Markman, radio psychologist Andrea Van Steenhouse, University of Denver psychologist Wyndol Furman, and Kristin Lindahl, now a psychologist and colleague, conducted a study to discover what happy couples were doing to develop and maintain what we called their "super marriages." In contrast to our other studies conducted in laboratory settings, this one was conducted through a local newspaper (*The Rocky Mountain News*), with the goal of getting many couples to share the secrets of their marriages. Couples who responded to the survey filled out over fifty questions on all aspects of their relationships, including satisfaction, commitment, communication, and just about anything else you could think of.

We were very surprised to find that, among all the variables, the amount of fun these partners had together emerged as the strongest factor in understanding their overall marital happiness. That's not to say that other things weren't going on in these relationships, but good relationships become great when you're preserving both the quantity and the quality of your fun times together.

In contrast to the couples in these super marriages, many couples don't continue having fun with much consistency. What makes this so puzzling is that fun plays a critical role in the development of most relationships during the courting period. Time spent playing together provides a relaxed kind of intimacy that strengthens the bond between two people. So why does fun go by the wayside for many couples when it's such a large part of developing the relationship in the first place? You'd think it'd be easy for couples to maintain something that's so pleasurable. Let's look at some barriers to fun in marriage; we'll then show you how to protect and enhance enjoyment in your relationship.

BARRIERS TO FUN

Most couples have a great deal of fun early in their relationships, but for too many, it fizzles out as time goes on. Here are some of the most common reasons for this that we hear from couples.

We're Too Busy

Couples often stop making the time for fun in their busy lives. Early in the relationship, they put a high priority on going to the movies, window shopping, walking hand in hand, going bowling, and so forth. That's the way it was for Miguel, twenty-eight, and Lucy, thirty. They'd spend many Saturdays together at the beach swimming and talking and lying in the sun. They'd take long walks in the sand and talk about their future together. When they got married, they continued to go to the beach, but less frequently. A few years later they had their first child and began to spend much less time having fun. Sure, their child, a girl named Amanda, was a delight for them, but it became rare for Miguel and Lucy to actually go out and have fun the way they used to.

Over time, they noticed that life wasn't as enjoyable as it used to be. They were happy together and their eight-year-old marriage was solid, but they'd let something slip away. It's really pretty simple. Life is more fun when you *do* have fun, and the rest of life will crowd fun out if you don't make time for it to happen. We want to encourage you to find the time to keep up the joy and playfulness that can make your relationship more delightful.

Karen and Frank are a good example of a couple who've preserved time for fun in their marriage. They've been married for twenty years and haven't let their playfulness slip away. Every Friday night, for most of those years, they've gone out on a date together. That's just one way they've preserved fun in their relationship. They've made use of babysitters and haven't let things come between them and this time together. It's a priority in their marriage.

They also vary what they do on these dates—dinner and a movie, swimming together, dance lessons, walking in the park and watching the sun set, and so forth. They've tried many things and made the time for each other, and their marriage has benefited. Their fun experiences have built a positive storehouse of pleasant times and memories. It's impossible to overestimate the value of that.

We're Married Now, So We're Not Supposed to Have Fun

One of the expectations people sometimes hold about marriage is that it's not supposed to be fun. Many of us vowed to love, honor, and obey, but where is fun mentioned in the wedding vows? It's as if once you get married, you have to be an adult, and adults don't—or shouldn't—have fun. Work and responsibilities are often emphasized over and above the legitimate need for rest and relaxation. There's nothing wrong with being a responsible member of society. In fact, we encourage it. But you also have to let your hair down and enjoy each other.

We were recently talking about fun and marriage when one husband mentioned that his wife was just too busy at work to plan any fun. Jeanne worked all the time. She'd feel guilty if she hadn't finished her projects at work, but there were so many projects that she was never done. Bob would ask her if she could go golfing or out to eat but she'd always have to work late. It's not that Jeanne didn't like to have fun, but her sense of responsibility to her work was so great that she and her marriage were suffering.

Does this sound like you or someone you know? These antifun ethics may date back to the puritan ideals that were so much a part of the early Anglo-American psyche. "Work hard and rewards will come," the saying goes. And, in fact, certain rewards do tend to come from hard work. But you also have to look at your overall priorities. How many couples do you know who worked hard their whole lives to build a home, send their kids to college, and have a retirement nest egg, but weren't able to reap the benefits because of death or divorce? At the end of life, when people are asked what they wish they'd done differently, hardly anyone says, "I wish I'd worked harder, sold another car, completed more projects." People usually wish they'd played more with the kids or spent more time with their spouse. Don't wait. Make sure that fun and play are an essential part of your relationship, now.

Play Is for Kids

Many preschool experts say that playing is the work that children do. Through play, children gain developmentally relevant social, emotional, and cognitive abilities. We believe that the developmental importance of play doesn't stop after childhood but continues throughout life. Fun and play allow release from all the pressures and hassles of being an adult.

The relaxed togetherness of playful times is important in the initial development of the bond between two people. That's because when we're engaged in fun through play, we're often relaxed and more our-selves. It's under these conditions that people fall in love—when one sees in the other the relaxed self in the context of fun times together. You rarely hear someone say, "I really fell in love with him when I saw how much he loved to work."

We mentioned how Miguel and Lucy used to go to the ocean early in their relationship. During their time there, they'd splash in the water, make sand castles together, rub suntan lotion on one another, and bury each other—they'd play together like kids! During these times, they'd frequently look at one another and smile in the delight of the moment. You can't put a price on time that builds such basic bonds. Miguel and Lucy still experience that kind of bond when they play with Amanda, but they could use a lot more of this kind of relax-ation together. As we said above, the couples in super marriages create opportunities to play together, which keeps refreshing the bond. So be a kid from time to time.

Conflict

As with friendship, which we discussed in the last chapter, mishandled conflict is a real killer of fun times together. In fact, we'll make the same point in the next chapter on sensuality, too. Poorly handled conflict can ruin the most enjoyable aspects of any relationship.

Noreen and David were a middle-aged couple we talked with who were making time for fun. That wasn't the problem, but all too often they'd be out to have a good time and some event would trigger an issue that would kill the playfulness of the moment. One night, they'd arranged for a sitter for the kids and went out to take a class in cou-ples' massage. They thought, "This will push us a bit to have some fun in a new way." Great idea! The instructor was making a point to the class about paying attention to their partner's reactions. David whis-pered to Noreen, "That's a great point." Noreen whispered back, "I've been trying to tell you that for years." David was instantly offended. He felt attacked and pulled away from Noreen, folding his hands across his chest in disgust.

This event triggered some hot issues for David and Noreen. For years, Noreen had felt that David didn't listen well to what she said, hitting a hidden issue of caring. She was hurt that he hadn't cared enough to remember her making the same point the instructor was making. On his part, David had been feeling that Noreen was critical about nearly everything and now was attacking him when he was really getting into this massage workshop with her. He felt rejected and dejected, wondering, "Can't she even lay off when we're out to have fun?" On this evening, they didn't recover well. David suggested that they leave the class early and go home. They did—in silence.

There will be occasions for all couples when conflict erupts during fun times. But if it begins to happen a lot, the fun times won't be so much fun anymore. The whole idea is to do something together that's relaxing and that brings out positive emotions you can share. Poorly handled conflict will disrupt these times. The sense that conflict could erupt at any moment isn't compatible with relaxed playfulness. We set ourselves to fail at fun when we carry over grievances or anger into our special fun times.

Now that we've discussed the barriers that can prevent fun from being a regular part of a relationship, we want to present some ideas for keeping it a significant part of yours.

A PRIMER FOR HAVING FUN IN MARRIAGE AND PROTECTING FUN TIMES

You may be thinking that you know how to enjoy yourselves together and don't need strategies and skills. That's great. But we think we have some pointers that can keep any couple on track. Here are some suggestions.

MAKING THE TIME

It's hard to have fun together without setting aside time for it to happen. Sure, you could have a moment of playfulness just about anywhere, anytime, if the mood strikes you both. Even a quick joke together or seeing something funny on TV can be enjoyable. But to get the full benefit, we suggest that you make this a priority so that you can get into the flow of it together. *This means you need to be serious about setting aside time to be less serious.*

Most people are so busy and harried that it takes them a while just to switch gears into the fun mode. That's why for many couples, the first day or two of a vacation can be more stressful than fun. A transition is taking place. The same holds true for shorter breaks. It's often hard to wind down enough to get relaxed. But once you're relaxed and playing together, the opportunities to draw closer through the bond of this positive emotion really come to life. We can think of no more powerful way to recharge the batteries in your relationship. In the language of Chapter Nine, you're making a significant investment in your marriage when you set aside time for fun.

To do this, you might actually have to pull out a schedule and arrange to make time together. That may not sound very spontaneous, but most couples have so much else going on that it takes a deliberate act to create free time. If you have children, you may need to arrange for a baby-sitter, and if you don't have a sitter you trust, this may be the time to look hard and find one. There's nothing that helps you relax more when you're out to have fun than knowing that your little ones are with someone you trust.

Last, if you're making the time for fun, try to eliminate the possibility of distractions. For example, if your job requires you to wear a beeper, do you have to wear it when you've carved out time to play with your spouse? It's not very relaxing to know you could get beeped at any moment. Set aside time and shut out the distractions of the rest of your life. It's worth it. It might even give you something to look forward to.

PROTECTING FUN FROM CONFLICT

As we said in our discussion of friendship in Chapter Eleven, the material on handling conflict that's presented in Chapters One through Six is critical if you're going to preserve fun in your relationship. You, as a couple, need to control the times and conditions for dealing with the difficult and conflictual issues in your relationship. When you've blocked out time to have fun, don't do conflict. Block out a separate time to handle the tricky issues.

Many couples finally buy into the wisdom of a "date night" to get away and enjoy each other. However, in our experience, many couples try to do too much with the time they've set aside. They try to have fun together *and* resolve difficult issues "while we have this time together."

Frank and Karen, mentioned earlier in this chapter, learned this the hard way before they got into the groove of doing fun right. Earlier in their marriage, they went through a period when they were so busy that they'd try to do everything in the little time they had together. They'd get a sitter, go out for fun, and mess up the evening with issues.

For example, one night they went out to an ice skating show. When they were seated and waiting for the show to start, Frank said, "We haven't had time to talk out that budget problem. Let's see what we can get done right now." Big mistake. Their budget was a serious conflict area between them, and it deserved far more focused time than they were going to have waiting for an ice show to start. As you can imagine, they didn't get anywhere on the budget in the time they had, and they only succeeded in becoming on edge with each other when they were out to have fun.

While it's understandable and expected that conflicts are occasionally going to come up during fun times, we don't understand why couples set aside time then deliberately spend some of it dealing with issues. That isn't compatible with the part of fun time that brings the greatest benefit to your relationship—being relaxed and upbeat with one another.

Deal with the important issues in your relationship in meetings arranged for that purpose—not during times set aside for fun. When issues are triggered during these times, table them. Call a Time Out. Come back to them later. It's not hard to do once you try it a few times. In our experience, there's no more powerful and rapid change that couples can make in their relationship than to agree to keep conflict out of time set aside for enjoyment. When you feel safe and confident that issues will be dealt with at the appropriate time and place, you'll find it much easier to relax and have fun.

SO WHAT CAN WE DO FOR FUN?

Okay, you've set aside time for fun and you've agreed to put conflicts aside to protect that time. Now what? For many couples who have gotten rusty at coming up with fun things to do together, this is a difficult question. Others, like the couples in the super marriages we described, have plenty of ideas. In many ways, being playful is a skill like all the other skills we're emphasizing in this book. You have to practice such skills if they're going to work for you. If you're rusty or want to keep your skills sharp, here are some ideas that might help.

Talking Can Be Fun

Talks about intimate topics are an important way to enjoy being together. This point is like one we made about friendship in the last chapter, but the focus here is on what's fun to talk about, not just what's of interest to you in terms of friendship. Usually, enjoyable talks are about topics that are engaging for both of you and that you both find humorous. Using a format like the Speaker-Listener Technique is not usually necessary for fun talks; that much structure is overkill and isn't needed if what you're talking about are really fun topics. We can think of several kinds of talks that couples tell us they enjoy.

Research by speech communication expert Fran C. Dickson at the University of Denver has revealed that most couples who've been married fifty years have been guided by a vision of shared relationship. That doesn't mean solving how to pay for that new house. Instead, it involves sharing goals and dreams, wishes, hopes, and worries—*into the future.* It's your future together that you're talking about, with the freedom to discuss fantasies you each might have about what the future will hold. These talks could be about any number of things, such as a dream home, a vacation you'd love to take, or your fantasy of what it'll be like when you retire. Sharing plans and dreams is important for maintaining your bond together. And it's fun.

You can also reminisce about the past—going backward into the future. Every couple has at least one good story about how they met or about something that happened when they were dating. It's important to talk about these kinds of memories to help you remember the fun times you've had as well as encourage you to have them in the future. When you look backward to remember these good times, you strengthen your ability to move forward. When you look backward to focus on bad times, you get stuck in the muck. As with sharing a vision for the future, there's real strength in looking at the positives in your shared history.

Share all kinds of fantasies. For example, what would it be like if you gave up your life as you know it and went to live on a Caribbean island for a couple of years? Not only do many couples love to talk about this sort of thing, but such sharing may spark ideas that you can actually carry out for the fun of it. For example, one couple told us that they'd shared fantasies about what the ideal romantic evening would be like. Then it occurred to them that nothing was stopping them from having that type of evening.

It's also important for couples to share silliness and have private jokes and language. One of us, Susan Blumberg, and her husband, Lewis, share a private joke that goes back to when Susan was in college. Lewis came to visit her, and they were at her dorm, dreamily gazing into each other's eyes. She thought that something really romantic was going to happen, like a proposal. Then, with a tremendous look of love and interest, he said, "Graham crackers." He wasn't looking at her at all; he was looking at a box of cookies on the desk behind her.

Although she was quite offended at first, over time it became a little phrase the two of them use that stands for "I love you." They drive florists crazy on birthdays and anniversaries by putting "graham crackers" on the card instead of "I love you."

Compliments Can Be Fun

Recently, Howard Markman was working with a client when he got a great idea for something fun for couples to do. As they were talking, the husband said, "In my family, growing up, no news was good news, so we only talked about the bad news. This made sense to me. So when I don't say anything to my wife, that means things are good."

Howard asked his wife, "When's the last time you heard a compliment?" She replied, "Twenty years ago!" The same is true for too many couples. The rationale is "If you don't hear anything, things are fine. If something's bad, I'll tell you—maybe." As with the media, we hear more about the bad news than the good news.

This can lead to a boring and stiff relationship centered on the negatives. What we've discovered is that couples can learn to push compliments as a way to increase fun. The key is to give your partner the good news—in headlines. Bad news may sell newspapers, but it bankrupts relationships.

Howard suggested that this couple make an enjoyable game out of pushing the positives. He told them to give each other one compliment every day. To do this yourself, start by thinking about something you really appreciate about your partner. Here are some sample compliments.

About your partner's work in or out of the home:

"I appreciate how hard you work to help our family."

"I sure like the way you work with me to keep the house looking good."

About your partner's parenting (if you are raising children):

"I think it's great how sensitive you are to what Joseph needs."

"You sure are a great father!"

About your partner's personality:

"You're such a warm and caring person."

"I like it that you think about what's important to me."

About your partner in the area of sensuality:

"I think it's great that you show so much enthusiasm for being with me in bed."

"You're very giving when we make love, and I really like that about you."

You get the idea. Push yourself a bit to give your partner a compliment every day. For Howard's couple, this took a lot of practice, because it went against the grain of their relationship. But soon, they became very good at compliments and had a great time playing the game. The compliment game is fun and it boosts the whole level of positive emotion in your marriage. So play it!

Brainstorming About Other Fun Activities

Of course, couples take part in many kinds of activities for fun. What do you do? Sit down together and think about the most enjoyable, interesting, and playful things you've ever done or would like to do together. Make a list to which you both contribute, putting down

RAGNAR STORAASLI

every idea you think of no matter how foolish or outrageous it may seem. Part of the fun is brainstorming about fun and throwing out the wackiest ideas you can. Avoid getting into a rut.

Ideas We've Heard from Couples

To help you get started, we'd like to mention some of the great ideas we've heard from couples over the years. Maybe one of them will cause a cascade of new ideas to form in your own mind.

Couples have suggested doing exercise, yoga, or massage together. Fun doesn't have to be something that's elaborate or costs money. These are activities you can do almost anywhere if you find them enjoyable. In contrast, skiing is wonderful, but it can be very expensive. However, if you have the time and the money, it can be great to spend the day together. Many couples enjoy going to the movies. That's not a very original idea, and you've probably already thought of it, but how long has it been since you've done it? Or if you go regularly, how long has it been since you made out in the back row of the theater? If you've never have kissed your way through a movie, give it a try.

You can bake cookies together and make a big mess. You can climb a mountain or collect sea shells. You can go swimming or play tag. How about renting a classic movie and cuddling on the sofa with a bowl of popcorn? How long has it been since you had a soda with two straws? Have you ever tried preparing a meal together, then fed it to each other?

Even things that seem like work can be turn into play if that's your attitude. According to one husband, "My wife and I found out that it was really fun to do yard work together. It's great to be together sprucing up our home, and at the end of the day, it's rewarding to see what we accomplished. And in the summertime, seeing the flowers we planted together bloom is something that gives us great pleasure and pride. These things are fun for us because it's us doing them together."

Over the years, we've noticed that when we have couples brainstorm about enjoyable things to do, sex usually isn't mentioned until many other matters have been mentioned. Couples tend to forget that sexual intimacy is one of the most fun things they can do together. Several variations, to suit your personal preference of course, should be on your list. How about setting aside an evening without the kids to make love?

We want you to reach a level where any fun time you have together is something to be eagerly anticipated! Be creative.

Getting Going

Make a personal fun deck by taking a deck of index cards and writing down on each card one of the items from your brainstorming sessions. We suggest listing twenty-five to thirty ideas to start with, and they can cover a whole range of topics. Once you've made the deck, set aside particular times to choose activities and do them. Don't let anything stop you.

Since you're going to have more fun if you're both eager to do the activities you choose, here's one way to make sure this happens when you use your fun deck. Each of you picks three cards from the deck describing things you'd enjoy doing in the time set aside that day. You trade cards, then each of you chooses one card from the three your partner picked and takes responsibility for making that one activity happen. That way, you're each picking something you know your partner will like, but since you get to choose from among the three, you're likely to like it too. Don't worry about which one your partner wants you to pick. If you don't get to it today, you'll have another chance tomorrow!

You can derive a lot of pleasure from rituals in your marriage—like dinner out every Thursday—but it's also important to stretch yourselves. A lot of times the most enjoyable things are novel, and the newness of the activity is a big part of the fun. Perhaps one week you can say, "You know, for a change, I'd really like to hire a baby-sitter and go out to a dinner theater instead of going to the movies. What do you think?" It might feel risky to try something new, and you don't know what your partner will say. But if you get into the spirit of fun together, your partner may say, "Great, when do we go?" Or your partner may have another idea you find even more appealing. The key is that you're able to work together to collaborate on choosing these activities.

You can also choose at times to intensify the effort. For example, you could try a slightly different approach with your fun deck in which you each pick three cards and then, over the next weekend, do all six of these activities. Break that fun barrier. You may think, "My goodness, I can't possibly do that." But if you think about it, you could go for a walk and watch the sunset (there's one), then go out to dinner (there's two), go to a movie (three), come home and make love (four), have breakfast in bed the next morning (that's five), and then take a shower together (there's six). So you can do six activities in the course of one evening and morning. When they are dating, couples commonly do many fun things together in a short period of time. If your priorities are on keeping your relationship vibrant, there's no reason not to keep doing this. Break the fun barrier!

If you follow the key points in this chapter, you'll be qualified for a degree in relationship fun. You can do it. Early in relationships, it comes easily. Even after many years in a marriage, it's not hard if you make the time, protect that time, and make fun happen.

Sensuality and sexuality can be fun, too. All too often, however, the sensual-sexual area also falls victim to the barriers against fun that we discussed earlier. Many professionals believe that sexual chemistry inevitably decreases over time. Yet many couples are able to sustain and even improve their sex lives. We don't believe that couples fall out of attraction. Instead, the biggest reason attraction dies down is that couples neglect the very things that built and maintained it in the first place, friendship and fun. But before we focus on the sensual and sexual side of things, we have some exercises to help you break the fun barrier.

 Exercises

We'd like you to go through the steps we discussed in this chapter. Here they are again.

1 Brainstorm about a list of fun things. Be creative. Anything goes, so have a good time coming up with ideas.

2. Write these ideas out on index cards to make your fun deck. It will come in handy when you don't have much time to decide what to do, but you're ready for some fun.

3. Set aside time. Pick out three things from the deck that you'd enjoy doing and hand them to your partner. Each of you should take responsibility for making one of your partner's three things happen in the time you've set aside. Go for it!

13

Enhancing Your Sex Life

P HYSICAL INTIMACY IS VERY IMPORTANT to most couples. In fact, couples commonly report that sexual concerns are among their top three problem areas. Therefore, it's important to work toward preserving and enhancing the quality of the physical intimacy between the two of you. In this chapter, we'll emphasize three major ideas: (1) the need to separate sexuality from sensuality, (2) the importance of protecting physical intimacy from anxiety and conflict, and (3) the need for partners to communicate clearly their sensual or sexual desires.

SEPARATING SEXUALITY FROM SENSUALITY

Think about sexuality. What comes to mind? For many, the first thought is of sexual intercourse and all the pleasurable acts that may come before and after. Anything else? Perhaps thoughts of what arouses you or your partner, or feelings you have when you want to make love with your partner.

Now think about sensuality. What comes to mind? Usually, some pleasant experience that involved touching, seeing, smelling, or feeling—for example, walking on the beach or being massaged with sweet-smelling oil. How about the roughness of a beard or silkiness of hair? The smell of your partner after a shower? Chocolate? You get the idea. These are sensual experiences, which are not necessarily goal-oriented or connected with sexuality.

We'd like to suggest that sensuality includes physical touch or other senses but is not always associated with making love. We'd include hugging, affectionate cuddling, nonsexual massages—all acts that provide physical pleasure in nonsexual ways. This distinction between sensuality and sexuality is important.

In the early stages of a relationship, touching, holding hands, hugging, and caressing are common. Unfortunately, many couples tend to bypass the sensual areas and move more exclusively to goals-oriented sexual behavior over time. Less attention is paid to the kinds of touching and sensing that were so delightful before. This leads to problems, because such touching is a basic, pleasurable part of overall intimacy. In fact, in a survey reported in her column, Ann Landers found that *both women and men preferred hugging to intercourse.* Holding and touching are that important to most people.

For example, Wanda and Eugene have been married for eight years. Like many other couples, they used to spend a lot of time just cuddling and caressing each other. As the years went by, they got busier with children, work, and home, and after a year or two of marriage, they'd settled into a pattern of having sex about twice a week. Because of time pressures and the other cares of life, less and less time was devoted to sensuality. At night, in bed, one or the other would initiate sex and they'd quickly have intercourse, usually finishing in about ten minutes.

Wanda and Eugene had become quite efficient at making love—or, rather, at having intercourse. They didn't have or make a lot of extra time, so they made do. In fact, they were making do rather than making love. Their focus on sexual intercourse instead of sensuality led to dissatisfaction for both of them. "What happened to all those times we'd lie around for hours together?" Wanda wondered. "It seems like Wanda used to be a lot more responsive when we made love," Eugene mused. We'll come back to them in a bit.

The fact is that there needs to be a place for sensual touching in your relationship—both in and out of the context of making love. This is similar to the distinction between problem discussion and problem solution. Just as the pressures of life lead many couples to the problem-solving stage prematurely, too many couples short-change their sensuality and prematurely focus on sex. That leads to sex that lacks the overall context of touching. As we learned from the classic studies of psychologist Harry Harlow, even baby chimps die without physical contact—and without touching, marriages die too.

Therefore, it's important to make sensual experiences a regular part of your relationship, apart from sexuality. Furthermore, sensual experiences set the stage for better sexual experiences. The whole climate for physical intimacy is better when you've preserved sensuality. Talk together about what's sensual for each of you. What do you enjoy? Make the time for sensual experiences, like massages, that don't necessarily lead to sex.

It's also important to keep sensuality as a regular part of your lovemaking. Keeping a focus on a variety of ways of touching preserves and elevates the importance of the whole sensual experience. Most couples prefer this broader sensual focus to a narrow focus on sex. It fosters a fuller expression of intimacy in your physical relationship. We'll give you some specific suggestions for preserving and enhancing sensuality in the exercises at the end of the chapter.

PROTECTING PHYSICAL INTIMACY FROM ANXIETY

Arousal is the natural process by which we're stimulated to sensual or sexual pleasure. It's a state of pleasurable excitement. While just about everyone is capable of being aroused, this pleasurable feeling can be short-circuited by anxiety. Numerous studies suggest that anxiety is the key factor inhibiting arousal. We'd like to discuss two key kinds of anxiety in this context: performance anxiety and the tension from conflict in your marriage.

THE BARRIER OF PERFORMANCE ANXIETY

Those who have studied the sexual relationship most intensely, like William Masters and Virginia Johnson, have described a particular type of anxiety that is virtually incompatible with good lovemaking. Performance anxiety is anxiety about how you're performing when you make love. Asking yourself questions such as "How am I doing?" or "Is my partner enjoying this?" on a regular basis reflects performance anxiety.

When you're keeping an eye on your performance, you put distance between you and your partner. You're focused on how you're doing rather than on being with your partner. Many people report feeling distant when making love, as if they're just watching what's going on instead of participating. This kind of detachment is believed to lead to a variety of sexual problems. The focus is no longer on the pleasure you're sharing; instead, your self-esteem feels at stake. It's as if the event of making love has triggered issues of acceptance and the fear of rejection.

The focus on performance interferes with arousal because you're distracted from your own sensations of pleasure. This distraction leads to many of the most common sexual problems people experience—premature ejaculation and problems with keeping erections for men and difficulty lubricating or having orgasms for women. You can't be both anxious and pleasantly aroused at the same time. And you can't be relaxed and enjoy being with your partner if you're concentrating on not making mistakes.

Consider Eugene and Wanda again. Eugene became aware over time that Wanda was less and less pleased with their lovemaking. Without a focus on sensuality and touching throughout their relationship, Wanda began to feel as if Eugene was just using her sexually. This feeling was intensified because he'd have orgasms every time they made love, but hers were less frequent. As unsatisfying as their lovemaking was for both of them, it seemed to Wanda that it was still better for Eugene, so her resentment grew.

Eugene knew that Wanda was resentful and wanted to make things better. But instead of talking it out and working on the problem together, he decided he'd just do a better job of making love to Wanda. This wasn't all bad as ideas go. However, it caused him to be more and more focused on performing—and his anxiety grew. Thoughts about performance became his constant companions during their lovemaking: "How's Wanda doing? Is she getting excited? Does she like this? I wonder if she thinks I'm doing this right? Man, I'd better try more of this for a while, I'm not sure she's ready."

Pretty soon he was pleasing Wanda more, but he was growing tenser and tenser about what he was doing when they made love. Sure, he was meeting some of her needs, but he wasn't feeling at all connected with her or satisfied in their lovemaking. He was performing! Wanda knew there was a change in Eugene's attention to her arousal, which pleased her to a degree. But she had a growing sense that Eugene was somewhere else when they made love. She was having more orgasms, but she didn't feel as if they were sharing a sensual experience.

The key for Wanda and Eugene was to rediscover the sensual side of their relationship. They had to talk out loud about what was going on. They had a great deal of love and respect for each other, so once they started dealing with the issues, things quickly got better. Here's how they started to talk about it:

WANDA: [bringing up the subject after the kids were in bed and they were relaxed and reading in bed] Can we talk for a minute about something?

EUGENE: Sure. What's up?

WANDA: I've been thinking that our lovemaking just isn't like it used to be.

EUGENE: [He feels a twinge of anxiety but decides to listen nondefensively. He turns toward Wanda to show his interest.] I agree. I'm really glad you're bringing it up. What's it been like for you?

WANDA: Well, lately, it seems like you're trying harder to please me, but for some reason I don't like what's going on that much more than before.

EUGENE: I know what you mean. It's just not relaxed like it used to be. Heck, I'm tense half the time we're together in the bedroom.

WANDA: I wonder why that is. Are you trying too much? It almost seems to me like you're not there with me.

EUGENE: Well, yes. I am trying hard to please you. I knew you weren't happy with what we've been doing, so I was trying to make things better for you. But that's been a drag. Now I'm worried so much about doing things well that it's no fun to make love.

WANDA: I appreciate that you've been trying to make things better for me. And I've sensed what you're saying about you working so hard at it that you're not having any fun. That's partly why I'm not happy with the whole thing. It's not like it used to be, when the two of us really enjoyed being together in bed.

EUGENE: It's pretty clear that what I'm doing isn't getting us back to the way things used to be. We used to enjoy our time in bed together so much—like that time in San Diego where it was just the two of us, alone, for the whole weekend. We used to spend more time touching and kissing, and I think that made the whole thing better.

WANDA: It sure did. That's what I really want more of, not what we're doing now. Like you say, we used to spend the time for it to be like that. I think time is our biggest problem here. Most of the time, now, it seems like we're in a hurry—like making love is something to get over with rather than something to enjoy. That's frustrating to me.

EUGENE: Me too. When there's time pressure, we don't spend the time to just caress each other and relax. I think that sets us up for having a frustrating time when we jump into making love.

As you can see, they didn't try to fix the problem prematurely. Each of them listened to the other's frustrations and desires for their physical relationship. They agreed that they'd been giving too little time to this important aspect of their marriage. As they moved on, they decided to make more time for lovemaking, and they pursued sensuality together in and out of the context of lovemaking. Later, they worked on just touching and massaging each other in different ways. These changes made a difference. They eliminated a lot of their fears about performance and reestablished a full and pleasurable physical relationship.

In the PREP approach, we emphasize that you can prevent problems from developing in the first place if you're willing to do so and you know what to do. It's the same for physical intimacy. You can do a lot to keep problems like Wanda and Eugene's from ever developing. For some of you, their story is very familiar. For others, your physical relationship hasn't deteriorated, and that's great. Your goal is to learn to keep things that way.

THE BARRIER OF RELATIONSHIP CONFLICT AND ANXIETY

Mishandled conflicts can destroy your physical relationship by adding tension both in and out of the bedroom. Let's face it, when you've been arguing and angry with each other, you usually don't feel like being sensual or making love. While for some, the sexual relationship is temporarily enhanced by conflict followed by making up, for most, poorly handled conflict adds a layer of tension that affects everything else in the relationship.

Tension isn't compatible with enjoyable, intimate lovemaking for most people. In fact, there may be no area of intimate connection that's more vulnerable to the effects of conflict and resentment than your physical relationship. If you're experiencing conflict in other areas of your relationship, it can be difficult to feel positive about sharing an intimate physical experience. Worse, these conflicts too often erupt in the context of lovemaking.

Even though touching sensually and making love are powerful ways to connect, destructive conflict builds barriers. If you can protect your times for physical intimacy from conflict, you can do a great deal to keep your physical relationship alive and well. To do this, you must work to handle conflict effectively—for example, by using the ground rules and the other techniques we've been stressing. *It's critical to agree to keep problems and disagreements off-limits during times you reserve to be together to touch or make love.* We can't think of anything more powerful for preserving your ability to enjoy physical intimacy.

Sometimes the conflicts affecting the physical relationship are about sensuality or lovemaking. Consider Don and Melissa, a couple we talked with on a break at a PREP workshop who wanted pointers on how to get unstuck in their physical relationship. They had been married just a few years and were worried that their closeness was slipping away. Their comments went something like this:

DON:	When I come home from work, I'd like to be able to hug and kiss Melissa for a moment, to say hello. That doesn't seem too unreasonable, does it?
MELISSA:	No, it isn't, but that's not what I see happening. You start putting your hands all over me without seeing if I'm in the mood or busy. I feel like I'm not even a person sometimes.
DON:	But it's like that in bed, too. I want to snuggle up to you and you pull away. I like to touch a lot, and you don't seem to anymore.
MELISSA:	I'd really like to, but it seems like we need to slow down, with you being more aware of what I want. And if you yelled at me earlier in the day, I'm not going to feel like touching or making love later on.

Don and Melissa had a positive relationship. They were at our workshop to learn how to keep it that way. Their physical relationship was one area where they were having trouble, and we were able to make some suggestions that helped them before real resentment built up.

We'd like you to notice several things in this example:

1. Don and Melissa had fallen into a pursuer-withdrawer pattern in regard to physical intimacy. It's not uncommon for men to withdraw from conflict but be the pursuer in physical intimacy. Any time there's a strong imbalance with one pursuing and one withdrawing, the situation is ripe for conflict.

2. What each of them did in this pattern was affected by the other. As Don pushed more, Melissa pulled back, and as she pulled back, he pushed more—just as we described for gender differences in Chapter Two. One partner's actions are rarely independent of the other's.

3. They each had developed some negative interpretations about what all this meant, which they hadn't been talking about constructively. Melissa started to believe that Don was just interested in sex, which turned out not to be the case, and he started to think that she wasn't interested in any touching, whether or not it led to sex.

Men often look to sexual intimacy as a way to connect with their wives, while women may more often turn to talking as a way to connect. While men and women may have different preferences for type of intimacy, we feel that both sexes want to connect in a variety of positive ways. Don and Melissa were both interested in talking, touching, and making love, but barriers were creeping into their marriage. They needed to start talking about what was going on, and that's what we encouraged them to do.

Obviously, a lack of communication about your physical relationship can cause barriers. If Don and Melissa hadn't been interested in preventing this pattern from going further, real problems with conflict could have crept into their relationship. In turn, the resulting anxiety and tension could have led to decreased arousal and interest in the physical relationship. When a couple allows that to happen, an area of delightful intimacy becomes something to avoid or get over with, to avoid conflict.

Physical intimacy is an area that's particularly ripe for triggering hidden issues of control, caring, and acceptance. For example, the way your partner pursues lovemaking may lead you to feel controlled. That's what Melissa was feeling when Don would touch her when she wasn't ready or interested. Or perhaps one partner avoids sex as a way to gain some control in the relationship. Likewise, it's very easy to feel uncared for if your partner doesn't show an interest in touching or making love in the ways that interest you the most. Don was beginning to believe that Melissa didn't care when she'd rebuff his attempts to hug her when he'd come home. To be rebuffed physically or sexually seems to be particularly stinging to most people. It's often seen as a deep rejection.

You can't prevent or repair such patterns unless you're handling conflict well and communicating openly and safely. It's just too easy to let resentments build if you don't open up about your concerns, especially when hidden issues are being triggered. Don and Melissa told us later that they had a great discussion about their problem and were able to develop real solutions for handling physical intimacy. In their discussion, she learned that he wasn't just trying to use her sexually, and that he truly cared a lot about keeping their physical relationship healthy. He learned that she was interested in their physical relationship but wanted some changes to make it better. She wanted him to take into account her needs and state of mind in his physical advances.

Melissa felt that he heard her concerns and was relieved as she saw his genuine desire to work on this part of their relationship. Don felt that he was being heard when he expressed how important the physical relationship was to him—not just for the sake of sex, but because this was a major avenue of intimacy together.

After having such a good discussion, they went on to some problem solving that really got them on track. For one thing, they decided to reemphasize their sensuality by planning times for touching when the focus wasn't on sex. This helped Melissa to relax about touching again and allowed her to see that Don wasn't focused on sex. They also agreed to some ground rules of their own about when and where certain kinds of touches were okay. They planned for a way to enjoy the pleasures of a long hug at the end of the workday, without either of them feeling any pressure to have sex.

Finally, they also agreed to plan times to make love that allowed for more sharing, verbally and nonverbally, about what they really liked. And that brings us to our last major point in this chapter.

COMMUNICATING DESIRES

It's critical for you to communicate about your physical relationship in ways that protect and enhance this important way of being intimate. This applies not only to handling potential conflicts about physical intimacy but also to letting each other know what you desire. We're talking about real communication here, not mind reading. Mind reading can cause many serious conflicts throughout a relationship, including conflicts about sensuality and sexuality. The problem is that people too easily assume that they know what their partner wants, and when.

YOU SHOULD KNOW WHAT I LIKE!

It's a mistake to assume that your partner will like whatever you like, or that you can read each other's minds. Would you go out to a restaurant and order for your partner without talking about what he or she would like? Of course not. It's also too easy for some people to assume that their partner won't like the things they like. Either way, you're

making assumptions. And since many couples have trouble communicating about their physical relationship, it's very easy for these assumptions to take control. You don't know what your partner's expectations are until you ask, and vice versa.

Of course, based on your previous experiences together, you can often assume correctly, and things can work out fine based on those assumptions. However, keep in mind that people change, so checking in with each other about desires and expectations is valuable for a good sexual relationship. We can't tell you how many couples we've talked with in which one partner expects the other to "know" what she or he likes most when making love. It's as if people believe: "It just isn't romantic or exciting if I have to tell you what I want. You should *know!*" That's an unreasonable expectation. If you hold this fantasy, you should probably challenge it for the health of your relationship.

Couples who have the best sexual relationships have ways of communicating both verbally and nonverbally about what they like. Furthermore, they usually have a genuinely unselfish desire to please one another. There's a strong sense of teamwork, even in lovemaking, where each gives to and receives from the intimacy they share. This giving, combined with direct communication, leads to great lovemaking.

We recommend that you communicate clearly about what feels pleasurable to you while you're touching or making love. Your partner won't know unless you say something. We're not suggesting that you have a Speaker-Listener discussion in the middle of making love (though if it excites you, let us know!).

Finally, look for ways to give to your partner in your physical relationship. If you're keeping conflict out of the bedroom, handling conflict well in the rest of your relationship, and taking the time and energy to preserve sensuality, this kind of communication will be much easier to do.

TAKING A RISK

Many people also have to overcome the fear of rejection that can occur when they ask for what they want. Your desires say something about who you are, so to ask is to risk being rejected. But you have to take the risk or you'll settle for less in your relationship. Again, don't expect your partner to read your mind. Just as important, don't take it as severe rejection if your partner isn't interested in some lovemaking behaviors that interest you. That's normal in any marriage. As in other areas, you must be sensitive to each other's needs and desires. While there may be some behaviors one of you would enjoy but the other wouldn't, there are probably many others that you're both very interested in and you'd both enjoy, including some you may not have tried or talked about before.

We'll give you an example. Sharon and Oliver (Oly, for short) had a lot of trouble communicating about what they wanted sexually. They both came from families where no one talked directly about wants and desires. Consequently, they had experienced a satisfying, though not very fulfilling, sexual relationship over their twenty-five years of marriage. In fact, they'd never had sex outside of the bedroom, and they'd rarely spent any time in prolonged, sensual lovemaking. Each had assumed that having intercourse once a week, in their bed with the lights out, for about five to ten minutes, was all that the other was interested in. Yet they both wanted more than that, though they'd never said anything.

Now, with their two daughters in college, they had more time for lovemaking. Sharon and Oliver listened to some of our tapes and were trying new things. As they used the Speaker-Listener Technique to communicate about physical intimacy, each was delighted to find out that the other wanted more from their lovemaking. Their assumptions had been way off. Here's a sample of how they opened up with one another about some of their desires and expectations:

OLY:	(Speaker) I've never felt I could say this before, but I've wanted to try some different things for years.
SHARON:	(Listener) So you've wanted to try some things, but hadn't felt you could say anything.
OLY:	(Speaker) [feeling accepted so far, and willing to open up more] Right. I think we've missed some ways we could really enhance our physical relationship, but it's hard to talk about because we came from families where you didn't do that.
SHARON:	(Listener) You think we've missed out some, and that it's hard for us to talk about these things since we came from families where that wasn't done.
OLY:	(Speaker) Yeah. For instance, there's times I've wished we'd just make love somewhere else in the house for a change— like on the sofa in the family room. That'd be a change. I've also thought of getting some massage oils and spending a whole evening touching and making love. But I've never told you these things because I wasn't sure how you'd react.
SHARON:	(Listener) [glad to hear him talking openly and working at listening well] So, you weren't sure how I might take it, so it's been hard to tell me that you wanted to try some different things like making love on the sofa.
OLY:	(Speaker) Exactly!

FLOOR SWITCH.

SHARON: (Speaker) [*feeling very good about how this talk is going*] I really like to hear these things. I've also felt we've been missing something but wasn't sure you felt the same way. It's great to hear that you *do*.

OLY: (Listener) It sounds like you're relieved to hear that we share these concerns.

SHARON: (Speaker) Yes. Relieved is a good word. In retrospect, it seems dumb that we didn't talk like this before.

OLY: (Listener) Are you saying you feel we should've known better?

SHARON: (Speaker) [*with just a touch of sadness*] Not really that we should've known better. More that while we've had a great marriage and I've enjoyed our physical relationship, I feel we've missed some opportunities.

OLY: (Listener) So you're feeling a bit sad that we missed some opportunities to build up this part of our relationship.

SHARON: (Speaker) That's it. It really seems rather simple to tell each other what we might like to try or do. For example, I also like the idea of massaging and touching more. It'd be really nice.

OLY: (Listener) You're feeling good that we're talking about this, and you like some of the ideas I mentioned—especially the one about massage.

SHARON: (Speaker) [*with a very upbeat tone*] Yes. In fact, I've got quite a few other ideas to share, too, now that we are getting this in the open.

OLY: (Listener) I'm all ears.

And on they went. Since they liked each other's ideas, the line between problem discussion and problem solving was rather blurry. That wasn't a negative here, though. As they shared a mutual desire for more in their physical relationship, some solutions became obvious.

IT'S NOT THAT I'M COMPLAINING HELGA, BUT COULDN'T WE TRY SOMETHING DIFFERENT?

As it turned out, they'd both been interested in taking much more time to touch in all kinds of ways and to make a full sensual experience out of their lovemaking.

For Oly and Sharon, the key was getting to the point where they could talk openly about their expectations and desires. What had always seemed like a good marriage became an even better marriage, and not just because of the improvements in their physical relationship. The increased openness throughout their marriage brought them closer than they'd felt since they were newlyweds.

Communication is the key. It also helps to try some new ideas to break out of ruts, as Oly and Sharon were able to do. Read a book on massage or sex together. This might help you to talk about these issues. Agree to surprise each other one night.

Try something new, even if just once. Exploring both the sensual and sexual sides of your relationship may relieve concerns about performance and help you to find even more pleasure.

We're not saying that every couple can have a wonderful physical relationship. You both have to want it, protect it, and nurture it. If things are going well in your physical relationship, keep them that way. If problems have developed, the ideas we're emphasizing here can help you to get back on track.

In this chapter we've emphasized several key ways to keep your physical relationship growing and vibrant. Now it's up to you. We don't intend this chapter to be a substitute for sex therapy if you have a history of significant sexual difficulties. If that sounds like you, we want to encourage you to work together to overcome the problems. Working with an experienced sex therapist can usually accomplish a great deal when there are significant problems. Our focus here has been more to help couples with satisfying physical relationships to keep things that way—and to make them even better.

This chapter was designed to help you maintain—and grow in—physical intimacy. As with so many areas we've discussed, working wisely on this aspect of your marriage can produce great benefits. Physical intimacy isn't all that marriage is about, but it's one of the areas, like fun and friendship, where you can develop a lasting, satisfying ability to connect. As we close this chapter, we offer exercises that can help you enhance your abilities to connect physically. They are exercises that have been tried successfully for years with many couples. If you're ready for sensual and sexual enhancement, read on. Then we'll move on to look at the implications of core belief systems for marriage.

🐾 Exercises

1. *Sensate-Focus.* Years ago, William Masters and Virginia Johnson began studying the various ways in which problems develop in sexual relationships. They created an exercise that can benefit you, whether or not you've struggled in your physical relationship. This exercise is called the Sensate-Focus. The purposes are twofold: (1) to keep you focused on sensuality and touching in your physical relationship and (2) to help you learn to communicate more openly and naturally about what you like and don't like in your lovemaking.

   This isn't the time for sexual intercourse. That would defeat the purpose, since we want you to focus on sensuality. Don't be goal-oriented, except toward the goal of relaxing and doing this exercise in a way that you each enjoy. If you want to make love following the exercise, that's up to you. But if you've been having concerns about feeling pressured sexually, we'd recommend that you completely separate out these practice times from times when you have sex. In fact, you shouldn't have sex unless both of you fully and openly agree to do so. No mind reading or assumptions!

The general idea is that you each take turns giving and receiving pleasure. The first few times, you are either the Giver or the Receiver until you switch roles halfway through the exercise. When you're in the Receiver role, your job is to enjoy the touching and to give feedback on what feels good and what doesn't. Your partner can't know this unless you say how you feel. You can give either verbal or hand-guided feedback. Verbal feedback means telling your partner what actions feel good, how hard to rub, or what areas you like to have touched. Hand-guided feedback consists of gently moving your partner's hand around the part of the body being massaged to provide feedback about what feels good.

As the Giver, your role is to provide pleasure by touching your partner and being responsive to feedback. Ask for feedback as often as necessary. Be aware of changes in how your partner is reacting: what feels good one minute may hurt the next. Focus on what your partner wants, not on what you think would feel good.

Choose roles and give a massage of your partner's hands or feet for about ten to twenty minutes, asking for and giving feedback. We recommend massages of areas like the hands, back, legs, or feet the first few times to get the hang of the technique. This also helps you relax if issues about sexuality exist between you. Then switch roles. Repeat as often as you like, but also remember to practice these roles in other aspects of your sensual and sexual relationship.

We recommend that you try the Sensate-Focus exercise over the course of several weeks, several times a week. As you work on the exercise over time, you can add in variations of the technique. Assuming that all is going well in your exercises, begin to move to other areas for touching. Wherever you want to be touched, including the sexual areas, is great.

As you continue with this exercise, you can drop the rigid emphasis on the Giver and Receiver roles and work on both of you giving and receiving at the same time, while still keeping an emphasis on sensuality and communication of desires. Or you can vary the degree to which you stay in these roles as you wish. Through practice, it will become easier for you to communicate openly about touch. It will also be easier for you to work together as you continue to keep physical intimacy vibrant and alive.

2. *Exploring the Sensual.* In addition to the Sensate-Focus exercise, set aside a specific time for sensual activities together. This works for all couples, regardless of whether or not they're engaging in sexual activity. Be sure you won't be interrupted (this is the time for baby-sitters or answering machines).

At the start of this exercise, talk about what's sensual for each of you and what you'd like to try doing to keep sensual experiences in your relationship. Here are some ideas:

- Give a massage to your partner, using the Sensate-Focus technique described above.

- Share a fantasy you've had about your partner.

- Cuddle and hug as you talk to your partner about the positive things you love about him or her.

- Plan a sensual or sexual activity for your next encounter.

- Plan a wonderful meal together. Prepare it together and sit close to each other. Share the meal.

- Wash your partner's hair.

- Spend some time just kissing.

14

The Importance of
Core Belief Systems

WE'VE JUST FOCUSED on how to enhance your relationship with a focus on friendship, fun, and physical intimacy. Now we're going to look at how spiritual or religious dimensions tend to affect and enhance the overall quality of relationships for many couples. While not everyone may be religious or spiritually inclined, there are key points of relevance here for any couple. Since for many people, the spiritual or religious realm embodies core belief systems, we'll use that as the focus for much of what we have to say. This has implications for any relationship, since all people have some core belief system.

If you aren't usually interested in religious or spiritual issues, you may be skeptical about the relevance of what we have to say. Or if you're very committed to a particular faith, you might see this chapter as watered down or too secular. Either way, we now invite you to explore the effect these dimensions can have on relationships. We want to point the way for you and your partner to participate in intimacy-enhancing discussions on these core issues.

We'll start with a focus on religion, since most of the relevant research has been conducted in that context. Then we'll look at what key research findings imply for any couple, regardless of belief. We'll ask you to consider these implications, whether you're Jewish, Christian, Islamic, an atheist, a follower of one of the eastern religions, an agnostic, or a follower of some other philosophical persuasion. Let's start with some definitions.

Webster's New World Dictionary defines *spiritual* as "of the spirit or the soul," with *spirit* having multiple definitions, including "the life principle"; "life, will, consciousness, thought, etc., regarded as separate from matter"; and "essential or characteristic quality." Hence, *spiritual* can be taken to pertain to the essence of the inner person, the core of life.

Religion is defined by *Webster's* as "any specific system of belief, worship, conduct, etc., often involving a code of ethics and a philosophy." A recent participant in one of our training workshops for professionals put it this way: "Religion is typically a structure in which people express their spirituality." Among other things, in religion people find codes and rituals—which we call structures in our model—that guide them in life. Hence, for many, though not all, people, their religious faith embodies central, core beliefs about life, its meaning, and how one should live. Furthermore, for many people, issues of the spirit are considered primarily from within the religious domain, while others hold views of spirituality quite apart from any particular religious tradition.

Most of the research we'll now describe for you is based on religious beliefs and practices rather than on spirituality. That's because you can't conduct research on things you can't measure, and while it's not hard to measure religious activity or even core beliefs, it's extremely difficult to measure spirituality. We're not saying that spirituality isn't important, it's just that most of the research is on religious behavior.

RESEARCH ON RELIGIOUS INVOLVEMENT

The impact of religion on marriage has been studied for years. Most of this research has been conducted with those involved in traditional religious systems, particularly within the Judeo-Christian spectrum. While you may not belong to one of those traditions, implications from these studies can benefit all couples. That's because many religions codify core beliefs, values, and practices that promote stability and health in relationships. Our goal here is to decode these findings and highlight key implications for all couples, whether they're religious or not.

WHO GETS MARRIED?

Religious people are more likely to get married in the first place. Bernard Spilka is a colleague of ours at the University of Denver who is an expert in the scientific study of religion. He attributes the lower rates of marriage among the nonreligious to two things. First, religious involvement brings people together. Even Ann Landers seems to regularly suggest that singles go to a church or synagogue to meet people.

Second, Spilka points out that, in general, people who are less religious conform less to society. They don't tend to see themselves fitting into a variety of traditional structures; therefore, they may be less interested in institutions such as marriage.

RELIGION AND MARITAL QUALITY

Numerous studies suggest that religion has a favorable impact on marriage. For example, couples who are more religious seem to be a bit more satisfied in their marriages. They're also less likely to divorce. In one of our studies, married subjects who rated themselves as more religious showed somewhat higher levels of satisfaction, lower levels of conflict about common issues, and higher levels of commitment.

Those who were more religious were also more likely to say that divorce is wrong, especially those who were conservative. They also were more likely to believe that if they had problems, they would encounter significant social pressure to stay together and make it work. And they were more likely to report being satisfied with sacrificing for one another and having a stronger sense of an identity as a team. These findings make sense, given the values that are emphasized in traditional religious groups.

A major survey by Tavris and Sadd, in 1975, found that more religious women reported greater sexual contentment in terms of both orgasmic frequency and openness of communication about sex with their husbands compared to moderately religious and nonreligious women. These same women also reported greater overall marital satisfaction.

It's not that more religious couples have substantially better marriages. The effects we're talking about are consistent and statistically significant, but the differences are also often rather small. It would be accurate to say that something about the factors associated with religious involvement gives religious couples an edge in keeping marriages strong. Before we look at this in more detail, let's consider research on a topic of major relevance for more and more couples—interfaith marriages.

INTERFAITH MARRIAGES

Because of changes in our society, people are now far more likely to marry out of their faith. One reason is that religion probably has less overall impact in our culture than it used to have, so people are less likely to take it into account when picking a mate. Also, with our society becoming more and more mobile, connections with religious communities become harder to maintain and intermarriage and divorce become more likely. In contrast, people who grow up with more religious education are more likely to marry within their faith. Finding someone who matches your faith probably becomes a higher priority when you are strongly grounded in it.

Whatever the reasons for intermarriage, research consistently shows that partners from different religions are much more likely to divorce. While no nationally representative studies have looked at this, various studies suggest that an increased risk exists for interfaith marriages. It seems likely that these effects would be related to the degree of commitment individuals have to their faith. When people of different backgrounds marry and have little allegiance to those backgrounds, we would assume that the risks for divorce are lower.

Many interfaith marriages start out just fine, with couples thinking that they can beat the odds and that "love will conquer all." While love can conquer a lot—especially if it's translated into loving and respectful behavior—the more there is to conquer, the greater the risk of failure. But, as with all couples, the way interfaith couples handle these differences in their relationships is the most critical factor in how they will get along in the future.

There are two key reasons why early optimism may give way to problems later. First, people tend to get more religious or spiritually inclined as they age—perhaps because death gets closer. Also, the challenges of life can change our perspective on religious or spiritual issues, so that what looks unimportant early in life can become more of an issue with age.

Second, when couples start thinking about children, they face a host of decisions about how the child is to be raised regarding religious and spiritual beliefs. This is when your past religious upbringing can become critical, even if you don't see yourself as a believer. Here are some of the key decisions and questions that come up:

- Do you have a boy circumcised by religious ceremony, by the doctor, or not at all?

- Does the baby get baptized? Dedicated? Does baptism happen later, at the age of accountability and personal belief, or now?

- What do you do about religious holidays like Christmas, Rosh Hashanah, Passover, Easter, Ramadan, or Earth Day?

- What about religious schooling? Parochial or public school? Sunday School? Hebrew School?

- What about Bar Mitzvahs, confirmations, dedications, and so on?

Marjorie and Simon married at twenty-three. They fell in love in college where he majored in marketing and she majored in English. The problem was that he was Jewish and she was Catholic. His parents were alarmed that he'd date a Gentile. Hers were concerned, but she'd dated so many guys in the past, they figured Simon for a passing fancy. He wasn't.

Marjorie's parents began to get pretty worried. They asked, "How could she not marry a Catholic boy?" Simon and Marjorie felt pressure from both families to break it off. But they really did love each other, so what did religion matter? Children? No problem: "We'll let them choose what to believe for themselves." Parents? No problem: "They'll learn to accept our marriage." Religious practice? No problem: Neither of them was particularly involved or observant at this point in life, so their belief was "You do your thing, I'll do mine."

They got married after college, and despite all threats from their families, both sets of parents showed up for the wedding, which was conducted by a judge in a lodge. Things went along fairly well for Simon and Marjorie until the fourth year of marriage, when Marjorie got pregnant. For her, the idea of having a child was wonderful but marred by concerns. She found herself asking, "What kind of world am I bringing this kid into?" These natural anxieties led her to a serious reevaluation of her faith. No other context seemed as relevant for grappling with such questions. Simon's vision of himself as a daddy also returned him to interest in his faith. He asked, "What if I have a son? I can't have a doctor do the circumcision."

Marjorie sought out a priest to talk with, and she began attending Mass again. Simon wondered whom to call about getting a circumcision done if he had a son. Having returned to church, Marjorie got to thinking about baptism. "Infants must be baptized," the priest had said. She now believed that this was critical. Things got pretty awkward between Marjorie and Simon. Suddenly, each had an interest in religious matters—for their child and themselves—that hadn't seemed important a few years before.

As it turned out, they had a son, Benjamin. They had decided to have him baptized as well as circumcised in religious ceremonies. The trouble was that the priest wanted her to commit to raising Benjamin as a Catholic in order to do the baptism. To make things more complicated, they couldn't find a mohel who would circumcise their son, since he was born to a Gentile woman who hadn't converted to Judaism. They ended up doing neither.

Compromises were made that worked for a couple of years. Both parents read Bible stories to Benjamin, and he certainly enjoyed celebrating both Hanukkah and Christmas. But it got tougher and tougher. By the time Benjamin turned four, both parents felt more and more pulled to see Benjamin educated in their own tradition. Conflicts became more frequent and more intense. They agreed that it would be confusing for Benjamin to expose him to different teachings, but they weren't willing to give up the idea of Benjamin learning their faith.

Simon and Marjorie became increasingly alienated as they experienced the great frustration of not being able to come to an agreement that made any sense. Negative feelings intensified to the point where their conflicts about Benjamin were erupting into all sorts of other relationship events. One by one, key areas of intimacy suffered under the weight of the conflict about Benjamin. Marjorie and Simon no longer had any safe place just to relax and enjoy each other's company.

From time to time, Marjorie suggested that they get some professional help. Simon said, "No, we can handle this ourselves." They couldn't talk things out with family members because they'd just hear, "I told you so." In frustration and isolation, they separated and moved toward the idea of divorce. They still didn't seek professional help but instead tried on their own to work out decisions of child custody, time-sharing with Benjamin, and religious practice for him.

As with most couples who separate, what they were unable to do when they were together they were equally unable to do when they were separated. This led to divorce and a nasty custody battle, in which the judge was eventually called upon to decide both who would be the custodial parent and which religion Benjamin would be raised in. That may sound shocking, but courts are now being asked to decide such questions.

Of course a great many interfaith marriages don't come to this, but you can readily understand the kinds of pressures that couples like Simon and Marjorie can go through. We know of other couples who have made interfaith marriages work well. The key difference is how they handle conflicts—religious or otherwise. Of course, this is a core theme of the PREP approach.

Here's a more positive illustrative story. Janet and Cameron came from different religious backgrounds, but they've made their marriage work. Janet grew up a Methodist and Cameron a Christian Scientist. Both had some commitment to their faiths, so it wasn't easy to work through the issues. The key for them was making their expectations extremely clear and using a lot of skill in dealing with the issues. The most difficult decisions were those concerning their children. They had two sons, Stephen and Philip, and they decided that both boys would be exposed to the teachings of each faith. They found two churches so the boys could attend Sunday school at one and children's church at the other. They also decided that the boys would each be encouraged to make their own decisions about faith as they grew older.

The issue of medical care was the hardest to resolve. As a Christian Scientist, Cameron believed that medical procedures were not desirable and that if you were ill you could be healed spiritually. Janet wasn't raised that way at all. She had a big problem with any notion that medical care would not be rendered if it seemed to be needed. Cameron and Janet were able to agree to a compromise that has worked for them. In the event of any serious condition such as a high fever or broken limbs, Janet could freely take the boys to the doctor. However, for more minor ailments, they both agreed to refrain from using traditional medicine. If some intervention was desired, Cameron would take the boys to a healing practitioner of his faith.

As Cameron and Janet's marriage demonstrates, couples can make mixed-faith marriages work. It just takes more work than other couples might have to do. But even that depends a lot on how committed each partner is to a belief system. If one or both partners in an interfaith marriage are not strongly committed—and if they don't become more committed later as a result of changes in their life—such differences in background will have much less potential to produce friction and conflict.

To summarize, here's what the findings about the religious influence on marriage indicate. Couples who are more religiously inclined and from same-faith backgrounds appear to have an edge in maintaining satisfying marriages and avoiding divorce. We would now like to offer an analysis of why this might be true, in hopes of stimulating you to consider ways to strengthen your own relationship.

While we'll focus our understanding on relatively down-to-earth explanations, we recognize that many of you may also consider more spiritual explanations for such effects. In our attempts to decode the meaning of these studies for all couples, we focus on two key factors: (1) the value of social support for your relationship and (2) the effect of having a shared worldview. Let's look at these in detail.

SOCIAL SUPPORT

No matter what else they may do, religious and spiritual beliefs bring groups of similarly minded people together. There's a clear benefit for most people in being part of a social group—religious or not—as long as they have a clear sense that they belong or "fit" into the group. In fact, research by our colleague, Ken Pargament, has found that church and synagogue members who fit well into their religious community have higher levels of mental health than those who don't.

Studies have consistently shown that people who are more isolated are at greater risk for emotional problems like depression and suicide, health problems, and poverty. Many studies in the field of stress management demonstrate how much more vulnerable you are if you have significant stressors but no social support system to help you. It's just not healthy for most humans to be isolated. To paraphrase John Donne: "No person is an island!"

Religious involvements bring ready-made social structures. Religions specify codes of behavior and rituals, many of which cause natural points of connection between those involved. For example, most religious and spiritual groups meet regularly for numerous activities. Spiritual activities include worship, prayer, reading, study, and discussion groups. Social activities can include coffee hours, ice cream socials, picnics, group outings, get-together dinners, softball leagues, and about anything else you can think of. Service activities are also common, including food drives, visits to shut-ins, ministries of service to disadvantaged groups, community outreach services, volunteer work, and support groups. Social links to a community are important for couples, no matter how they're obtained.

For example, William and Sandra are a couple who met in the church where they later got married. They had been involved for years in the denomination before they decided to tie the knot, and they invited the entire congregation as well as their friends and family. The turnout was large, and the outpouring of support was very clear. They didn't just get married in front of friends, but in front of a whole community who knew them, supported them, and would be regularly involved in their lives.

As you can imagine, such a couple has a tremendous support system. Sandra and William are involved in weekly meetings, church on Sunday, and numerous other activities based in their religious community. Their relationship is supported and encouraged in the social network and by teachings that place great value on marriage and commitment, and especially on dedication.

Of course, there are other ways for people to get together in our culture, such as neighborhood get-togethers, political groups, interest groups, sports events, support groups, and clubs. *Our key point is that it's important for all couples to have a strong support system for their relationships.* Are you socially connected to a group that supports and somehow helps your relationship? If not, do you want to be? These are important questions for you and your partner to address directly.

A number of couples we've met haven't been interested in becoming part of a religious group, but have seen the need for a support system for their marriages. One such couple, John and Marsha, got involved with an organization called ACME, which stands for the Association for Couples in Marriage Enrichment. ACME is a national support network for couples that offers programs where couples can meet regularly for friendship, encouragement, and support directed at keeping their marriages vibrant and growing.

For John and Marsha, ACME has been just what they wanted. The focus is on support for marriage. Since neither of them is religious, this involvement has been a great way to meet their need for support and connection. The friends they've made and the group activities in ACME have helped them through some tough spots in their marriage. Such social support is critical for relationships.

Now we turn to other key implications of the research we've described. When you consider the spiritual or religious realm, you are dealing with core beliefs about your worldview—in other words, how you make sense of life. Everyone has some explanation for the big questions, whether it's simple or complex, religious or not. Hence, everyone has some core belief system. When you, as a couple, share such a belief system, you have a shared worldview.

A SHARED WORLDVIEW

As we mentioned in our discussion of fun in Chapter Twelve, University of Denver communication expert Fran Dickson's studies show that couples who have stayed together for fifty years have a shared *relationship vision* that includes personal dreams and goals for the future. A shared belief system—including mutual understanding about the meaning of life, death, and marriage—makes it easier to develop a relationship vision. In turn, having a relationship vision supports the long-term view of commitment.

Most religions have a common understanding and language system for thinking and talking about core beliefs. So another explanation for the benefit of religious involvement is that these religious couples have a belief system that facilitates developing and maintaining the shared worldview. Experts in the study of religion Bernard Spilka, Ralph Hood, and Richard Gorsuch put it this way in their book, *The Psychology of Religion* (1985): "Since it is fairly likely that the religious feelings of spouses tend to be similar, among the more religious, who probably come from religious homes, there may be a *supportive complex of perceptions* leading to increased marital satisfaction" (p. 105, emphasis added). That is, a shared worldview.

One important factor for *all* couples to consider is the impact of their worldviews on the marriage. Do you share a core belief system? How are the similarities and differences in views being handled? Think about these questions as we look at three specific areas where your worldview can have an effect on your marriage: core relationship values, moral judgments, and expectations. Then we'll take a look at how different couples might handle these issues.

CORE RELATIONSHIP VALUES

Let's focus on four key values that are emphasized in many belief systems, values with obvious positive implications for relationships such as marriage: *commitment, respect, intimacy,* and *forgiveness*. When you and your partner have similar core beliefs systems, it's likely that you'll have a similar understanding about these values and about how you can give life to them in your marriage. Regardless of core beliefs, we see the need for all couples to have some way to reinforce such values.

Commitment in its various aspects is strongly emphasized in many belief systems, in terms of both dedication and constraint. While there are great differences among belief systems about the morality of divorce, there would be wide agreement across beliefs about the value of commitment. Long-term relationships need a sustained sense of commitment. It's so important that we took two chapters to present it.

Respect is a core value emphasized in most religious or spiritual groups. While various religions hold to specific beliefs that others may reject, respect for the value and worth of others is still emphasized in most systems. Respect is a core need of all people; as a couple, your value system needs to have a strong emphasis on respect for each other.

In the PREP approach, even if you have significant disagreements and differences, you can show respect for one another by the way you communicate. This is validation. You show interest in and respect for your partner even when you see things quite differently. You can't have a good relationship without basic respect.

Intimacy is prized in most religious and spiritual systems. While it may be understood differently, it's usually emphasized and encouraged, especially in marriage. All of the traditional religious systems in Western cultures seem to place a high value on the importance of marriage and the relationship between the two partners.

One way to think about everything we're saying in this book is that couples need to have clear ways to maintain and enhance intimacy. Furthermore, poorly handled conflict can do great damage to all that is intimate. All couples seeking long-term, satisfying marriages need to value intimacy and the importance of preserving and protecting it.

Forgiveness is a core theme for relational health. Long-term, healthy relationships need an element of forgiveness. Otherwise, emotional debts can be allowed to build in ways that destroy the potential for intimacy and teamwork. That's why we spent an entire chapter just dealing with that topic. Marriages need forgiveness to stay healthy over the long term.

The PREP approach is quite specific and skill-oriented. Underlying that focus, we hope that you can see how the four core values discussed here are reflected in the skills and attitudes we encourage. Religious belief systems have been emphasizing these values for thousands of years in ethics, codes of conduct, and standards for dealing with others. In doing so, these belief systems have reflected the importance of commitment, respect, intimacy, and forgiveness.

Our understanding of marital success and failure leads us to emphasize these same values. In essence, the PREP approach teaches ways of thinking and acting that enable couples to put these values into action. They are relevant for every couple. As you practice and put into effect the kinds of strategies and structures we advocate, you are building positive relationship rituals for the future health of your marriage.

In contrast to these four relationship values, other aspects of people's worldviews that are based on individual core belief systems—specifically, moral judgments and expectations—vary a great deal. Depending on how they are handled, such differences can have a positive or negative impact on a marriage.

MORAL JUDGMENTS

How two partners view what is and isn't moral can have a bearing on their ability to develop a shared worldview. Consider the following list of moral questions:

- Where is the line between personal responsibility and community responsibility? Why do people do wrong?

- Is capital punishment morally right?

- What is our responsibility toward our fellow humans? Toward animals? What about the environment?

- What is appropriate sexual behavior? Why? On what do you base your judgment?

- How about drug and/or alcohol use? What's okay? Why?

This is just a sampling of the questions people grapple with in life. Many partners derive similar moral views from a shared religious belief system. Likewise, for nonreligious or less religious couples, a similar philosophy of life would enhance their shared worldview in this regard.

But what is the impact on a couple when moral views aren't shared? These are the kinds of questions that spark the greatest controversy and conflict in our culture. In marriage, such issues can be discussed in ways that enhance intimacy, or they can lead to conflicts. For some couples, agreement may never come on some moral issues that affect society. The ability to talk openly together about moral matters that you disagree on leads to greater understanding of who each of you is. In fact, these are the kinds of topics many friends talk about because it can be quite interesting. Being able to handle such differences well has the most to do with a couple's ability to communicate, enjoy each other as friends, and keep these kinds of differences from triggering hidden issues of acceptance and rejection.

One couple we worked with in a research project came from very different viewpoints on such moral issues. Jan was a conservative Republican and Richard was a liberal Democrat. They came from similar, but not identical, religious backgrounds—his more liberal and hers more conservative. They greatly disagreed on many moral issues. Nevertheless, they could have talks that maintained their friendship rather than damaging it. For example, in discussing capital punishment, this is how they would communicate:

RICHARD: Did you see that they just executed that guy down in Texas? It just doesn't make sense to me.

JAN: I know it's not something you agree with. It makes perfect sense to me.

RICHARD: But I can't accept that the taking of human life is ever justified. To me, it shows a cultural disrespect for the value of life.

JAN: I hear you, but that's exactly why I'm for capital punishment. The way our society treats some of these murderers shows a total disregard for the value of the life of the victim.

RICHARD: I know you and a lot of others see it that way. But to me, it cheapens life when anyone takes another's life. I mean, who are we to take someone else's life?

JAN: I can see why that bothers you. I think there's a big distinction between the government taking on this responsibility and an individual citizen taking a life—even of a murderer.

RICHARD: It's amazing to me that we both argue this from a position of respect for life, but reach such a different conclusion.

JAN: Good observation. That's not the only reason I favor capital punishment, though. I think it's just.

RICHARD: You mean like an eye for an eye? I just don't think I could ever see it that way. To me that's vengeance.

JAN: But even that phrase can be taken to mean that the punishment should fit the crime, not to mean simple vengeance.

RICHARD: I don't think too many people make that distinction. It strikes me as culturally sanctioned violence.

JAN: In a way, I think it is. But it makes sense.

RICHARD: Not to me. I wish our society would come around to seeing the wrong that's being done in this.

JAN: I can see how frustrating it is for you that more people don't agree that it's wrong.

And on they go. The key to maintaining your friendship in such conversations is to keep the focus off agreement or a need to solve such moral dilemmas and focus instead on learning more about how your partner thinks. After all, to what degree does your marriage depend day to day on your sharing the same viewpoint on such matters? These differences only threaten your marriage if they trigger deeper issues of acceptance and rejection.

If you could hear Jan and Richard having such talks, you wouldn't hear any defensiveness or attacking. Even when they attack each other's position, they maintain an air of respect in their talks on such subjects, so much so that they actually enjoy them, most of the time. We'll come back to add some points about how such differences are handled, after discussing the last factor related to worldview—expectations.

EXPECTATIONS

Another way in which your worldview can significantly impact your marriage is in shaping your expectations in areas such as child rearing and discipline, intimacy, dealing with in-laws, and marital roles. In contrast to the moral viewpoints discussed above, this aspect of your worldview has very significant implications for your marriage on a daily basis.

The potential for differences in expectations to spark conflict is so great that we spent an entire chapter (Chapter Seven) encouraging you to make such expectations clear—no matter where they come from. When two people share a perspective on key relationship expectations, they're going to have an easier time negotiating life. Shared expectations lead to shared rituals and routines that guide couples more smoothly through the transitions and trials they must confront every day.

In religious systems, such viewpoints tend to be very clear and codified in the beliefs and rituals; this may make it easier to have a shared worldview in terms of everyday expectations. This also could explain, in part, the research findings showing that couples who are more religious and those with similar belief backgrounds have a somewhat easier time in marriage. Sharing a structured belief system simplifies dealing with many expectations, in that they don't have to be worked out or negotiated. Presumably, couples who aren't religiously involved can derive this same benefit if they share some philosophical viewpoint that makes it easier to maintain a shared viewpoint on expectations.

THREE TYPES OF COUPLES

Whatever your backgrounds and beliefs, you shouldn't take agreement for granted in your relationship. Key similarities and differences in your viewpoints must be identified and talked about in ways that will help you work together as a team. Let's look at three different kinds of couples before we recommend some exercises for you to do.

Type 1: A Shared View

For many couples, similar core beliefs lead to a lower likelihood of conflict for the various reasons outlined above. There is simply less to work out in all sorts of areas. However, all couples still must clarify their key expectations about how they will handle various marital and family matters. It's best when such differences are discussed early on and decisions made that will form the default settings for your relationship. This means that there's basic agreement about how various things will be handled—the default—so that you aren't constantly adjusting to differences in your worldviews in the context of events.

Type 2: Nonshared but Respected Views

These couples have a significant difference of opinion on core beliefs, but they handle the differences with respect. The differences don't produce alienation and may, in fact, be a source of intimacy if the partners are able to enjoy the exchange of different perspectives, like Richard and Jan, whom we discussed earlier.

To accomplish this, couples need at least two things: (1) the skills needed to maintain respect in light of their differences and (2) enough personal security about their core beliefs to not be overly threatened by the absence of agreement. The views and expectations of these couples aren't shared in the sense of being similar, but they can be shared in the sense that there's open expression that doesn't trigger hidden issues of acceptance and rejection.

Type 3: Nonshared Views with Conflict

These partners don't share the same perspective and this sparks conflict that is generally not handled well. Such couples aren't able to talk freely about the differences in their views and maintain mutual respect at the same time. Either they argue unpleasantly about these differences or avoid talking about them. It's easy to trigger hidden issues of basic acceptance. The differences in core beliefs become a barrier, with the partners being unable to share openly their perspectives on the deepest issues of life.

Simon and Marjorie, discussed earlier in this chapter, fall into this last category. While they shared many core beliefs, having a child brought up significant differences in their expectations for their son—expectations that were rooted in their core belief systems. If they hadn't both gotten more interested in the beliefs and practices of their religions, there probably wouldn't have been much conflict. But key life transitions, such as marriage, birth, and death, have a habit of placing us more in touch with our core beliefs, and in fact most religions specify key rituals for such events.

We'd suggest that having a shared worldview is most beneficial to your relationship when you're going through a major life transition. At such times, a similarity in core beliefs guides you through with less stress and disruption. These transitions would also be the times when having social support is most critical. Without a shared view, the next best thing you can do is to be clear about your expectations and agree how you will proceed as a couple. Anticipate life's key transitions so that you can talk together about how you will handle things.

In summary, you and your partner may come from different perspectives, even if you were raised similarly. When you think about religious and spiritual differences, a lot is at stake. The same is true for any core belief system, such as a philosophy of life. Everyone has beliefs, and it's not likely that a couple exists where both partners line up perfectly on all dimensions. The point is that you need to grapple with the effects on *your* relationship. The exercises for this chapter are designed to help you do just that—grapple. We want you to explore your beliefs on religious or spiritual dimensions and talk them over together.

Exploring and sharing clearly what you believe and expect about some of these key questions can be an enriching if not eye-opening experience in your relationship. Talking about these issues with respect can be a very intimate experience. Try it and see what we mean. Then go on to the last chapter, in which we'll talk about some strategies to pull together everything you've learned in this book.

🐞 Exercises

There are three exercises for this chapter, in which we follow the key themes used to explain the research findings regarding the impact of religion and spiritual values on relationships. First, we ask you to consider what your core values are, where they come from, and how they affect your marriage. Second, we ask you to take stock of your social support system. Third, we want you to explore your core belief systems and the expectations specifically related to them. You will each need a separate pad of paper to do these exercises.

1. We'd like you to consider what your core values are in life. What values are central for you? Where did these values come from? Spend some time thinking about this individually. Jot down some notes on it. Then share with each other what you've been thinking about.

   You may have some additional ideas after you work on the next exercise. In addition to other ideas that come up for you, specifically discuss together your views of the core relationship values mentioned in this chapter: commitment, respect, intimacy, and forgiveness. What is your view of these values?

2. Talk together about your social support system. Do you have a strong support system of people you can rely on, who encourage you, and who hold you accountable at times? Are you involved in a community that supports and nurtures your growth in your marriage? Do you want to be? What could you do as a couple to build up more support if you see the need to do that?

3. Now, we want you to explore on your own and share with your partner issues that are relevant to your core belief system. For many people, religious faith or spiritual orientation reflects or determines core philosophical, moral, and cultural beliefs and practices. If that's the case for you, it will make the most sense to answer these questions in that light. For others, these questions may seem less religiously oriented and more philosophical.

Either way, it can be very important for partners to understand one another's core belief system, whether it's based in spiritual or religious beliefs or other philosophies of life. This exercise will help you to accomplish this goal. It's very much like the exercise you did in Chapter Seven, but focused on the area of core belief systems.

The following questions are designed to get you thinking about a broad range of issues related to your beliefs. There may be other important questions that we've left out, so feel free to answer questions we don't ask as well as those we do ask. We'd like you to write down an answer to each question as it applies to you, on your own pad of paper. This will help you think more clearly about the issues and will also act as a guide when it comes time to talk with your partner about them. As you think about and answer each question, it can be especially valuable to note what you were taught as a child versus what you believe or expect now as an adult.

QUESTIONS FOR REFLECTION

a. What is your core belief system or worldview? What do you believe in?

b. How did you come to believe in this viewpoint?

c. What is the meaning or purpose of life in your core belief system?

d. What was your belief growing up? How was this core belief practiced in your family of origin? In religious practice? Some other way?

e. Do you make a distinction between spirituality and religion? What is your view on these matters?

f. What is the meaning of marriage in your belief system?

g. What vows will you say, or what vows did you say? How do they tie in to your belief system?

h. What is your belief about divorce? How does this fit in with your belief system?

i. How do you practice, or expect to practice, your beliefs as part of your relationship? (This could mean religious involvement, spiritual practices, or other behaviors, depending on your belief system.) How do you want to practice your beliefs?

j. What do you think the day-to-day impact of your belief system should be on your relationship?

k. Are there specific views on sexuality in your belief system? What are they? How do they affect the two of you?

l. If you have or plan to have children, how are they being raised or will they be raised with respect to your belief system?

m.   Do you give, or expect to give, financial support to a religious institution or other effort related to your belief system? How much? How will this be determined? Do you both agree?

n.   Do you see potential areas of conflict regarding your belief systems? What are they?

o.   What do you believe about forgiveness in general? How does forgiveness apply in a relationship such as the one you have with your partner?

p.   In your belief system, what is your responsibility to other human beings?

q.   How do you observe or expect to observe religious holidays?

r.   What is the basis in your beliefs for respecting others?

s.   Are there any other questions you can think of and answer?

After you and your partner have finished the entire exercise, begin to plan time to spend together discussing these expectations. You should plan on a number of discussions. Discuss the degree to which you each felt that the expectation being discussed had been shared clearly in the past. Use the Speaker-Listener Technique if you'd like some additional structure to deal with these sometimes difficult issues. If any new expectations come up, talk out the degree to which you both feel that they're reasonable or unreasonable, and discuss what you want to agree to do about them.

15

Positive Steps for Keeping Your Relationship Strong

WE'VE COVERED MANY CONCEPTS in this book, including communication and conflict management, commitment, forgiveness, friendship, fun, sensuality, and, in the last chapter, the impact of core belief systems and social support on your relationship. We're confident that these ideas and techniques of the PREP approach can go a long way toward helping you keep your marriage strong.

You could think of this book as providing a recipe for a solid, lasting, satisfying relationship. The ingredients are in place—your love, attraction, and friendship, and the skills outlined in our approach. All you need to do is to blend these ingredients with your commitment in order to make a great marriage happen. Based on our experience with couples, we've provided recommendations for keeping your relationship strong and vital for years to come. Now we have some final and important points to make.

YOU ARE NOT ALONE

When people have problems in relationships, the mistakes they make are fairly similar across couples: escalation and withdrawal, invalidation, and negative interpretations. In contrast, there are many ways to have a good relationship. Happy, healthy couples can look very different from other couples who are doing well, and yet all of them may have great marriages with intimacy and teamwork. In other words, couples who are struggling look more alike than couples who are doing well.

During a workshop we recently conducted, a man's eyes lit up when he heard that other couples were making the same mistakes he and his wife were making. He was happy to hear that they weren't alone. In fact, this is a common reaction when we work with couples. They're frustrated about whatever negative patterns they have going but relieved because they can say, "Even though our marriage is pretty good, we blow it from time to time like everyone else."

You're in good company if you have some of the negative patterns and attitudes discussed throughout this book. We all do. They're common. But divorce is common, too, so it's important to be concerned about the negative patterns. It's even more important to do something about your concern.

Fortunately, the news is good. There's hope for couples who are invested in stopping negative patterns and preserving all the great things in marriage. Our research shows that you can prevent such problems from building up and harming your relationship, but you have to work at it. This leads us to the issue of motivation.

MOTIVATION

Our principles, knowledge base, research, and techniques aren't going to work for you unless you're motivated to do what it takes to have a good relationship. Sometimes it's hardest to motivate the couples who can do the most to prevent serious problems from developing in the first place—engaged and newlywed couples. There's just too much else going on. When you're still new to the relationship, it's hard to imagine having serious trouble later on. If that's your situation, please keep in mind that working to implement the kinds of strategies recommended here can do a lot to keep your relationship vibrant.

If you've been together for some time, you probably fall into one of three categories:

1. Those who are doing great and want to keep it that way

2. Those who are having some struggles and are in need of a tune-up

3. Those who have been having significant problems and need major changes to get back on track

Whatever category you're in, you can't get the most out of this approach with a halfhearted effort. Even though we emphasize relatively straightforward techniques and ideas, it still takes work to make any kind of meaningful change in life.

BUT MY PARTNER WON'T TRY THESE THINGS

What if your partner isn't motivated to learn some of the techniques we've presented? That can be a very frustrating problem if you really like the ideas. You could try several approaches.

Work on Yourself First

It's wisest to begin working on what you can change about how you handle yourself in the relationship, regardless of what your partner is willing to do. It's too easy for all of us to get focused on what our partners can do. Instead, focus your attention on where you have the most control—yourself!

Do you have a tendency to make negative interpretations? Do you tend to withdraw from talking about issues? Do you bring up gripes when you're out to have a fun evening with your partner? You can make substantial changes in such patterns no matter what your partner is doing. There are many ways in which you can work on maintaining and demonstrating your dedication without your partner ever reading this book.

You can also demonstrate some of the ground rules without necessarily working on them together. For example, if you're out together and begin to discuss some conflict, you could say, "You know, we're out to have fun tonight. Let's deal with that tomorrow when we have more time so we can focus on relaxing together this evening." Most partners would get the idea even if they've never heard of PREP or ground rules. It's really pretty basic, yet powerful, to make some of these changes.

While all the things we've suggested work best when you're working together, you can accomplish a lot on your own if you're willing to try and your partner isn't actively working to damage the relationship.

PREPlite: Tastes Great, Less Filling

You might try to get your partner interested in some of the lighter topics we've discussed, such as fun or friendship. Chapters Eleven and Twelve have many ideas that you could suggest to your partner as a start. They might initiate some potent and positive changes that could open up interest in other features of this program. As you may have noticed, many of the key ideas about fun and friendship don't depend on a knowledge of the other key concepts in this book.

There's More Than One Way to Skin a Cat

If the ideas above fail to spark your partner's interest, then you have a choice to make. Give some thought to the significance of your partner's reluctance. It could simply mean that he or she is less interested than you in a particular approach to strengthening your marriage. If that's the case, it would be a serious and inaccurate negative interpretation to assume that your partner wasn't as interested as you are in keeping your marriage strong.

In fact, we often talk to couples where one partner—more often the woman—thinks that the other isn't doing enough for their marriage, while the other—more often the man—brings up all sorts of things that he feels he's doing because he does care for the relationship. One couple we saw in counseling had a big problem with this kind of thinking. The wife loved to read self-help books and the husband didn't. The wife interpreted his lack of interest as a lack of motivation in the marriage, yet the husband was doing all sorts of other things that showed his investment—being actively involved in counseling, wanting to go out and spend time together, and being a reliable provider for the family.

So be careful how you interpret your partner's reluctance. Try to talk together about the ways you each think you can make progress as a couple. Your partner may have very different ideas about what's best for the marriage and how to get there. Listen up!

But My Partner Really Isn't Interested

If, on the other hand, you're convinced that your partner is substantially less motivated to work on the relationship in any way, you have a tougher situation. What you choose to do is up to you, but we still recommend that to give your relationship the best chance, you do the best you can to strengthen your marriage according to the kinds of principles we're advocating here.

As we said above, one person can cause substantial changes in a marriage. It's just a lot easier and more fun when you're working together. If you value your marriage, your own positive investment gives you the best chance of getting the changes you desire. Just keep in mind that sometimes the most positive investment you can make is to confront any problems you see head-on. You might need to sit your partner down and say something like this: "I've been concerned for some time about where we're headed. I'm really committed to making this a great marriage, not just one where we get by. I'm willing to do what it takes to make that happen. I'm hoping we can work together and I want you to know that I'll be trying hard. Let me know if you want to try some of the same things."

WHEN HELP IS DESIRED

Though we think that nearly all couples can benefit from the educational approach we've outlined, there are times when couples can benefit from professional help, times when motivation alone isn't enough to get you on a better path. We wish that everyone could work on *preventing* serious problems from developing so there wouldn't be such a demand for marital counselors. But as marital therapists as well as researchers, we recognize that there are times when couples can really benefit from a professional's skill.

We're not intending the PREP approach to be a substitute for therapy when that's what's really needed. There are many reasons why a couple or individual might wisely seek professional guidance—for example, in cases of physical abuse, substance abuse, depression, or ongoing conflict that never gets resolved. These are danger signs that would indicate that the educational approach may not be enough.

The most common reason couples seek professional help is that they feel stuck; they want or hope for significant changes to occur but aren't able to make them happen. For example, you might both read this book, love the approach, and try some of the techniques, but still find that you're having trouble changing your ingrained patterns.

Good therapists can help you in numerous ways. They can give you different perspectives on a problem. They can provide a structured, safe place to talk about difficult issues—much like the structure provided by some of the techniques we recommend. They can hold you more accountable for making certain changes happen. They can coach you in learning skills you may be having trouble with on your own. And they can also help you explore the effect of different family backgrounds and expectations on your relationship.

If you decide that seeing a professional may be something for you to consider, seek help sooner rather than later. Studies show that people live through up to seven years of stress before they start seeking help. That's a really long time to wait. It's easier to change patterns earlier than later, especially if you wait so long that one of you has given up. If you're at a point where you think professional help might be useful, read our tips for finding a competent couples' counselor in the resource section at the end.

WHAT TO DO NOW

Bill Coffin, a colleague and prevention specialist who works for the U.S. Navy, suggests that couples think about relationship fitness the way they might think about physical fitness. Just as physical fitness experts recommend that you work out three or four times a week for twenty to thirty minutes, couples should devote at least that much time to working on their relationships. This doesn't mean just having couple's meetings, but also planning fun times together, having friendship talks, making love, giving a back rub, hanging out together reading a book in the same room, listening to music, or playing with the children. Make the time to regularly renew your relationship in these ways.

If you're serious about putting some of these key ideas into practice, here are a few important points to keep in mind.

REVIEW

To get the most out of what we've presented here, be sure to review the material. We all learn better when we go over key concepts again and again. Perhaps you've highlighted key sections in this book as you've read them. Go back and read those sections again. For example, this would be a great time to go back to Chapter Five and review the ground rules. Are you using them? Have you kept at it?

It would be especially valuable to review the rules for the Speaker-Listener Technique, problem solving, and principles for forgiveness. None of these rules or ideas is all that complicated, but you'll want to master them to get the greatest benefit in your marriage. Better yet, read through the whole book again, together.

PRACTICE

The PREP approach is a very specific, skill-oriented model for building solid relationships. The key to such an approach is to practice the skills and ways of thinking we've recommended. It's not enough just to review the ideas; you need to make them a part of your life. Practice the techniques and strategies so that you can put them into practice. We know they'll feel artificial at first—they're not like your usual behaviors. But if you practice enough, the solid skills, techniques, and ways of thinking we're emphasizing will become regular habits in your relationship.

RITUALS AND ROUTINES

One way to think about the PREP approach is as a model in which the kinds of patterns that work for happy couples can be applied to all couples, including unhappy couples. Too many couples find that relationship problems control them. We want them to take control. Rituals are well-organized habits that guide people in life. A colleague of ours, Bob Weiss, at the University of Oregon, says that the benefit of rituals is that they place you under *rule control* rather than *stimulus control.* To be under stimulus control means that you're constantly reacting to the things happening around you—the stimuli of your life. We've given you some pretty good rules, but it's up to you to make them habits. In effect, we're suggesting that you not fall into the pattern of reacting to events, but instead, that you build rituals into your lifestyle that give you, as a couple, control over important aspects of your life.

Many rituals take place during important life transitions. That's because transitions—like birth, weddings, leaving the nest, and death—are stressful. Rituals and routines can reduce stress by providing some structure during these times of change. For example, almost all cultures have ritualized ways of dealing with death and mourning. Rituals provide a map or structure to help in handling these transi-

... AND DO YOU PROMISE TO USE THE SPEAKER-LISTENER TECHNIQUE...?

tions. But the daily conflicts that come up in life are stressful, too, and rituals and routines provide the same stress-reducing benefits here.

You may already have many rituals in your relationship, simple routines for getting ready for bed or handling special meals on holidays. Clearly, young children benefit from routines for family life. But it's not just kids who benefit from structure. For example, if you're having a weekly couple's meeting to deal with issues in your relationship, you've begun a ritual that we believe will have a very positive payoff over the long term. Meeting regularly helps to prevent destructive conflict and enhance intimacy. It gives you a routine for anticipating issues that may come up—like those concerning upcoming holidays or child rearing.

We're not suggesting that you get weighed down by all sorts of rules. We are suggesting that some solid, commonsense skills can make all the difference in the world in how the tougher issues affect your relationship. You'll get the greatest benefit when such skills and ways of thinking become routine. Some of the powerful rituals we're recommending here include:

1. Using the Speaker-Listener Technique

2. Separating problem discussion from problem solving

3. Working through the forgiveness model when you need to

4. Having a weekly couple's meeting

5. Agreeing to keep fun and friendship times off-limits for arguments and discussions of issues

6. Making time to practice the skills that will help you keep your marriage strong

Preserve spontaneity and creativity in the more wonderful aspects of your relationship. Structure conflict, and let loose with fun.

ENGAGING THE SKILLS

As you consolidate your skills through practice and the development of positive rituals, the most important thing is for you to be able to engage the skills when you need them. Knowing how to use the Speaker-Listener Technique or the problem-solving model is great, but the real benefit comes from using these skills when they're most needed. Unfortunately, the times when you need the most skill are usually the times when it's hardest to use them, so being able to make the shift to engage more skill is critical. That's where practice and good habits really pay off.

It's hardest to engage the skills the first few times you try. For example, working on Ground Rule No. 1—Time Out—will be harder at the start than after you've used it a few times. When you start using Time Out, it can seem like avoidance, but the habit will get stronger as you see that it works, and your relationship will benefit from your increased control over how and when you deal with difficult issues.

REINFORCE, REINFORCE, REINFORCE

When we train other professionals and paraprofessionals to work with couples, we emphasize over and over the need to be active in reinforcing the positive steps couples make as they learn the skills we teach. It's very important to reinforce new skills as well as the positive things that are already happening.

We make the same suggestion to you. As you work on learning new patterns and ways of thinking, reinforce each other. Praise your partner for trying things out, for listening, for working with you to handle issues well, for being committed, and so forth. Don't take each other for granted. Show your appreciation for a positive effort. And don't dwell on the past. In other words, don't ask, "Why couldn't you have done this seven years ago?" *Instead, focus on reinforcing the positive changes that are occurring now!*

When was the last time you said, "Gee, honey, I sure like how you do that?" or "I really felt great the other night when you dropped what you were doing and spent time just listening to me talk about my concerns at work"? It's not hard to say "thanks" or "great job" or "I really appreciated the way you did that." The effects on your relationship can be dramatic. Too often we focus only on the negative. Instead, try looking for ways to reward the positive. That's the best way to encourage more positive behavior in the future.

In general, our entire culture greatly underestimates the power of verbal reinforcement. Maybe that's because we're so focused on material rewards here in America. Don't succumb to this cultural tendency. Positive verbal reinforcement is the most potent change agent ever devised. Use it. If you like what you see going on, say so. Reinforce, reinforce, reinforce!

IN CLOSING, WE'D LIKE TO SAY . . .

If we can train the best military in the world (sure, we're a bit biased), you'd think we could train couples to have good marriages. But, in fact, marriage is in trouble in our culture. We don't think it has to stay this way. If you have the know-how and the will to have a great marriage, you stand a good chance of making it happen. We don't pretend to know everything about marriage and relationships, but we think the material in this book will give you a good start.

We started our work with couples who were happy and planning marriage. As researchers and therapists, our chief goal was to help them prevent the kinds of pain and damage all too many people experience in marriage. You can't prevent marriage from being hard work at at times, but if you work together, you can make your relationship the kind that deepens and grows over the years, whatever comes your way.

We've detailed our approach in this book. We've tried to provide tools that you can use to build a relationship that brings long-term fulfillment, and to protect your relationship from naturally occurring storms. But, like anything else, once you have the tools, it's up to you what you do with them.

As the ad says: *"Just do it."*

Resource: Finding a Counselor When You Need One

IN MOST AREAS, there are so many potential therapists and counselors to choose from that it's hard for many couples to know how to find the best help. How do you find a good couples' therapist out of all the psychologists, marital therapists, professional counselors, psychiatrists, and social workers listed in the Yellow Pages? The best way is to try to get names from some source you trust—a friend, a physician, a member of the clergy. If all else fails, you can write to us for referrals of people in your area who have been trained in the PREP approach, if any. If you want to do that, send a self-addressed, stamped envelope to us at:

> PREP, Inc./Referrals
> P.O. Box 102530
> Denver, Colorado 80250–2530

Or you can write to:

> American Association of Marriage
> and Family Therapists
> 1100 17th Street N.W., 10th Floor
> Washington, DC 20136

Ask them to send you a list of certified marriage and family therapists in your area. You can also call your state's marriage and family therapy association, psychological association, or social work association. You might even have a trusted radio talk-show psychologist or therapist in your area. These people usually know of some of the best resources in their communities because they have to be prepared to refer a lot of people for help.

Getting two or more names is a good idea. Then be an active consumer: call them up and ask about their training, experience, approach, fees, license, and billing policies. If you really like the kind of approach taken in this book, you might ask for a therapist who specializes in what is called the cognitive-behavioral approach. You can and should ask a potential therapist directly about these matters and about anything else that's important to you, such as the therapist's religious or cultural background, viewpoint on codependency issues, or experience with a very specific issue like the effect of having a seriously ill child on marriage. You get the idea.

It's very important to ask if the therapist specializes in working with couples or mostly does individual therapy. Many individually oriented therapists will gladly do marital therapy, but that doesn't mean they're skilled at it. Some members of all the professions listed above specialize in marital or couples' work. Again, you're a consumer, and many locations have dozens of therapists you could consider seeing. If you don't like the answers to your questions, move on and try another name.

If you begin to see a therapist, keep the above issues in mind. If, after a few sessions, you don't feel as though this person can help you, you may be right. You're going to spend a lot of money with a therapist, so don't persist very long with someone you don't feel right about.

It's probably most important to get a sense of the connection and fit you may have with the potential therapist. One of the best predictors of success in couples' therapy, as in all other therapy, is the quality of the relationship you have with the therapist. Do you think this is someone you can trust and respect?

Last, what if you want to get professional help but your spouse isn't interested? Here's what psychologist and colleague Andrea Van Steenhouse often suggests on her radio call-in show. Say something like this to your partner: "I've been concerned about some of the issues in our relationship, and I think we could benefit from some help. I've made an appointment with a therapist for Wednesday at 4:00 P.M. I'd really like you to come with me. I want to do this together. But if you don't want to, I want to let you know that I plan to go anyway. I want to do what I can to get this situation turned around for both our sakes."

This kind of strategy shows your positive intent. It also shows how serious you are about getting help. It may not work, but then again, it just might. It takes some courage to get help when you need it. If you need it, we hope you'll do just that.

Recommended Reading

W E PROVIDE THE FOLLOWING LIST for those interested in further reading in the fields of study underlying this work. Some of the works, like this book, were written for the typical reader. Some were written for researchers and students who are interested in deeper study. The works written for the more academically inclined reader are identified by an asterisk and would make a great start for those who'd like to study further the kinds of research used in preparing this book.

Baucom, D. H., & Epstein, N. (1990). *Cognitive-behavioral marital therapy.* New York: Brunner/Mazel.*

Beach, S.R.H., Sandeen, E. E., & O'Leary, K. D. (1990). *Depression in marriage.* New York: Guilford Press.*

Blumberg, S. L. (1991). *Premarital intervention programs: A comparison study.* Unpublished doctoral dissertation, University of Denver, Denver, CO.*

Dickson, F.C. (in press). The best is yet to be: Research on long-lasting marriages. In J. Wood and S. Duck (Eds.), *Off the beaten track: Understudied relationships.* Newbury Park, CA: Sage.

Epstein, N. (1982). Cognitive therapy with couples. *American Journal of Family Therapy, 8,* 417–428.*

Gottman, J. (1979). *Marital interaction: Empirical investigations.* San Diego, CA: Academic Press.*

Gottman, J. M., & Krokoff, L. J. (1989). Marital interaction and satisfaction: A longitudinal view. *Journal of Consulting and Clinical Psychology, 57,* 47–52.*

Gottman, J., Notarius, C., Gonso, J., & Markman, H. (1976). *A couple's guide to communication.* Champaign, IL: Research Press.*

Guerney, B. G., Jr. (1977). *Relationship Enhancement: Skills training programs for therapy, problem prevention, and enrichment.* San Francisco: Jossey-Bass.

Hahlweg, K., & Markman, H. (1988). The effectiveness of behavioral marital therapy: Empirical status of behavioral techniques in preventing and alleviating marital distress. *Journal of Consulting and Clinical Psychology, 56,* 440–447.*

Jacobson, N. S., & Margolin, G. (1979). *Marital therapy: Strategies based on social learning and behavior exchange principles.* New York: Brunner/Mazel.*

Johnson, D. J., & Rusbult, C. E. (1989). Resisting temptation: Devaluation of alternative partners as a means of maintaining commitment in close relationships. *Journal of Personality and Social Psychology, 57,* 967–980.*

Johnson, M. P. (1982). The social and cognitive features of the dissolution of commitment to relationships. In S. Duck (Ed.), *Personal relationships: Dissolving personal relationships.* San Diego, CA: Academic Press.*

Knox, D. (1971). *Marriage happiness.* Champaign, IL: Research Press.*

Levinson, R., & Gottman, J. M. (1983). Marital interaction: Physiological linkage and affective exchange. *Journal of Personality and Social Psychology, 45,* 587–599.*

Markman, H. J., Floyd, F. J., Stanley, S. M., & Jamieson, K. (1984). A cognitive/behavioral program for the prevention of marital and family distress: Issues in program development and delivery. In K. Hahlweg & N. Jacobson (Eds.), *Marital interaction: Analysis and modification.* New York: Guilford Press.*

Markman, H. J., Floyd, F. J., Stanley, S. M., & Lewis, H. (1986). Prevention. In N. Jacobson & A. Gurman (Eds.), *Clinical handbook of marital therapy.* New York: Guilford Press.*

Markman, H. J., Floyd, F. J., Stanley, S. M., & Storaasli, R. D. (1988). Prevention of marital distress: A longitudinal investigation. *Journal of Consulting and Clinical Psychology, 56,* 210–217.*

Markman, H. J., & Kraft, S. A. (1989). Men and women in marriage: Dealing with gender differences in marital therapy. *The Behavior Therapist, 12,* 51–56.*

Markman, H. J., Renick, M. J., Floyd, F. J., Stanley, S. M., & Clements, M. (1993). Preventing marital distress through communication and conflict management training: A 4- and 5-year follow-up. *Journal of Consulting and Clinical Psychology, 61,* 1–80.*

Markman, H. J., Stanley, S. M., & Blumberg, S. (1991). *Fighting for your marriage: The PREP approach.* Videotape or audiotape series. Denver, CO: PREP Educational Videos. 1-800-366-0166.

Masters, W., & Johnson, V. (1970). *Human sexual inadequacy.* Boston: Little, Brown.

Miller, S., Miller, P., Nunnally, E. W., & Wackman, D. (1991). *Talking and listening together.* Littleton, CO: Interpersonal Communication Programs.

Napier, A. Y. (1988) *The fragile bond: In search of an equal, intimate and enduring marriage.* New York: Harper Perennial.

Notarius, C., & Markman, H. J. (1993). *We can work it out: Making sense of marital conflict.* New York: Putnam.

Notarius, C., & Vanzetti, N. (1984). The Marital Agenda Protocol. In E. Filsinger (Ed.), *Marital and family assessment.* Newbury Park, CA: Sage.*

Pargament, K. I., Tyler, F. B., & Steele, R. E. (1979). Is fit it? The relationship between the church/synagogue member fit and the psychosocial competence of the member. *Journal of Community Psychology, 7,* 243–252.

Rausch, H. L., Barry, W. A., Hertel, R. K., & Swain, M. A. (1974). *Communication, conflict, and marriage.* San Francisco: Jossey-Bass.*

Renick, M. J., Blumberg, S. L., & Markman, H. J. (1992). The Prevention and Relationship Enhancement Program (PREP): An empirically based preventive intervention program for couples. *Family Relations, 41,* 141–147.*

Rosenthal, R., & Jacobsen, L. (1968). *Pygmalion in the classroom: Teacher expectations and pupils' intellectual development.* Troy, MO: Holt, Rinehart & Winston.*

Rubin, L. (1983). *Intimate strangers.* New York: HarperCollins.

Rusbult, C. E. (1983). A longitudinal test of the investment model: The development (and deterioration) of satisfaction and commitment in heterosexual involvements. *Journal of Personality and Social Psychology, 45,* 101–117.*

Sager, C. J. (1976). *Marriage contracts and couple therapy: Hidden forces in intimate relationships.* New York: Brunner/Mazel.*

Schwartz, J. C., Sharpsteen, D. J., & Butler, J. M. (1987). *Regulation of intimacy in conversations between same-sex close friends.* Unpublished manuscript, University of Denver, Denver, CO.*

Snyder, M., & Swann, W. B. (1978). Behavioral confirmation in social interaction: From social perception to social reality. *Journal of Experimental Social Psychology, 14,* 148–162.*

Spilka, B., Hood, R., & Gorsuch, R. (1985). *The psychology of religion: An empirical approach.* Englewood Cliffs, NJ: Prentice-Hall.*

Stanley, S. M., & Markman, H. J. (1992). Assessing commitment in personal relationships. *Journal of Marriage and the Family, 54,* 595–608.*

Stanley, S. M., Markman, H. J., St. Peters, M., & Leber, D. (1995). Strengthening marriages and preventing divorce: New directions in prevention research. *Family Relations, 44,* 392–401.*

Tannen, D. (1990). *You just don't understand: Women and men in conversation.* New York: Ballantine.

Tavris, C., & Sadd, S. (1975). *The* Redbook *report on female sexuality.* New York: Dell.

Thibaut, J. W., & Kelley, H. H. (1959). *The social psychology of groups.* New York: Wiley.*

Index

More Information on the PREP Approach and How You Can Fight for Your Marriage

WORKSHOPS

For information on *Fighting* for *Your Marriage* workshops put on by us in Denver or on workshops by us or others around the country, please write us. We will be glad to give you information about seminars (for counselors or couples) or products.

You can write to us at:
> Fighting *for* Your Marriage
> *c/o* PREP, Inc.
> P.O. Box 102530
> Denver, Colorado 80250–2530

AUDIO AND VIDEO TAPES

To order *Fighting for Your Marriage* audio or video tapes, please call (800) 366-0166. (This number is for product sales only.)

We have a complete, six-hour audiotape set covering roughly the same content as this book. We also have a videotape series, which at this time covers key communication and conflict-management concepts. We are planning to add other videos to the series in the future.

THE AUTHORS

Howard Markman is a professor of psychology and co-director of the Center for Marital and Family Studies at the University of Denver. He received his Ph.D. degree (1977) in clinical psychology from Indiana University. He is internationally known for his work on the prediction and prevention of divorce and marital distress; among his many published works on the subject is *We Can Work It Out: Making Sense of Marital Conflict*, which he co-authored with Clifford Notarius. Markman has often appeared in the media, including on *20/20, The Oprah Winfrey Show,* and *48 Hours,* in segments on the PREP approach.

Scott Stanley is co-director of the Center for Marital and Family Studies at the University of Denver and adjunct associate professor of marital and family therapy at Fuller Theological Seminary. He received his Ph.D. degree (1986) in clinical psychology from the University of Denver. He is the author of numerous research articles on relationships and an expert on marital commitment. Along with Markman and Blumberg, he has developed the video- and audiotape series "Fighting *for* Your Marriage: The PREP Approach." He contributes regularly to both broadcast and print media.

Susan L. Blumberg is a psychologist in private practice who specializes in working with couples, families, and children. She received her Ph.D. degree (1991) in clinical psychology from the University of Denver. She provides PREP seminars for couples in the Denver area and has been actively involved in doing research on PREP and developing professional training materials for PREP workshops. She also consults with businesses and organizations about providing PREP in corporate settings.